OpenLayers 3.x Cookbook
Second Edition

Over 50 comprehensive recipes to help you create
spectacular maps with OpenLayers 3

Peter J. Langley

Antonio Santiago Perez

[PACKT] open source
PUBLISHING   community experience distilled

BIRMINGHAM - MUMBAI

OpenLayers 3.x Cookbook
Second Edition

First published: August 2012

Second edition: March 2016

Production reference: 1180316

Published by Packt Publishing Ltd.
Livery Place
35 Livery Street
Birmingham B3 2PB, UK.

ISBN 978-1-78528-775-6

www.packtpub.com

Credits

Authors

Peter J. Langley

Antonio Santiago Perez

Reviewer

Jorge Arévalo

Commissioning Editor

Veena Pagare

Acquisition Editor

Kirk D'costa

Content Development Editor

Rashmi Suvarna

Technical Editor

Kunal Chaudhari

Copy Editor

Priyanka Ravi

Project Coordinator

Judie Jose

Proofreader

Safis Editing

Indexer

Tejal Daruwale Soni

Production Coordinator

Manu Joseph

Cover Work

Manu Joseph

About the Authors

Peter J. Langley has been developing websites ever since he owned his first computer. He has been working professionally for many years as a lead web developer for various companies and industries as an employee & freelancer. As the influx of available technologies and capabilities in web browsers continues to increase, he has been fortunate enough to play a leading role in the software engineering of some sophisticated solutions, such as web-based GIS applications for Britain's mapping agency, Ordnance Survey.

Peter is passionate about the Internet, computing, and software engineering principles. He enjoys working on engaging projects in vibrant atmospheres that quickly deliver value to consumers. He has been sharing how-to guides on his website, www.codechewing.com, for many years. This is a demonstration of his personal desire to encourage people to passionately unite knowledge and thrive from each other's experiences, interests, and perspectives.

I would like to thank my partner, Alanna, for all her dependable support and positivity during the undertaking of this book.

Antonio Santiago Perez is a computer science professional with more than 10 years of experience in designing and implementing systems. Since the beginning of his professional life, his work has been always related to the world of meteorology while working for different companies as an employee or a freelancer. He has experience in development of systems that collect, store, transform, analyze, and visualize data, and he is actively interested in any GIS-related technology with a preference for data visualization. His main field of experience is the Java ecosystem, and he has also actively worked with many related web technologies while looking to improve the client side of web applications. He is a firm believer in software engineering practices and is a follower of agile methodologies, involving customers as the main key to the project's success.

About the Reviewer

Jorge Arévalo is a computer engineer from Universidad Autónoma de Madrid, UAM. He started developing web applications with JS, PHP, and Python in 2007. In 2010, he began collaborating with PostGIS and GDAL projects after participating in GSoC 2009, creating the PostGIS Raster GDAL driver. He currently works as a technology trainer and Python/Django developer. He also organizes hackathons with others at `http://hackathonlovers.com/`. He has cowritten the book *Zurb Foundation 4 Starter*, for Packt Publishing. He has also worked as a reviewer for the books, *PostGIS 2.0 Cookbook*, *OpenLayers 3: Beginner's Guide*, *Memcached*, *Speed Up Your Web Application*, and *QGIS Cookbook*. All of these were published by Packt Publishing.

I want to thank my wife, Elena, for her continuous love and support while reviewing this book.

www.PacktPub.com

eBooks, discount offers, and more

Did you know that Packt offers eBook versions of every book published, with PDF and ePub files available? You can upgrade to the eBook version at www.PacktPub.com and as a print book customer, you are entitled to a discount on the eBook copy. Get in touch with us at customercare@packtpub.com for more details.

At www.PacktPub.com, you can also read a collection of free technical articles, sign up for a range of free newsletters and receive exclusive discounts and offers on Packt books and eBooks.

https://www2.packtpub.com/books/subscription/packtlib

Do you need instant solutions to your IT questions? PacktLib is Packt's online digital book library. Here, you can search, access, and read Packt's entire library of books.

Why Subscribe?

- ▶ Fully searchable across every book published by Packt
- ▶ Copy and paste, print, and bookmark content
- ▶ On demand and accessible via a web browser

Table of Contents

Preface

Geographical awareness is an exciting and reassuring concept in general for many people. If a friend were to ask you where you live, you'd normally have a genuine desire to describe where. Better yet, you could show them where you live on a (digital) map. Not only is this exciting, but it's also often extremely relevant and useful to include spatial data in products or services to reveal exactly where something is. We live in a time where information is in abundance, and a lot of this information is susceptible to being represented geographically.

The ubiquity of the Web and the improvement in various browsers' performance has made it possible for the Web to become a major player in the GIS field. It can rival desktop applications because of its capabilities. Browsers now allow us to show data visualizations to the masses, create online data editors, and so on.

Nowadays, OpenLayers isn't without its competing libraries. However, with the new API (v3), it's better focused for mobile, and it remains a comprehensive mapping library to create any kind of web mapping application. In addition to offering a great set of components, such as maps, layers, or controls, OpenLayers also offers access to a great number of data sources using many different data formats and implements many standards from the Open Geospatial Consortium (OGC) (`http://www.opengeospatial.org`).

What this book covers

Chapter 1, *Web Mapping Basics*, demonstrates how creating a simple full-screen map is made easy with OpenLayers. This chapter will take a look at some basic map options and controls that help a user get around the map and view different locations. You will gain an understanding of the basic concepts behind a web-based map.

Chapter 2, *Adding Raster Layers*, talks about integrating with external services for data and how mapping imagery is an integral part of any mapping application on the Web. You will learn how to utilize tiles and WMS mapping services from a variety of external providers and customize the URL requests being made to these third parties. You will also discover how to customize animation effects for map interactions and modify default layer properties, which include simple performance techniques to preload data.

Chapter 3, Working with Vector Layers, teaches you how to integrate detailed GIS data from external sources into your own map layers to build useful sets of information for users. You will learn how to create custom layers with performance strategies for high volumes of data, how to integrate with sources in a variety of different formats, how to package layer data for export, how to interact with features on these layers, and also some basic feature manipulation.

Chapter 4, Working with Events, explains how you need to know how to handle triggered events like in any other JavaScript Web application. You will learn how to create event handlers for a variety of different events that are sourced from map navigation, feature modifications, keyboard interaction, and more.

Chapter 5, Adding Controls, teaches you how to create capabilities for users to get on with their intended tasks around a customized mapping application. You will learn new ways to interact with the map and manipulate features on layers. You will also learn how to customize the mapping experience for your target users by adding helpful map controls to achieve known tasks.

Chapter 6, Styling Features, will help you create a personalized mapping application that can be fully customized to meet users' expectations. You will learn how to set static layer-wide styling rules, as well as dynamic styling that is based on geometry types or feature attributes. You will take advantage of styling features differently during specific user actions, such as on selection, when dragged, or while being drawn.

Chapter 7, Beyond the Basics, shows you how to take the foundational skills that you learned in the previous chapters to the next level by taking on new and advanced functionality to create full-featured mapping applications. You will learn what the canvas renderer is capable of, how to build a custom version of the library, how to create features in freehand mode directly on the map, and how to work with other projections.

What you need for this book

The fact that OpenLayers is a JavaScript library, which must be integrated within HTML pages, implies that the user must be familiar with these technologies.

To successfully view all the recipes in this book in action, you need to have Node.js (`https://nodejs.org`) installed on your machine, as we use an HTTP server written in Node.js. Please follow the `README.md` instructions inside the bundle for more details, where you'll be instructed to install the required Node.js packages (these are listed in the `package.json` file).

Once you've installed these dependencies and initiated the server, you can access a chapter topic from any browser at `http://localhost:3000/ch03/ch03-gml-layer`.

All library dependencies required by the code of various recipes, such as OpenLayers or jQuery, are included in the bundle itself.

Who this book is for

This book is ideal for GIS-related professionals who need to create web-mapping applications. From basic to advanced topics, the recipes of this book cover the most common issues a user may find during their career in a direct way.

Sections

In this book, you will find several headings that appear frequently (Getting ready, How to do it, How it works, There's more, and See also).

To give clear instructions on how to complete a recipe, we use these sections as follows:

Getting ready

This section tells you what to expect in the recipe, and describes how to set up any software or any preliminary settings required for the recipe.

How to do it...

This section contains the steps required to follow the recipe.

How it works...

This section usually consists of a detailed explanation of what happened in the previous section.

There's more...

This section consists of additional information about the recipe in order to make the reader more knowledgeable about the recipe.

See also

This section provides helpful links to other useful information for the recipe.

Conventions

In this book, you will find a number of text styles that distinguish between different kinds of information. Here are some examples of these styles and an explanation of their meaning.

Code words in text are shown as follows: "The `map.getLayers()` method returns the collection of map layers." Folder names, filenames and pathnames are shown in this format: `ch02/ch02-zoom-effect`.

A block of code is set as follows:

```
var view = new ol.View({
    zoom: 7, center: [3826743, 4325724]
});
```

Any command-line input or output is written as follows:

cd ch07/ch07-custom-openlayers-build

New terms and **important words** are shown in bold. Words that you see on the screen, for example, in menus or dialog boxes, appear in the text like this: "However, if they click on **OK**, the logic in the `click` event handler executes, adding the features to a new vector layer."

[Warnings or important notes appear in a box like this.]

[Tips and tricks appear like this.]

Reader feedback

Feedback from our readers is always welcome. Let us know what you think about this book—what you liked or disliked. Reader feedback is important for us as it helps us develop titles that you will really get the most out of.

To send us general feedback, simply e-mail `feedback@packtpub.com`, and mention the book's title in the subject of your message.

If there is a topic that you have expertise in and you are interested in either writing or contributing to a book, see our author guide at `www.packtpub.com/authors`.

Customer support

Now that you are the proud owner of a Packt book, we have a number of things to help you to get the most from your purchase.

Downloading the example code

You can download the example code files for this book from your account at `http://www.packtpub.com`. If you purchased this book elsewhere, you can visit `http://www.packtpub.com/support` and register to have the files e-mailed directly to you.

You can download the code files by following these steps:

1. Log in or register to our website using your e-mail address and password.
2. Hover the mouse pointer on the **SUPPORT** tab at the top.
3. Click on **Code Downloads & Errata**.
4. Enter the name of the book in the **Search** box.
5. Select the book for which you're looking to download the code files.
6. Choose from the drop-down menu where you purchased this book from.
7. Click on **Code Download**.

Once the file is downloaded, please make sure that you unzip or extract the folder using the latest version of:

- WinRAR / 7-Zip for Windows
- Zipeg / iZip / UnRarX for Mac
- 7-Zip / PeaZip for Linux

Downloading the color images of this book

We also provide you with a PDF file that has color images of the screenshots/diagrams used in this book. The color images will help you better understand the changes in the output. You can download this file from `https://www.packtpub.com/sites/default/files/downloads/OpenLayers3xCookbook_ColorImages.pdf`.

Errata

Although we have taken every care to ensure the accuracy of our content, mistakes do happen. If you find a mistake in one of our books—maybe a mistake in the text or the code—we would be grateful if you could report this to us. By doing so, you can save other readers from frustration and help us improve subsequent versions of this book. If you find any errata, please report them by visiting `http://www.packtpub.com/submit-errata`, selecting your book, clicking on the **Errata Submission Form** link, and entering the details of your errata. Once your errata are verified, your submission will be accepted and the errata will be uploaded to our website or added to any list of existing errata under the Errata section of that title.

To view the previously submitted errata, go to `https://www.packtpub.com/books/content/support` and enter the name of the book in the search field. The required information will appear under the **Errata** section.

Piracy

Piracy of copyrighted material on the Internet is an ongoing problem across all media. At Packt, we take the protection of our copyright and licenses very seriously. If you come across any illegal copies of our works in any form on the Internet, please provide us with the location address or website name immediately so that we can pursue a remedy.

Please contact us at `copyright@packtpub.com` with a link to the suspected pirated material.

We appreciate your help in protecting our authors and our ability to bring you valuable content.

Questions

If you have a problem with any aspect of this book, you can contact us at `questions@packtpub.com`, and we will do our best to address the problem.

1
Web Mapping Basics

In this chapter, we cover the following topics:

- ▸ Creating a simple fullscreen map
- ▸ Playing with the map's options
- ▸ Managing the map's stack layers
- ▸ Managing the map's controls
- ▸ Moving around the map view
- ▸ Restricting the map's extent

Introduction

This chapter shows us the basics and the important things that we need to know when we start creating our first web-mapping application with OpenLayers.

As we will see in this and the following chapters, OpenLayers is a big and complex framework, but at the same time, it is also very powerful and flexible.

Although we're now spoilt for choice when it comes to picking a JavaScript mapping library (as we are with most JavaScript libraries and frameworks), OpenLayers is a mature, fully-featured, and well-supported library.

In contrast to other libraries, such as *Leaflet* (`http://leafletjs.com`), which focuses on a smaller download size in order to provide only the most common functionality as standard, OpenLayers tries to implement all the required things that a developer could need to create a web **Geographic Information System** (**GIS**) application.

One aspect of OpenLayers 3 that immediately differentiates itself from OpenLayers 2, is that it's been built with the **Google Closure library** (`https://developers.google.com/closure`). Google Closure provides an extensive range of modular cross-browser JavaScript utility methods that OpenLayers 3 selectively includes.

OpenLayers 3 packs a smaller footprint than its predecessor and targets the latest HTML5 and CCS3 capabilities. The trade off, of course, is that legacy browsers will not be as fully featured (primarily, Internet Explorer lower than version 9). As the rate of modern browser adoption ever increases, this disadvantage will soon become a moot point.

The main concept in OpenLayers is, rightly, the map. It represents the view where information is rendered. The map can contain multiple layers, which can be raster or vector layers. Each layer has a data source that serves data with its own format: a `.PNG` image, a `.KML` file, and so on. In addition, the map can contain controls, which help interact with the map and its contents; these are pan, zoom, feature selection, and so on.

Let's get started with learning OpenLayers by examples.

Creating a simple fullscreen map

When you work in mapping applications, the first and foremost task is the creation of the map itself. The map plays a core role in your application, and this is where you will add and visualize data.

This recipe will guide you through the process of creating our first and very simple web map application.

Getting ready

Programming with OpenLayers mainly boils down to writing HTML, CSS, and, of course, JavaScript. We simply need a text editor to start coding up our recipes. There is a wide variety of text editors available, so just take your pick!

Our HTML file will include some OpenLayers library assets. Although you'll see our examples referencing these assets, we won't show you the file contents of these large files in this book. In order to follow along, begin by downloading the latest OpenLayers source code (`http://openlayers.org/download/`).

You can find the source code for this example in `ch01/ch01-full-screen-map/`.

How to do it...

1. Let's start by first creating a new HTML file with the following content:

```html
<!doctype html>
<html>
<head>
  <meta charset="utf-8">
  <title>Creating a simple full screen map | Chapter
    1</title>
  <link rel="stylesheet" href="ol.css">
  <link rel="stylesheet" href="style.css">
</head>
<body>
  <div id="js-map" class="map"></div>
  <script src="ol.js"></script>
  <script src="script.js"></script>
</body>
</html>
```

You'll notice that the OpenLayers files being linked to here are `ol.css` and `ol.js`. Our own custom files are `style.css` and `script.js`.

The OpenLayers CSS (`ol.css`) contains CSS3 animations and styling for HTML elements, such as map controls, that is, the map zooming buttons, and much more.

Using best practices, the OpenLayers JavaScript (`ol.js`) and our own custom JavaScript file has been included just before the closing `</body>` tag to avoid blocking page rendering. Another positive outcome of this is that we can be assured the DOM has loaded before executing our JavaScript.

2. Next, create a stylesheet (`style.css`) with the following content:

```css
.map {
  position: absolute;
  top: 0;
  bottom: 0;
  left: 0;
  right: 0;
}
```

This combined set of CSS rules results in expanding `div` so that it completely fills the page's available space. Using the `.map` class selector means that this will target our `<div>` element that was created earlier:

```html
<div id="js-map" class="map"></div>
```

Downloading the example code

You can download the example code files for all Packt Publishing books that you have purchased from your account at `http://www.packtpub.com`. If you purchased this book elsewhere, you can visit `http://www.packtpub.com/support` and register to have the files e-mailed directly to you.

You can download the code files by following these steps:

- Log in or register to our website using your e-mail address and password.
- Hover the mouse pointer on the SUPPORT tab at the top.
- Click on Code Downloads & Errata.
- Enter the name of the book in the Search box.
- Select the book for which you're looking to download the code files.
- Choose from the drop-down menu where you purchased this book from.
- Click on Code Download.

Once the file is downloaded, please make sure that you unzip or extract the folder using the latest version of:

- WinRAR / 7-Zip for Windows
- Zipeg / iZip / UnRarX for Mac
- 7-Zip / PeaZip for Linux

3. Lastly, create our custom JavaScript file (`script.js`) and place the following content in it:

```
var map = new ol.Map({
  view: new ol.View({
    center: [-15000, 6700000],
    zoom: 5
  }),
  layers: [
    new ol.layer.Tile({
      source: new ol.source.OSM()
    })
  ],
  target: 'js-map'
});
```

Open the file in your browser and witness the result. You will see a map that fills the page with some controls in the top-left corner and map attribution in the bottom-right corner, which is similar to what's shown in the following screenshot:

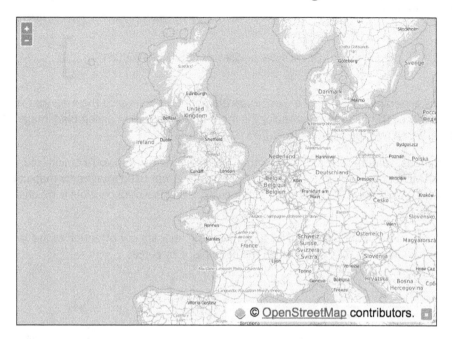

How it works...

It's pleasing to realize that creating a map with OpenLayers can be quickly achieved with minimal code. However, we aren't reading this book to stand back in awe, we'd rather try to understand how JavaScript has accomplished this.

Initially, it's worth examining the HTML because OpenLayers has been busy making amendments. You'll need to open up your browser development tools. This is normally as easy as right-clicking anywhere on the page and selecting **Inspect Element** from the context menu. Scroll down to our `<div>` element that we originally created. It should look similar to the following screenshot:

```
▼<div id="js-map" class="map">
  ▼<div class="ol-viewport" style="position: relative; overflow: hidden; width: 100%; height: 100%;">
    <canvas class="ol-unselectable" width="1197" height="861" style="width: 100%; height: 100%;">
    <div class="ol-overlaycontainer"></div>
    ▶<div class="ol-overlaycontainer-stopevent">…</div>
  </div>
</div>
```

You'll notice that OpenLayers has modified the content of our previously empty `<div>`, and inserted a `<div class="ol-viewport">` child element, which expands to the total dimensions of the parent element, which we set to fill the screen. You control the size of the map completely through CSS.

 OpenLayers prefixes its CSS hooks with `ol-`.

Within this generated `<div>` lies a `<canvas>` element that makes up the map that you see before you. The HTML5 canvas technology is more performant than assembled image DOM elements, which was the default structure in OpenLayers 2.

For the curious, venture further into the other `<div>` elements, and you'll quickly stumble into the HTML for the map controls. Unlike OpenLayers 2 that used images for map controls, OpenLayers 3 uses only CSS. This means that customizing the map controls is much easier than before.

Let's pull ourselves out of the HTML for a moment and relocate our attention to the JavaScript that got this all working. We'll go through the code piece by piece:

```
var map = new ol.Map({
   // ...
});
```

The `ol.Map` constructor is our entry point to create a map. On instantiation, part of what happens involves the creation of the HTML elements that we looked over earlier. At a minimum, the constructor requires a view, one or more layers, and a target as it's arguments:

```
view: new ol.View({
   center: [-15000, 6700000],
   zoom: 5
}),
```

To help us understand the separate steps required to create a map, let's imagine the following analogy. Let's suppose that the map is a vast and scenic world that you're only able to view through binoculars and `ol.View` is the binoculars. You can tilt your head and spin around (view rotation), move your line of sight to point to somewhere else (changing your view center) and adjust focus for varying objects at a distance (zoom/resolution).

With this analogy in mind, we use our binoculars (the view) to set the starting position. The center xy coordinates are passed in via an array (we'll explore coordinates and projections in more detail as this book progresses). We also provide a zoom level. We have selectively created a subset viewport of the world.

```
layers: [
   new ol.layer.Tile({
```

```
      source: new ol.source.OSM()
    })
  ],
```

The `layers` property of `ol.Map` expects an array, as you can include multiple layers per map.

The `ol.layer.Tile` constructor is a subclass of `ol.layer.Layer`, but it is specifically designed for prerendered tiled images that are structured in grids and organized by zoom levels for specific resolutions.

The source of the tiled layer is derived from the `ol.source.OSM` constructor, which enables us to effortlessly use the OpenStreetMap tile service. This constructor is a subclass of `ol.source.XYZ`, which is the format that OSM uses.

```
  target: 'js-map'
```

Lastly, the `target` property of `ol.Map` can either be a string (which must represent the ID of the HTML element), or you can pass in a DOM element instead. Our string, `'js-map'`, matches up with our HTML element:

```
<div id="js-map" class="map"></div>
```

Alternatively, we could have passed in the DOM element:

```
  target: document.getElementById('js-map')
```

Now that we've covered all the parts of this puzzle, we hope that you've been able to get a better insight behind what's actually going on. This basic knowledge will help you build a solid foundation as we keep moving forward.

There's more...

In our first example, we used up as much of the web page as possible, but we all know that this is not quite the definition of fullscreen! To actually go properly fullscreen, OpenLayers can make use of the HTML5 fullscreen API.

You can find the source code for this example in `ch01/ch01-html5-full-screen-map/`.

Keep the HTML and CSS exactly the same as the previous version, but modify the JavaScript so that it matches the following:

```
var map = new ol.Map({
  view: new ol.View({
    center: [-15000, 6700000],
    zoom: 5
  }),
  layers: [
    new ol.layer.Tile({
```

```
      source: new ol.source.OSM()
   })
 ],
 controls: ol.control.defaults().extend([
   new ol.control.FullScreen()
 ]),
 target: 'js-map'
});
```

The watchful among you may have noticed that regardless of the fact that we didn't pass in any controls to our previous version of the map, it still contained the zoom and attribution controls. This is because OpenLayers adds some default controls if none are specified.

```
controls: ol.control.defaults().extend([
  new ol.control.FullScreen()
]),
```

We have decided to extend the default controls that OpenLayers normally provides and append the fullscreen control. The extend utility method comes from the Google Closure library, which extends an object with another object in place.

Open the file in your browser and you'll see the new fullscreen control at the top-right corner of the map. Click the button to go fullscreen!

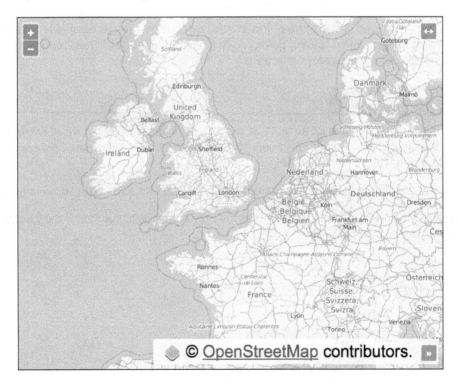

If we wanted to just enable the fullscreen control with no others, we can use the following code:

```
controls: [
        new ol.control.FullScreen()
],
```

Although we're passing in just a single control, OpenLayers expects a collection, so it's wrapped inside an array.

We finish this topic having learned how to create a new map from scratch with some custom controls. It's time to move on to the next topic!

Playing with the map's options

When you create a map to visualize data, there are some important things that you need to take into account: the projection to use, the available zoom levels, the default tile size to be used by the layer requests, and so on. Most of these important pieces are enclosed in the map's properties.

This recipe shows you how to set some common map properties. You can find the source code for this recipe in `ch01/ch01-map-options/`.

Getting ready

When you instantiate a new `ol.Map` instance, you have the option to pass in all the properties as an object literal—this is what we did in the first recipe. In the next recipe, you will take a look at a different way of achieving a similar result through the use of setter methods.

How to do it...

1. Just like we did in the first recipe, create an HTML page to house the map, include the OpenLayers dependencies and, add our custom CSS and JavaScript files. This time, place the following CSS into your custom style sheet:

    ```
    .map {
      position: absolute;
      top: 0;
      bottom: 0;
      left: 0;
      right: 0;
    }
    .ol-mouse-position {
      top: inherit;
      bottom: 8px;
      left: 8px;
    ```

```
      background-color: rgba(255,255,255,0.4);
      border-radius: 2px;
      width: 100px;
      text-align: center;
      font-family: Arial, sans-serif;
      font-size: 12px;
   }
```

2. Put the following in your custom JavaScript file:

```
var map = new ol.Map({
   layers: [
     new ol.layer.Tile({
        source: new ol.source.OSM()
     })
   ]
});

var mousePositionControl = new ol.control.MousePosition({
   coordinateFormat: ol.coordinate.createStringXY(2),
   projection: 'EPSG:4326'
});

map.addControl(mousePositionControl);
map.setTarget('js-map');

var view = new ol.View({
   zoom: 4,
   projection: 'EPSG:3857',
   maxZoom: 6,
   minZoom: 3,
   rotation: 0.34 // 20 degrees
});

view.setCenter([-10800000, 4510000]);

map.setView(view);
```

If you now open this file up in your browser, you'll see something similar to the following screenshot:

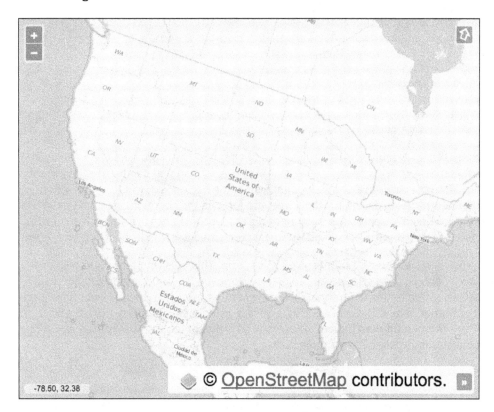

How it works...

Aside from the CSS to create the fullscreen map, we've also added some new CSS rules that style the mouse position control on the map (bottom-left). This demonstrates the ease of styling map controls with a bit of simple CSS. The default class name for the mouse position control is `.ol-mouse-position`, which we use to override the default CSS.

We've introduced some new methods and properties in this recipe, so let's go over the JavaScript together:

```javascript
var map = new ol.Map({
  layers: [
    new ol.layer.Tile({
      source: new ol.source.OSM()
    })
  ]
});
```

When instantiating a new instance of `ol.Map`, we've passed in only the `layers` property at this point and saved a reference to the map instance in a variable named `map`.

```
var mousePositionControl = new ol.control.MousePosition({
    coordinateFormat: ol.coordinate.createStringXY(2),
    projection: 'EPSG:4326'
});
```

There's quite a bit going on in this snippet of JavaScript that we haven't seen before. When instantiating this new mouse position control, we passed in an object containing some additional settings.

The `coordinateFormat` property allows us to alter how the coordinates are displayed. This property expects an `ol.CoordinateFormatType` function that can be used to format an `ol.coordinate` array to a string. In other words, the `ol.coordinate.createStringXY` function returns the expected function type and formats the coordinates into a string, which we see onscreen. We specify the number of digits to include after the decimal point to 2. Coordinates can get rather long, and we're not concerned with the level of accuracy here!

Let's take a look at the next property, `projection`. This tells OpenLayers to display the coordinates in the `EPSG:4326` projection. However, the default map projection is `EPSG:3857`. Due to this difference, OpenLayers must transform the projection from one type to another behind the scenes. If you were to remove this property from the control, it'll inherit the default map projection and you'll be presented with very different looking coordinates (in the `EPSG:3857` projection).

The `EPSG:4326` and `EPSG:3857` projections are boxed up with OpenLayers as standard. When you start dealing with other worldwide projections, you'll need to manually include the projection conversions yourself. Don't worry because there's a library for exactly this purpose, and we'll cover this later in this book.

```
map.addControl(mousePositionControl);
```

We then add the mouse position control to the map instance using the `addControl` method. This implicitly extends the default map controls.

```
map.setTarget('js-map');
```

We use one of the map setter methods to add the `target` property and value.

```
var view = new ol.View({
    zoom: 4,
    projection: 'EPSG:3857',
    maxZoom: 6,
    minZoom: 3,
    rotation: 0.34 // 20 degrees
});
```

We've introduced some new view properties with this instantiation of the view: `projection`, `maxZoom`, `minZoom`, and `rotation`.

The `projection` option is used to set the projection that is used by the map view to render data from layers. The projection of `EPSG:3857` actually matches the default projection, and it is also the projection that OpenStreetMap uses (which is important, as you need to be sure that the tile service accepts the type of projection). We've explicitly set it here only for demonstration purposes.

Setting the `maxZoom` and `minZoom` properties creates a restricted zoom range. This means that the user can only view a subset of the available zoom levels. In this case, they cannot zoom further out than zoom level 3, and further in than zoom level 6.

The `rotation` property rotates the map by a specified amount in radians. You'll notice that once you've set a rotation, OpenLayers automatically adds a rotation control to the map. In the case of this example, it appeared at the top-right. If you're feeling disorientated you can click this button and it will reset the map rotation back to O for you.

```
view.setCenter([-10800000, 4510000]);
```

As we stored the `view` instance in a variable, we can easily add additional properties just like we did for the `map` instance. Here, we use a setter method on `view` to set the initial center position of the map.

```
map.setView(view);
```

Finally, we add the completed `view` instance to the map instance using another helpful map method, `setView`.

> For projections other than `EPSG:4326` and `EPSG:3857`, you need to include the `Proj4js` project (`http://proj4js.org`) in your web application. This is discussed later in this book.
>
> EPSG codes are a way to name and classify the set of available projections. The site Coordinate Systems Worldwide (`http://epsg.io/`) is a great place to find more information about them.

There's more...

The `EPSG:4326` projection is also known as *WGS84*, which is measured in degree units. The `EPSG:3857` projection is also know as *Spherical Mercator*, which is in meter unit coordinates.

Imagery from sources such as Google Maps or OpenStreetMap are special cases where the pyramid of images is previously created with the Spherical Mercator projection—`EPSG:3857`. This means that you can't set the projection when requesting tiles because it is implicit.

If you put a layer in a different projection other than the one used by the map view, then it won't work as expected.

 Services such as Google Maps and OpenStreetMap have prerendered rasterized images or tiles, that make up the extent of the world. This saves servers from rendering images on demand, which means that more requests can be processed in a timely manner. The images form a pyramid tiling pattern, whereby at the smallest scale, there are fewer tiles (top of the pyramid), and as the scale is increased, more tiles make up the region (bottom of the pyramid). You can find a good explanation and also some interesting history behind this pattern's inception here: `https://www.e-education.psu.edu/geog585/node/706`.

See also

- ▸ The *Managing the map's stack layers* recipe
- ▸ The *Managing the map's controls* recipe
- ▸ The *Working with projections* recipe in *Chapter 7, Beyond the Basics*.

Managing the map's stack layers

An OpenLayers map allows us to visualize information from different kinds of layers, and it brings us methods to manage the layers that are attached to it.

In this recipe, we'll learn some techniques on how to control the layers: adding, grouping, managing the stack order, and other layer manipulation. Learning these very common operations is important because these types of tasks will be required on almost every web-mapping application.

The application will display a map on the left and a control panel on the right with a list of layers, which can be dragged, that you'll be able to sort. Here's what we'll end up with:

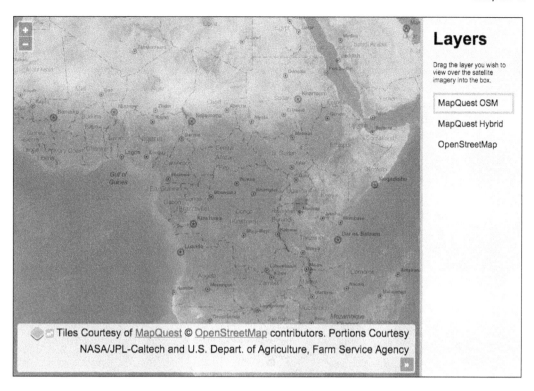

You can find the source code for this recipe in `ch01/ch01-map-layers/`.

When creating widgets such as a sortable list in this recipe, we're going to use the jQuery UI library (`https://jqueryui.com`), which has a single dependency on jQuery (`https://jquery.com`). Doing so will help us focus our attention towards the OpenLayers code, rather than the general JavaScript code that is used to create advanced UI components.

How to do it...

1. We start by creating an HTML file to organize the application layout and link to resources:

```
<!doctype html>
<html>
<head>
  <meta charset="utf-8">
  <title>Managing map's stack layers | Chapter 1</title>
  <link rel="stylesheet" href="ol.css">
```

```
    <link rel="stylesheet" href="style.css">
</head>
<body>
    <div id="js-map" class="map"></div>
    <div class="pane">
        <h1>Layers</h1>
        <p>Drag the layer you wish to view over the satellite imagery
into the box.</p>
        <ul id="js-layers" class="layers"></ul>
    </div>
    <script src="ol.js"></script>
    <script src="jquery.js"></script>
    <script src="jquery-ui.js"></script>
    <script src="script.js"></script>
</body>
</html>
```

2. Create the CSS file, `style.css`, and add the following content in it:

```
.map {
    position: absolute;
    top: 0;
    bottom: 0;
    left: 0;
    right: 20%;
}

.pane {
    position: absolute;
    top: 0;
    bottom: 0;
    right: 0;
    width: 20%;
    background: ghostwhite;
    border-left: 5px solid lightsteelblue;
    box-sizing: border-box;
    padding: 0 20px;
}

.layers {
    cursor: move;
    list-style: none;
    padding: 0;
```

```css
  position: relative;
}

.layers::before {
  content: '';
  display: block;
  position: absolute;
  top: 0;
  height: 30px;
  width: 100%;
  border: 4px solid lightsteelblue;
  z-index: 0;
}

.layers li {
  z-index: 1;
  position: relative;
  line-height: 38px;
  display: block;
  height: 38px;
  padding: 0 10px;
}
```

3. Create the `script.js` JavaScript file and add the following in it:

```javascript
var map = new ol.Map({
  layers: [
    new ol.layer.Tile({
      source: new ol.source.MapQuest({
        layer: 'sat'
      }),
      opacity: 0.5,
      zIndex: 1
    })
  ],
  view: new ol.View({
    zoom: 4,
    center: [2120000, 0]
  }),
  target: 'js-map'
});

var layerGroup = new ol.layer.Group({
  layers: [
```

```
      new ol.layer.Tile({
        source: new ol.source.MapQuest({
          layer: 'osm'
        }),
        title: 'MapQuest OSM'
      }),
      new ol.layer.Tile({
        source: new ol.source.MapQuest({
          layer: 'hyb'
        }),
        title: 'MapQuest Hybrid',
        visible: false
      }),
      new ol.layer.Tile({
        source: new ol.source.OSM(),
        title: 'OpenStreetMap',
        visible: false
      })
    ],
    zIndex: 0
});

map.addLayer(layerGroup);

var $layersList = $('#js-layers');

layerGroup.getLayers().forEach(function(element, index, array) {
  var $li = $('<li />');
  $li.text(element.get('title'));
  $layersList.append($li);
});

$layersList.sortable({
  update: function() {
    var topLayer = $layersList.find('li:first-child').text();

    layerGroup.getLayers().forEach(function(element) {
      element.setVisible(element.get('title') === topLayer);
    });
  }
});
```

How it works...

The HTML contains the markup for the map and the control panel. As mentioned earlier in this recipe, we've linked to local copies of jQuery UI and jQuery. If you're not using the provided source code, you'll need to download these libraries yourself in order to follow along.

The CSS organizes the layout so that the map takes up 80% width of the screen with 20% left over for the control panel. It also provides the styling for the list of layers so that the first item in the list is outlined to represent the layer that is currently in view. We won't go into any more detail about the CSS, as we'd like to spend more of our time taking a closer look at the OpenLayers code instead.

Let's begin by breaking down the code in our custom JavaScript file:

```
var map = new ol.Map({
  layers: [
    new ol.layer.Tile({
      source: new ol.source.MapQuest({
        layer: 'sat'
      }),
      opacity: 0.5,
      zIndex: 1
    })
  ],
  view: new ol.View({
    zoom: 4,
    center: [2120000, 0]
  }),
  target: 'js-map'
});
```

We've introduced a new layer source here, `ol.source.MapQuest`. OpenLayers provides easy access to this tile service that offers multiple types of `layers`, from which we've chosen type `sat`, which is an abbreviation of satellite. We're going to use this layer as our always-visible backdrop. In order to produce this desired effect, we've passed in some properties to `ol.layer.Tile` to set `opacity` to 50% (`0.5`) and `zIndex` to 1.

The reason why we set `zIndex` to 1 is to ensure that this layer is not hidden by the layer group that's added on top of this layer. This will be better explained when we continue looking through the next piece of code, as follows:

```
var layerGroup = new ol.layer.Group({
  layers: [
    new ol.layer.Tile({
      source: new ol.source.MapQuest({
```

```
        layer: 'osm'
      }),
      title: 'MapQuest OSM'
    }),
    new ol.layer.Tile({
      source: new ol.source.MapQuest({
        layer: 'hyb'
      }),
      title: 'MapQuest Hybrid',
      visible: false
    }),
    new ol.layer.Tile({
      source: new ol.source.OSM(),
      title: 'OpenStreetMap',
      visible: false
    })
  ],
  zIndex: 0
});
```

We instantiate a new instance of `ol.layer.Group`, which expects a layers collection. One useful benefit of creating a layer group is when you want to apply the same actions against many layers at once, such as setting a property.

We instantiate three new instances of `ol.layer.Tile`, two of which are different layer types offered from `ol.source.MapQuest` (osm and hyb). The other tile service source is the familiar `ol.source.OSM` layer source (OpenStreetMap) from previous recipes.

We have set the `visible` property on two of the three tile layers to `false`. When the page loads, the `MapQuest osm` layer will be the only visible layer from this layer group.

Optionally, we could have set the `opacity` to 0 for the layers that we didn't want to display. However, there's a performance benefit from setting the visibility to `false`, as OpenLayers doesn't make any unnecessary HTTP requests for the tiles of layers that aren't visible.

The `title` property that we set on each layer isn't actually part of the OpenLayers API. This is a custom property, and we could have named it almost anything. This allows us to create arbitrary properties and values on the `layer` objects, which we can later reference in our application. We will use the title information for some layer-switching logic and to display this text in the UI.

Lastly, a customization has been applied to all the layers inside the `layer` group by setting the `zIndex` property to 0 on the layer group instance. However, why have we done this?

Internally, OpenLayers stores `layers` in an array, and they are rendered in the same order that they are stored in the array (so the first element is the bottom layer). You can think of the map as storing layers in a stack and they are rendered from bottom to top, so the above layers can hide beneath the below layers depending on opacity and extent.

With this in mind, when this layer group is added to the map, it'll naturally render above our first layer containing the satellite imagery. As the layers in the group are all opaque, this will result in hiding the satellite imagery layer. However, by manually manipulating the map layer stack order, we force the layer group to be at the bottom of the stack by setting `zIndex` to `0`, and we force the satellite imagery layer to the top of the stack by setting `zIndex` to `1` so that it'll render above this layer group.

> The default `zIndex` property for a layer group is `0` anyway. This means that we could have just set the `zIndex` property of the satellite layer to `1`, and this would leave us with the same result. We've explicitly set this here to help explain what's going on.

As we always want our satellite imagery on top, it's also worth mentioning that `ol.layer.Layer` offers a `setMap` method. The tile layer (`ol.layer.Tile`) is a subclass of `ol.layer.Layer`, so if we added the satellite imagery tile layer to the map via the `setMap` method, we wouldn't need to manually adjust the `zIndex` property ourselves because it would automatically appear on top. In any case, this was a good opportunity to show `zIndex` ordering in action.

```
map.addLayer(layerGroup);
```

The layer group is simply added to the map instance. You'll notice that this method can be used to add a single layer or a group of layers.

```
var $layersList = $('#js-layers');
layerGroup.getLayers().forEach(function(element, index, array) {
  var $li = $('<li />');
  $li.text(element.get('title'));
  $layersList.append($li);
});
```

Now, we begin to take advantage of the jQuery library in order to perform some DOM operations. We store the element of the `js-layers` ID into a variable, namely `$layersList`. Prefixing the variable with a dollar symbol is a convention to represent the result as a jQuery object. This selector will target this HTML from earlier:

```
<ul id="js-layers" class="layers"></ul>
```

In order to populate the list of layers dynamically in the panel, we use a method from the layer group instance called `getLayers`. This returns a list (`ol.collection`) of all the layers for the given group, which we then chain to the `forEach` method (another method available from `ol.collection`).

Internally, the `forEach` method calls a utility method from the Google Closure library. The available parameters within this `forEach` method are element, index, and array. The element is the layer at iteration, index is the position of this layer within the group at iteration, and array is the group of layers that we're looping over. In our case, we only make use of the element parameter.

We use jQuery to create a `li` element and set the text content. The text value is derived from the layer's title value—this is the custom property that we gave to each layer in the group in order to identify them. OpenLayers provides a handy `get` method for the retrieval of this value. We then use jQuery to append this `li` element to the `ul` element.

```
$layersList.sortable({
  update: function() {
    var topLayer = $layersList.find('li:first-child').text();

    layerGroup.getLayers().forEach(function(element) {
      element.setVisible(element.get('title') === topLayer);
    });
  }
});
```

In order to enable list items to be reordered, we use the jQuery UI sortable widget and apply it to the list of layers in the HTML. Once an item on the list has been moved, the update event is triggered; this is where we perform some OpenLayers logic.

The text content of the topmost layer is fetched, as this is the layer the user wishes to see. The text is stored inside the `topLayer` variable. This text will correspond to one of the layer titles.

We use the same `getLayers` method on the layer group and the `forEach` method on the `ol.collection` as before. Depending on whether or not the text matches the layer title, we toggle the layer visibility accordingly with the `setVisible` method.

There's more...

For this recipe, we chose to display only one other additional layer at a time. If you need to keep all layers visible and instead dynamically change the stack order of layers, you can use the layer `setZIndex` method to manage which layers are above other layers.

With a collection of layers, such as what's returned with `ol.Map.getLayers()`, you can use the `setAt` method on the `ol.collection` layers object to reorder layers, which, subsequently, alters their stacking order. This is effectively the same as changing the `zIndex` property.

There are plenty of other methods to manipulate map layers. We have seen only a few in this recipe: adding, setting standard and arbitrary properties, layer stack ordering, and so on. However, you can find more methods, such as layer/layer group removal, changing the layer source, and much more.

See also

▶ The *Managing the map's controls* recipe

▶ The *Moving around the map view* recipe

▶ The *Restricting the map extent* recipe

Managing the map's controls

OpenLayers comes with lots of controls to interact with the map, such as pan, zoom, show overview map, edit features, and so on.

In the same way as `layers`, the `ol.Map` class has methods to manage the controls that are attached to the map.

We're going to create a way to toggle map controls on or off. The source code can be found in `ch01/ch01-map-controls/`. Here's what we'll end up with:

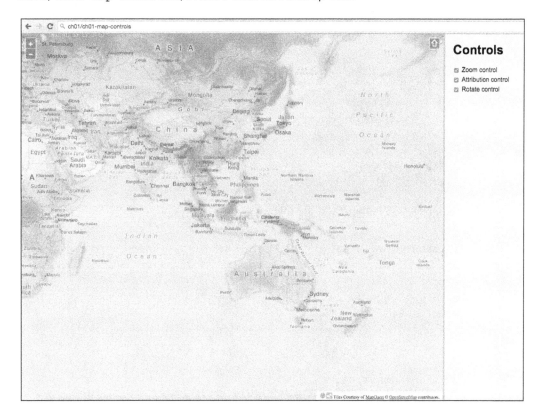

How to do it...

1. Create a new HTML file and add the OpenLayers dependencies as well as the jQuery library. In particular, add the following markup to the body:

```
<div id="js-map" class="map"></div>
<div class="pane">
  <h1>Controls</h1>
  <ul id="js-controls">
    <li>
      <label>
        <input type="checkbox" checked value="zoomControl">
        <span>Zoom control</span>
      </label>
    </li>
    <li>
      <label>
        <input type="checkbox" checked value="attributionControl">
        <span>Attribution control</span>
      </label>
    </li>
    <li>
      <label>
        <input type="checkbox" checked value="rotateControl">
        <span>Rotate control</span>
      </label>
    </li>
  </ul>
</div>
```

2. Create a new CSS file and add the following:

```
.map {
  position: absolute;
  top: 0;
  bottom: 0;
  left: 0;
  right: 20%;
}

.pane {
  position: absolute;
  top: 0;
  bottom: 0;
  right: 0;
```

```
    width: 20%;
    background: ghostwhite;
    border-left: 5px solid lightsteelblue;
    box-sizing: border-box;
    padding: 0 20px;
}
```

3. Create a new script file and create the map, as follows:

```
var map = new ol.Map({
  layers: [
    new ol.layer.Tile({
      source: new ol.source.MapQuest({
        layer: 'osm'
      })
    })
  ],
  view: new ol.View({
    center: [12930000, -78000],
    zoom: 3
  }),
  target: 'js-map',
  controls: []
});
```

4. Create some controls and add them to the map, as follows:

```
var zoomControl = new ol.control.Zoom({
  zoomInTipLabel: 'Zoom closer in',
  zoomOutTipLabel: 'Zoom further out',
  className: 'ol-zoom custom-zoom-control'
});

var attributionControl = new ol.control.Attribution({
  collapsible: false,
  collapsed: false
});

var rotateControl = new ol.control.Rotate({
  autoHide: false
});

map.addControl(zoomControl);
map.addControl(attributionControl);
map.addControl(rotateControl);
```

5. Finally, enable the control toggle logic:

```
$('#js-controls').on('change', function(event) {
  var target = $(event.target);
  var control = target.val();

  if (target.prop('checked')) {
    map.addControl(window[control]);
  } else {
    map.removeControl(window[control]);
  }
});
```

How it works...

Our HTML and CSS divide up the page so that it contains the map and a control panel. Within this panel are three checkboxes that correspond to the three controls that will be added to the map. Toggling the checkboxes will, in turn, add or remove the selected controls.

It's important to note that the value of the checkboxes match up with the variable names of the controls in the JavaScript. For example, `value="zoomControl"` will link to the map control variable named `zoomControl`.

Let's pick apart the OpenLayers code to find out how this works:

```
var map = new ol.Map({

// ...
  controls: []
});
```

This map instantiation code will be familiar from the previous recipes, but note that because we don't want OpenLayers to set any default controls on the map, we explicitly pass an empty array to the `controls` property.

```
var zoomControl = new ol.control.Zoom({
  zoomInTipLabel: 'Zoom closer in',
  zoomOutTipLabel: 'Zoom further out',
  className: 'ol-zoom custom-zoom-control'
});
```

We store a reference to the zoom control inside the `zoomControl` variable. We've decided to customize the tool tips that appear for the plus and minus buttons. The `className` property has also been modified to include both the default class name for the zoom control (`ol-zoom`) in order to inherit the default OpenLayers styling and a custom class of `custom-zoom-control`. We can use this custom class name as a CSS hook for any of our own styles that override the defaults.

```
var attributionControl = new ol.control.Attribution({
  collapsible: false,
  collapsed: false
});
```

We store a reference to the attribution control inside the `attributionControl` variable. This control normally allows the user to collapse the attribution, and it's initial state is collapsed by default. By specifying these two properties, we have inverted the defaults.

```
var rotateControl = new ol.control.Rotate({
  autoHide: false
});
```

We store a reference to the rotate control inside the `rotateControl` variable. Normally, this control is only displayed when the map rotation is anything other than 0. We explicitly set this control to not automatically hide itself.

```
map.addControl(zoomControl);
map.addControl(attributionControl);
map.addControl(rotateControl);
```

All three controls are added to the `map` instance.

```
$('#js-controls').on('change', function(event) {
  var target = $(event.target);
  var control = target.val();

  if (target.prop('checked')) {
    map.addControl(window[control]);
  } else {
    map.removeControl(window[control]);
  }
});
```

We take advantage of event bubbling in JavaScript and attach a single change event listener to the HTML containing the list of layers; this is more efficient than attaching an event listener to each input element.

When a checkbox is toggled, this event handler is executed. The event target (the checkbox) is cached inside the `target` variable as it's used more than once. The value of the checkbox (which is also the name of the map control) is stored inside the `control` variable.

The new state of the checkbox for this control is passed into the `if` statement. If this is enabled, we add the control to the map with the `ol.Map` method, `addControl`. Otherwise, we remove the control from the map with the opposite `ol.Map` method, `removeControl`.

We use the checkbox value to select the matching OpenLayers control from the `window` object using array notation. The control's variable name (for example, `zoomControl`) will be the same as the checkbox value (for example, `zoomControl`), which is how this link is forged.

All controls are a subclass of `ol.control.Control`. This means that any controls extended off this class will inherit the `ol.Object` methods (such as `get` and `set`), as well as other functions, such as `getMap`, which informs you which map this control is attached to. The `ol.control.Control` class makes creating custom controls much easier—a recipe that's covered later on in this book.

See also

▸ The *Managing the map's stack layers* recipe

▸ The *Moving around the map view* recipe

Moving around the map view

Unless you want to create a completely static map without the controls required for users to pan, zoom or rotate, you would like the user to be able to navigate and explore the map.

There can be situations when the built-in controls are not enough. Imagine a web application where the user can search for a term, such as *'Everest'*, and the application must find its location and pan to it. In this case, you need to navigate by code and not using a control.

This recipe shows you some programmatic ways to move around the map without using the default controls. The source code can be found in `ch01/ch01-moving-around`, and here's what we'll end up with:

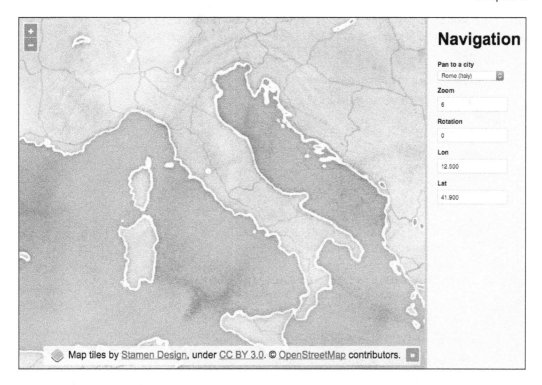

The application contains a selection of European cities, which when changed will pan the map to the selected city. The current zoom, rotation, longitude, and latitude values are kept up-to-date with map interactions. These input fields can also be manually edited to update their respective map properties.

We've omitted the full HTML and CSS code that is necessary to create the application layout; so, if you are interested in the complete code, you can take a look at the source code available on the Packt Publishing website.

How to do it...

1. Create an HTML file with OpenLayers dependencies. Most of the HTML will be self explanatory, but in particular, here's the HTML for the city selection menu (this will help our understanding of the JavaScript later on):

```
<select id="js-city">
  <option value="12.5,41.9">Rome (Italy)</option>
  <option value="30.517,50.45">Kiev (Ukraine)</option>
  <option value="-9.183,38.7">Lisbon (Portugal)</option>
```

```
    <option value="-0.117,51.5">London (England)</option>
    <option value="14.417,50.083">Prague (Czech Rep)</option>
</select>
```

2. Create a `map` instance, as follows:

```
var map = new ol.Map({
  layers: [
    new ol.layer.Tile({
      source: new ol.source.Stamen({
        layer: 'watercolor'
      })
    })
  ],
  target: 'js-map',
  view: new ol.View({
    zoom: 6,
    center: ol.proj.fromLonLat([12.5, 41.9])
  })
});
```

3. Cache some DOM elements to reusable variables:

```
var citySelect = document.getElementById('js-city');
var zoomInput = document.getElementById('js-zoom');
var rotateInput = document.getElementById('js-rotate');
var lonInput = document.getElementById('js-lon');
var latInput = document.getElementById('js-lat');
```

4. Add some event listeners to the map view along with an event handler function:

```
var updateUI = function(event) {
  var view = event && event.currentTarget || map.getView();
  zoomInput.value = view.getZoom();
  rotateInput.value = view.getRotation();

  var centerLonLat = ol.proj.toLonLat(view.getCenter());
  lonInput.value = centerLonLat[0].toFixed(3);
  latInput.value = centerLonLat[1].toFixed(3);
};
updateUI();

map.getView().on([
  'change:center',
  'change:resolution',
  'change:rotation'
], updateUI);
```

5. Create a helper function to set the new map view center:

```
var setCenter = function(lon, lat) {
  map.getView().setCenter(ol.proj.fromLonLat([
    parseFloat(lon), parseFloat(lat)
  ]));
};
```

6. Create an event listener and handler for input field updates:

```
window.addEventListener('keyup', function(event) {
  switch(event.target.id) {
    case 'js-zoom':
      map.beforeRender(ol.animation.zoom({
        resolution: map.getView().getResolution(),
        duration: 150
      }));
      map.getView().setZoom(parseInt(event.target.value, 10));
    break;

    case 'js-rotate':
      map.beforeRender(ol.animation.rotate({
        rotation: map.getView().getRotation(),
        duration: 250
      }));
      map.getView().setRotation(parseFloat(event.target.value));
    break;

    case 'js-lon':
      setCenter(event.target.value, latInput.value);
    break;

    case 'js-lat':
      setCenter(lonInput.value, event.target.value);
    break;
  }
});
```

7. Create the event listener and handler for city selections:

```
citySelect.addEventListener('change', function() {
  map.beforeRender(ol.animation.pan({
    source: map.getView().getCenter(),
    duration: 500
  }));
  setCenter.apply(null, this.value.split(','));
});
```

How it works...

There's a fair bit going on here, as we've introduced manual control over a range of map navigation methods. We've also hooked into map events, animations and projection conversions. It's time to take a closer look at what's going on:

```
new ol.layer.Tile({
  source: new ol.source.Stamen({
    layer: 'watercolor'
  })
})
```

The tile service for this recipe is from the *Stamen* source with the watercolor layer style. This is another source that OpenLayers has built-in support for and is made easy to include.

```
view: new ol.View({
  zoom: 6,
  center: ol.proj.fromLonLat([12.5, 41.9])
})
```

For this recipe, we are using longitude and latitude values to navigate around the map. However, the default projection for the map view is `EPSG:3857` (Spherical Mercator) and longitude and latitude is in the `EPSG:4326` projection. We need a way to convert these longitude and latitude coordinates.

Luckily for us, `ol.proj` has many helpful methods, one of which is to convert coordinates from longitude and latitude to `EPSG:3857`, which we've just used. You can also pass a target projection as the second parameter to `fromLonLat`, but the default target projection is `EPSG:3857` anyway, so we don't need to bother.

```
var citySelect = document.getElementById('js-city');
var zoomInput = document.getElementById('js-zoom');
var rotateInput = document.getElementById('js-rotate');
var lonInput = document.getElementById('js-lon');
var latInput = document.getElementById('js-lat');
```

The DOM elements that the user interacts with have been cached into variables for efficiency. We refer to these elements in order to retrieve and update values.

```
var updateUI = function(event) {
  var view = event && event.currentTarget || map.getView();
  zoomInput.value = view.getZoom();
  rotateInput.value = view.getRotation();

  var centerLonLat = ol.proj.toLonLat(view.getCenter());
  lonInput.value = centerLonLat[0].toFixed(3);
```

```
        latInput.value = centerLonLat[1].toFixed(3);
    };
    updateUI();
```

A function called `updateUI` has been created in order to synchronize the input fields with the current map state. This function will either be called upon page initialization or as an event handler. To account for both these scenarios, the map view will derive from either the event argument if it is available (`event.currentTarget` will be the map view in this case), or we grab it ourselves (`map.getView()`). Of course, we could have used `map.getView` in both scenarios, but it's good to familiarize ourselves with some of the available map event properties.

Updating the zoom and rotation values are easy with simple `get` methods offered from the view (`getZoom` and `getRotation`).

The center positions need a little more work. Remember that the map view projection is in `EPSG:3857`, but we want to display the coordinates in longitude and latitude. We do the opposite of what we did before when setting up the view using the `ol.proj.toLonLat` method to convert the coordinates from Spherical Mercator to `EPSG:4326`. This method accepts a second parameter to identify the source projection. The default source projection is `EPSG:3857`, which matches our map view projection anyway, so we can skip specifying this.

The result returns an array, which we store in `centerLonLat`. We then retrieve the respective values for display in the input field and constrain the decimal points to `3`.

```
    map.getView().on([
      'change:center',
      'change:resolution',
      'change:rotation'
    ], updateUI);
```

The `ol.View` class has an `on` method which enables us to subscribe to particular events from the view and specify an event handler. We attach three event listeners to `view`: `center`, `resolution`, and `rotation`. The resolution event listener is for changes in the zoom level. When any of these view properties change, our `updateUI` event handler is called.

```
    var setCenter = function(lon, lat) {
      map.getView().setCenter(ol.proj.fromLonLat([
        parseFloat(lon), parseFloat(lat)
      ]));
    };
```

Within this recipe, we need to set a new center position from a range of different places in the code. To make this a bit easier for ourselves, we've created a `setCenter` function, which takes the `lon` and `lat` values. It converts the provided longitude and latitude coordinates into map projection coordinates and sets the new center position.

As the longitude and latitude values will come from input elements as strings, we pass the values into the `parseFloat` JavaScript method in order to ensure they're in the expected type format for OpenLayers.

```
window.addEventListener('keyup', function(event) {
  switch(event.target.id) {
```

We attach a global `keyup` event listener to the window object rather than adding individual event listeners per input field. When this event handler is called, we determine what actions are performed by inspecting the target element ID attribute through a `switch` statement.

For example, if the zoom input field value is modified, then the target ID will be `js-zoom` because the HTML markup is `<input type="number" id="js-zoom">`:

```
case 'js-zoom':
  map.beforeRender(ol.animation.zoom({
    resolution: map.getView().getResolution(),
    duration: 150
  }));
  map.getView().setZoom(parseInt(event.target.value, 10));
break;
```

The first switch case is for the zoom input field. Instead of simply setting the new zoom level on the map view, we'd prefer to animate the transition between zoom levels. To do this, we add functions to be called before rendering the zoom change via the `ol.Map.beforeRender` method. It expects one or more functions of type `ol.PreRenderFunction`, `ol.animation.zoom` method returns this particular function type, which animates the resolution transition.

The `resolution` property of `ol.animation.zoom` provides the starting point of the animation, which is the current resolution. The `duration` property is given in milliseconds, so this will be a quick and snappy animation.

After we've attached the prerender function, we take the user input value and set the final zoom level (`setZoom`) via the `parseInt` JavaScript method, which ensures that the input field string is converted to the expected number type for OpenLayers.

```
case 'js-rotate':
  map.beforeRender(ol.animation.rotate({
    rotation: map.getView().getRotation(),
    duration: 250
  }));
  map.getView().setRotation(parseFloat(event.target.value));
break;
```

This switch case catches the rotation input field. Similar to the previous zoom control, we want to animate the transition again. To do this, we create a prerender function with `ol.animate.rotate`. We pass in the current rotation of the view and also a custom duration of `250` milliseconds. After this, we set the new rotation amount from the input field value with the `setRotation` map view method. Again, we ensure the input string is converted to a float value for OpenLayers via the `parseFloat` method.

```
case 'js-lon':
  setCenter(event.target.value, latInput.value);
break;

case 'js-lat':
  setCenter(lonInput.value, event.target.value);
break;
```

These switch cases match the longitude and latitude input field changes. Along with the longitude and latitude changes, we've decided to snap to the new center position rather than animate it. We call our own `setCenter` method that was discussed earlier with the longitude and latitude values to use. As the longitude and latitude values are paired, the one that wasn't changed is grabbed from the respective input field.

```
citySelect.addEventListener('change', function() {
  map.beforeRender(ol.animation.pan({
    source: map.getView().getCenter(),
    duration: 500
  }));
  setCenter.apply(null, this.value.split(','));
});
```

Finally, we attach a `change` event to the city selection menu. We've decided to animate the panning from the old center position to the new one. Just like the zoom and rotation transitions, we use the pan-specific `ol.animation.pan` method. We provide the `source` property with the starting position and set a duration of half a second.

Once the prerender function is in place, we can set the new center position. Once again, we call our custom `setCenter` function to do this for us.

The HTML for a specific option in the city selection menu contains the longitude and latitude values as a string. For example, if we want to pan to London, the value inside the option is a comma delimited `string`: `<option value="-0.117,51.5">London (England)</option>`. We convert this string (`"-0.117,51.5"`) into an array with the JavaScript `split` method to provide a distinct separation of the values. However, our `setCenter` function expects two parameters, not an array of values. To get around this, we use the JavaScript `apply` method, which calls `setCenter` with an array of arguments, producing the same result.

This completes a thorough look at how to navigate around the map without the default controls, offering a great deal of flexibility.

 ▸ The *Managing the map's stack layers* recipe

 ▸ The *Restricting the map's extent* recipe

Restricting the map's extent

Often, there are situations where you are interested in showing data to the user, but only for a specific area, which your available data corresponds to (a country, a region, a city, and so on).

In this case, there is no point in allowing the user to explore the whole world, so you need to limit the extent the user can navigate.

In this recipe, we present some ways to limit the area that a user can explore. You can find the source code in `ch01/ch01-map-extent/`. We'll end up with a restricted extent of the USA like in the following screenshot:

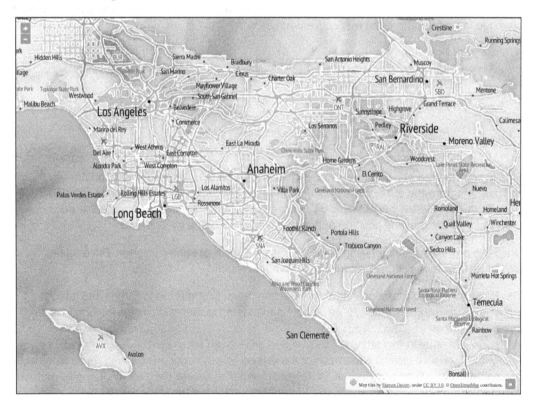

How to do it...

1. Create the HTML to house the map and include the OpenLayers dependencies.

2. Create your JavaScript file and set up a geographic extent:

```
var extent = ol.proj.transformExtent(
  [-125.0011, 24.9493, -66.9326, 49.5904],
  'EPSG:4326', 'EPSG:3857'
);
```

3. Create the map instance with some layers and a restricted view, as follows:

```
new ol.Map({
  layers: [
    new ol.layer.Tile({
      source: new ol.source.Stamen({
        layer: 'watercolor'
      })
    }),
    new ol.layer.Tile({
      source: new ol.source.Stamen({
        layer: 'terrain-labels'
      }),
      extent: extent
    })
  ],
  target: 'js-map',
  view: new ol.View({
    zoom: 6,
    minZoom: 5,
    center: [-12100000, 3400000],
    extent: extent
  })
});
```

How it works...

When you launch this recipe on your web browser, you'll notice that you cannot pan outside the restricted extent. Let's take a look at how this was accomplished:

```
var extent = ol.proj.transformExtent(
  [-125.0011, 24.9493, -66.9326, 49.5904],
  'EPSG:4326', 'EPSG:3857'
);
```

We've put together a bounding box which covers the United States. This extent is in longitude and latitude coordinates, but the map view is in a different projection (EPSG:3857). We need to convert our longitude and latitude extent into the map view projection.

The `ol.proj.transformExtent` projection helper method provides such a utility. We pass in the array of coordinates as the first parameter. The second parameter informs OpenLayers that the provided coordinates are in longitude and latitude (EPSG:4326). The final parameter tells OpenLayers what we'd like the coordinates to be converted into (EPSG:3857). This returns with an `ol.Extent` array we can use on the map. We store this array in a variable, namely `extent`, as we'll use it in a few places around the code:

```
new ol.Map({
  layers: [
    new ol.layer.Tile({
      source: new ol.source.Stamen({
        layer: 'watercolor'
      })
    }),
    new ol.layer.Tile({
      source: new ol.source.Stamen({
        layer: 'terrain-labels'
      }),
      extent: extent
    })
  ],
```

When we create the new `map` instance, we make use of the `Stamen` tile services. The background layer is made up of the `watercolor` layer, and the foreground layer is made up from the `terrain-labels` layer.

For the `terrain-labels` layer, we restrict the extent of the layer with our custom bounding box. It means that this layer will not request for tiles outside this extent.

```
view: new ol.View({
  zoom: 6,
  minZoom: 5,
  center: [-12100000, 3400000],
  extent: extent
})
```

When we create the view, we pass our bounding box into the `extent` property of the view. Passing the `extent` to `view` is where the navigation restriction gets enforced. If we hadn't passed the `extent` to `view`, the user could pan around the map as they wish.

We also set `minZoom` to 5, which accompanies the extent restriction quite well. It prevents the user from zooming far out and beyond the USA (our extent). This retains the user within the points of interest.

See also

▶ The *Moving around the map view* recipe

2
Adding Raster Layers

In this chapter we will cover the following topics:

- ▸ Using Bing imagery
- ▸ Using OpenStreetMap imagery
- ▸ Adding WMS layers
- ▸ Changing the zoom effect
- ▸ Changing layer opacity
- ▸ Buffering the layer data to improve map navigation
- ▸ Creating an image layer
- ▸ Setting the tile size in WMS layers

Introduction

Imagery is one of the most important kinds of data to work with in a GIS system. An eye-catching map with beautiful cartography can make an immediate difference to the appeal of a mapping application.

This chapter is all about working with different types of raster layers. We have tried to summarize, with a set of recipes, the most common and important use cases you can find day to day when working with OpenLayers and third-party layer providers.

OpenLayers offers several classes to integrate with different imagery providers, from proprietary providers, such as Bing Maps, and MapQuest, to open source ones, such as OpenStreetMap, and Stamen, or even any **Web Map Service** (**WMS**) service provider.

The base class for any layer type is `ol.layer.Base`, which offers a set of common properties and defines the common behavior for other layer classes. The `ol.layer.Layer` class further extends the base class with some extra methods and creates sub-classes, such as `ol.layer.Tile`, which we'll frequently use during this chapter.

The layer itself is decoupled from the layer source. The base class for any layer source is `ol.source.Source`. This class is extended through other sub-classes, such as `ol.source.Tile`, and furthermore with `ol.source.TileImage`, which offers many sub-classes that lay the foundations for the raster layer sources that we'll be using in this chapter later on.

In addition to this, many layer sources inherit from the `ol.source.XYZ` class, which divides the layer into zoom levels. This way, each zoom level covers the same area but uses a greater set of tiles. For example, at level zero, a grid with one tile covers the whole world; at level one, a grid with four tiles covers the whole world; and so on. As we can see, on each level, the number of tiles and their resolution increases.

This chapter introduces you to some of the built in raster layers from OpenLayers, as well as taking a look at arbitrary WMS layers, and how to manage some common layer properties.

Using Bing imagery

Bing Maps is the mapping service provided by Microsoft. OpenLayers makes integration with this tile service very easy with the class `ol.source.BingMaps`. We'll explore the variety of imagery Bing Maps offers.

We're going to create a map with a panel containing a list of layers you can switch between. The source code can be found in `ch02/ch02-bing-maps/`. We will end up with something similar to the following screenshot:

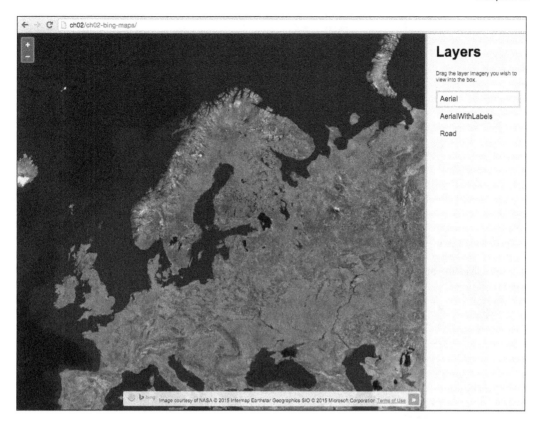

Getting ready

Bing Maps requires you to register as a consumer user in order to access their REST tile service. Once registered, you'll be able to view your personal API key which is needed to initialize the OpenLayers Bing Maps source layer. Your API key is used to authenticate you against the Bing Maps service.

> You can find out how to register for an API key at `https://www.bingmapsportal.com`.
>
> In addition to this, you can learn about the imagery that Bing Maps offers at `https://msdn.microsoft.com/en-us/library/ff701716.aspx`.

From this point on, it is assumed that you have an API key to be used in the upcoming code.

How to do it...

In this section, we will see how to use Bing Maps imagery. Here are the steps to follow:

1. Create an HTML file and add the OpenLayers dependencies, as well as jQuery and jQuery UI (responsible for the sortable list of layers).

2. Add the DOM elements to hold the map and layers panel, as follows:

```
<div id="js-map" class="map"></div>
<div class="pane">
  <h1>Layers</h1>
  <p>Drag the layer imagery you wish to view into the
  box.</p>
  <ul id="js-layers"></ul>
</div>
```

3. Within your custom JavaScript file, create this map instance:

```
var map = new ol.Map({
  view: new ol.View({
    zoom: 4,
    center: [2520000, 8570000]
  }),
  target: 'js-map'
});
```

4. Store your API key into a variable, as follows:

```
var apiKey = 'your_api_key';
```

5. Create a layer group with some Bing layers and add it to the map:

```
var layerGroup = new ol.layer.Group({
  layers: [
    new ol.layer.Tile({
      source: new ol.source.BingMaps({
        key: apiKey,
        imagerySet: 'Aerial'
      }),
      title: 'Aerial'
    }),
    new ol.layer.Tile({
      source: new ol.source.BingMaps({
        key: apiKey,
        imagerySet: 'AerialWithLabels'
      }),
      title: 'AerialWithLabels',
```

```
          visible: false
        }),
        new ol.layer.Tile({
          source: new ol.source.BingMaps({
            key: apiKey,
            imagerySet: 'Road',
            culture: 'en-GB'
          }),
          title: 'Road',
          visible: false
        })
      ]
    });

    map.addLayer(layerGroup);
```

6. Dynamically populate the list of layers in the UI:

```
    var $layersList = $('#js-layers');

    layerGroup.getLayers().forEach(function(element) {
      var $li = $('<li />');
      $li.text(element.get('title'));
      $layersList.append($li);
    });
```

7. Update the layer to be displayed on the map when the layers are reordered in the UI:

```
    $layersList.sortable({
      update: function() {
        var topLayer = $layersList.find('li:first-
        child').text();

        layerGroup.getLayers().forEach(function(element) {
          element.setVisible(element.get('title') ===
          topLayer);
        });
      }
    });
```

How it works...

The HTML and CSS divide the page into two sections: the map to the left and a slim layer-switching panel to the right. We won't go into anymore detail here, as we want to focus on the OpenLayers JavaScript code:

```
var map = new ol.Map({
  view: new ol.View({
    zoom: 4,
    center: [2520000, 8570000]
  }),
  target: 'js-map'
});
```

We create the map instance with properties `view` and `target`. We set up the layers property momentarily.

```
var apiKey = 'your_api_key';
```

We set up a variable to store our key inside, namely `apiKey`. Replace the `'your_api_key'` string with your own API key, which will be a long random string.

The code moves on to build out a layer group containing three different imagery layers from Bing Maps. Let's examine these layers individually:

```
new ol.layer.Tile({
  source: new ol.source.BingMaps({
    key: apiKey,
    imagerySet: 'Aerial'
  }),
  title: 'Aerial'
})
```

Each Bing Maps layer is an instance of the `ol.layer.Tile` class, of which the source is an instance of `ol.source.BingMaps`. The mandatory properties are `key` and `imagerySet`. The layer type for this one is `Aerial`, which provides impressive satellite imagery of the world.

We set a custom title property of `'Aerial'` for this layer. This name will be displayed in the layers list of the UI and is used for some JavaScript logic later on. You'll see that we give a custom title to each of our Bing Maps layers in order to identify them.

```
new ol.layer.Tile({
  source: new ol.source.BingMaps({
    key: apiKey,
```

```
      imagerySet: 'AerialWithLabels'
    }),
    title: 'AerialWithLabels',
    visible: false
  })
```

Similar to the first Bing Maps layer, this layer type is `AerialWithLabels`. This imagery extends the `Aerial` imagery with some useful labels. We've also given this layer a custom title and set its visibility to false. This is because we only want to display a single layer at any one time. This will ensure OpenLayers doesn't make any unnecessary tile requests when a layer is out of sight.

```
new ol.layer.Tile({
  source: new ol.source.BingMaps({
    key: apiKey,
    imagerySet: 'Road',
    culture: 'en-GB'
  }),
  title: 'Road',
  visible: false
})
```

The final Bing Maps layer is of type `Road`. It comes as no surprise that this layer provides road details, great for navigation guidance. Familiar properties aside (`title` and `visible`), we've set a new property culture with the `'en-GB'` value. Bing Maps attempts to localize street names into the local culture if applicable. So, if you were to request a location in Great Britain (`en-GB`), it will load localized data wherever available for this layer. For other supported culture codes, visit `https://msdn.microsoft.com/en-us/library/hh441729.aspx`.

```
  map.addLayer(layerGroup);
```

The group of Bing layers is added to the map:

```
var $layersList = $('#js-layers');

layerGroup.getLayers().forEach(function(element) {
  var $li = $('<li />');
  $li.text(element.get('title'));
  $layersList.append($li);
});
```

We cache the layers list (`<ul id="js-layers" class="layers"></ul>`) into a variable, namely `$layersList`. We then loop over each layer of the layer group and dynamically add the layer name into the list for display. The handy `get` method is used to fetch the title of the layer we set during initialization.

```
$layersList.sortable({
  update: function() {
    var topLayer = $layersList.find('li:first-child').text();

    layerGroup.getLayers().forEach(function(element) {
      element.setVisible(element.get('title') === topLayer);
    });
  }
});
```

jQuery UI enables the list of layers to be sorted. When an item is dragged into a new position in the list, the update event fires. Within our event handler, we cache the name of the top layer in the list (`topLayer`). After this, we loop over all the layers on the map and display the corresponding layer. All other layers get hidden (by setting their visibility to false). We are able to link the two sets of layers via their title property.

See also

▸   The *Adding WMS layer* recipe

Using OpenStreetMap imagery

OpenStreetMap (`http://www.openstreetmap.org`) is built by an open community of mappers who contribute and maintain geospatial data. This means that even you and I can get involved if we want to! This data is openly available to the public as long as you provide credit to OpenStreetMap and its contributors.

In earlier recipes, we only took a look at the standard layer type from OpenStreetMap, but there are many, many more layer styles that have been created on top of the OpenStreetMap data. We will show you three different OpenStreetMap sources: **Humanitarian OSM**, **MapQuest Open**, and **Transport Dark OSM**.

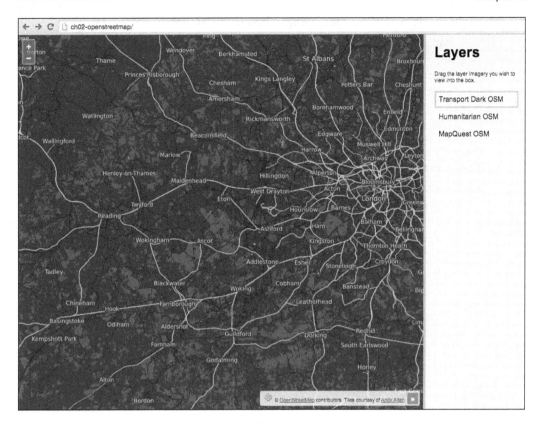

The preceding map shows the Transport Dark OpenStreetMap layer style from Andy Allen. The source code for this recipe can be found in `ch02/ch02-openstreetmap/`.

How to do it...

Let's produce this recipe using the steps outlined as follows:

1. Create the HTML page with OpenLayers dependencies, jQuery and jQuery UI. In particular, split the page into two sections for the map and layer switching panel:

    ```
    <div id="js-map" class="map"></div>
    <div class="pane">
      <h1>Layers</h1>
      <p>Drag the layer imagery you wish to view into the
      box.</p>
      <ul id="js-layers"></ul>
    </div>
    ```

2. In your custom JavaScript file, create a new map instance:

```javascript
var map = new ol.Map({
  view: new ol.View({
    zoom: 4,
    center: [4158174, 4392988]
  }),
  target: 'js-map'
});
```

3. Create the first OpenStreetMap layer, Humanitarian, and add it to the map:

```javascript
map.addLayer(new ol.layer.Tile({
  source: new ol.source.OSM({
    attributions: [
      new ol.Attribution({
        html: 'Tiles courtesy of ' +
        '<a href="http://hot.openstreetmap.org">' +
        'Humanitarian OpenStreetMap Team</a>'
      }),
      ol.source.OSM.ATTRIBUTION
    ],
    url: 'http://{a-
    c}.tile.openstreetmap.fr/hot/{z}/{x}/{y}.png'
  }),
  title: 'Humanitarian OSM'
}));
```

4. Create the MapQuest OpenStreetMap layer and add it to the map:

```javascript
map.addLayer(new ol.layer.Tile({
  source: new ol.source.OSM({
    attributions: [
      new ol.Attribution({
        html: 'Tiles courtesy of ' +
        '<a href="http://www.mapquest.com/">MapQuest</a>' +
        '<img src="https://developer.mapquest.com/' +
        'content/osm/mq_logo.png">'
      }),
      ol.source.OSM.ATTRIBUTION
    ],
    url: 'http://otile{1-3}.mqcdn.com/tiles/1.0.0/' +
      'osm/{z}/{x}/{y}.png'
  }),
  title: 'MapQuest OSM',
  visible: false
}));
```

5. Create the final layer of Transport Dark OpenStreetMap and add it to the map:

```
map.addLayer(new ol.layer.Tile({
  source: new ol.source.OSM({
    attributions: [
      new ol.Attribution({
        html: 'Tiles courtesy of ' +
        '<a href="http://www.thunderforest.com">Andy
        Allan</a>'
      }),
      ol.source.OSM.ATTRIBUTION
    ],
     url: 'http://{a-c}.tile.thunderforest.com/transport-   dark/'
+'{z}/{x}/{y}.png'
  }),
  title: 'Transport Dark OSM',
  visible: false
}));
```

6. Dynamically populate the list of layers in the UI, as follows:

```
var $layersList = $('#js-layers');

map.getLayers().forEach(function(element) {
  var $li = $('<li />');
  $li.text(element.get('title'));
  $layersList.append($li);
});
```

7. Add the logic to switch layers with the help of jQuery UI:

```
$layersList.sortable({
  update: function() {
    var topLayer = $layersList.find('li:first-
    child').text();

    map.getLayers().forEach(function(element) {
      element.setVisible(element.get('title') ===
      topLayer);
    });
  }
});
```

How it works...

This is the first recipe so far in this book that has seen layer creation with such granularity. We've declared properties, such as custom URLs, and attributions, for the first time.

We'll gloss over the more familiar parts of this recipe, such as the HTML, CSS, and JavaScript, to create the map instance and layer switching with jQueryUI so that we can take a deeper look at the newer components of this recipe: the OpenStreetMap layers:

```
map.addLayer(new ol.layer.Tile({
    source: new ol.source.OSM({
        attributions: [
          new ol.Attribution({
            html: 'Tiles courtesy of ' +
                  '<a href="http://hot.openstreetmap.org">' +
                  'Humanitarian OpenStreetMap Team</a>'
          }),
          ol.source.OSM.ATTRIBUTION
        ],
        url: 'http://{a-c}.tile.openstreetmap.fr/hot/' +
             '{z}/{x}/{y}.png'
    }),
    title: 'Humanitarian OSM'
}));
```

As the three layers follow the same pattern, we'll thoroughly walk through the first layer instantiation only, then simply point out any noteworthy differences against the other two layers.

We create the new `ol.layer.Tile` instance within the `addLayer` method for convenience. Our tile layer source is an instance of the built-in OpenStreetMap source (`ol.source.OSM`), which we pass a configuration object into.

The first property of the configuration object that we customize is `attributions`. This property expects an array of many `ol.Attribution` instances. The list of attributions gives credit to the appropriate parties, and this means that we adhere to the terms of usage. The content that we put in here makes up the attributions map control content (placed bottom-right of the map as standard).

The `ol.Attribution` constructor just requires a string of HTML to be passed in via the `html` property. We've populated a string of HTML that covers our usage of the Humanitarian OpenStreetMap layer. Concatenation of the string has been used to break it up over multiple lines for readability.

The second item in the attributions array (`ol.source.OSM.ATTRIBUTION`) is an already prepared instance of `ol.Attribution` from OpenLayers that contains the following HTML: `'&copy; <a href="http://www.openstreetmap.org/copyright">OpenStreetMap</a> contributors.'`. This is what gets implicitly added whenever you use `ol.source.OSM()` without supplying any custom attributions yourself.

The `url` property contains a string, which has the endpoint for the HTTP tile requests for this layer. You'll notice some curly braces within the string. These are template placeholders, which will be replaced by meaningful values for the request by OpenLayers.

This tile service supports three sub subdomains, namely a, b, or c. The `{a-c}` attribute is replaced with a letter within the range at random. So, our tile requests could go out to _a.tile. openstreetmap.org_, _b.tile.openstreetmap.org_ or _c.tile.openstreetmap.org_. The `{x}`, `{y}` and `{z}` attributes are also replaced by OpenLayers with the relevant grid coordinates to complete the request URL.

Using a template string, we can avoid having to pass in multiple URLs for differently named subdomains. However, if it's necessary for you to manually pass in multiple URLs, then you can alternatively use the `urls` property with an array of URL strings instead.

Finally, for the `ol.layer.Tile` options, we provide a custom title for this layer so that we can use it for display in the UI and also for some layer matching logic later on.

We go on to create another two OpenStreetMap based layers: MapQuest Open, and Transport Dark. These layers follow the same blueprint. Note that we set the visibility of these layers to false, as we only want to display one layer at a time.

 The MapQuest Open URL string for the HTTP requests contains a numbered range for their sub subdomain (`{1-3}`). This behaves in the same way as the letter range, and so, a number from 1 to 3 will be selected at random.

Once all the layers are in place, we dynamically populate the list of layers in the HTML and add some logic to show or hide layers depending on their position in the list. We won't go into detail about how this works, as this has been properly discussed during earlier recipes.

There's more...

The `ol.source.OSM` class is a subclass of `ol.source.XYZ`. This particular source type is for tile data with URLs in a set XYZ format that we saw defined in the string template. This structure follows the widely-used Google grid system. The `ol.source.XYZ` class provides some additional properties such as projection and methods, such as `setUrl`.

There are many more uniquely-designed tile services built on top of OpenStreetMap data, and this book simply can't demonstrate them all. The OpenStreetMap community is vibrant and creative, and I'm sure there will be lots more choice to come. I encourage you to take a look at the OpenStreetMap collection from `http://www.thunderforest.com` and the Stamen collection at `http://maps.stamen.com`, and then go expand your searches even further.

Big mapping companies, such as MapQuest, have embraced OpenStreetMap data and shown their support by openly providing great layers we can consume, like the one seen in this recipe. If you're interested to learn more about MapQuest, visit this informational link that provides some further insight: `http://wiki.openstreetmap.org/wiki/MapQuest`.

See also

- The *Using Bing imagery* recipe
- The *Managing map's stack layers* recipe

Adding WMS layers

Web Map Service (WMS) is a standard developed by the **Open Geospatial Consortium** (**OGC**) implemented by many geospatial servers, among which we can find the free and open source projects GeoServer (`http://geoserver.org`) and MapServer (`http://mapserver.org`). More information on WMS can be found at `http://en.wikipedia.org/wiki/Web_Map_Service`.

As a very basic summary, you can understand a WMS server as a normal HTTP web server that accepts requests with some GIS-related parameters (such as projection, bounding box, and so on), and returns map tiles forming a mosaic that covers the requested bounding box. Here's the finished recipe outcome using a WMS layer that covers the extent of the USA (source code can be found in `ch02/ch02-wms-layers/`):

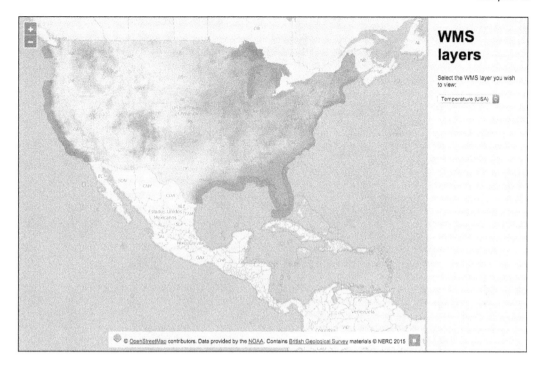

 We are going to work with remote WMS servers, so it is not necessary you have one installed yourself. Note that we are not responsible for these servers and that they may have problems, or may not be available any longer when you read this section.

Any other WMS server can be used, but the URL and layer name must be known.

How to do it...

We will add two WMS layers to work with. To do this, perform the following steps:

1. Create an HTML file and add the OpenLayers dependencies. In particular, create the HTML to hold the map and the layer panel:

```
<div id="js-map" class="map"></div>
<div class="pane">
  <h1>WMS layers</h1>
  <p>Select the WMS layer you wish to view:</p>
  <select id="js-layers" class="layers">
```

```
      <option value="-10527519,3160212,4">Temperature
      (USA)</option>
      <option value="-408479,7213209,6">Bedrock (UK)</option>
   </select>
</div>
```

2. Create the map instance with the default OpenStreetMap layer:

```
var map = new ol.Map({
  view: new ol.View({
    zoom: 4,
    center: [-10527519, 3160212]
  }),
  target: 'js-map',
  layers: [
    new ol.layer.Tile({
      source: new ol.source.OSM()
    })
  ]
});
```

3. Add the first WMS layer to the map:

```
map.addLayer(new ol.layer.Tile({
  source: new ol.source.TileWMS({
    url: 'http://gis.srh.noaa.gov/arcgis/services/' +
      'NDFDTemps/MapServer/WMSServer',
    params: {
      LAYERS: 16,
      FORMAT: 'image/png',
      TRANSPARENT: true
    },
    attributions: [
      new ol.Attribution({
        html: 'Data provided by the ' +
        '<a href="http://noaa.gov">NOAA</a>.'
      })
    ]
  }),
  opacity: 0.50
}));
```

4. Add the second WMS layer to the map:

```
map.addLayer(new ol.layer.Tile({
  source: new ol.source.TileWMS({
    url: 'http://ogc.bgs.ac.uk/cgi-bin/' +
```

```
          'BGS_Bedrock_and_Superficial_Geology/wms',
        params: {
          LAYERS: 'BGS_EN_Bedrock_and_Superficial_Geology'
      },
      attributions: [
        new ol.Attribution({
          html: 'Contains <a href="http://bgs.ac.uk">' +
          'British Geological Survey</a> ' +
          'materials &copy; NERC 2015'
        })
      ]
    }),
    opacity: 0.85
}));
```

5. Finally, add the layer-switching logic:

```
document.getElementById('js-layers')
    .addEventListener('change', function() {
      var values = this.value.split(',');
      var view = map.getView();
      view.setCenter([
        parseFloat(values[0]),
        parseFloat(values[1])
      ]);
      view.setZoom(values[2]);
    });
```

How it works...

The HTML and CSS divide the page into two sections: one for the map, and the other for the layer-switching panel. The top part of our custom JavaScript file creates a new `map` instance with a single OpenStreetMap layer—this layer will become the background for the WMS layers in order to provide some context.

Let's spend the rest of our time concentrating on how the WMS layers are created.

WMS layers are encapsulated within the `ol.layer.Tile` layer type. The source is an instance of `ol.source.TileWMS`, which is a subclass of `ol.source.TileImage`. The `ol.source.TileImage` class is behind many source types that we've already covered in this chapter, such as Bing Maps, and custom OpenStreetMap layers that are based on XYZ format.

When using `ol.source.TileWMS`, we must at least pass in the URL of the WMS server and a layers parameter. Let's breakdown the first WMS layer as follows:

```
map.addLayer(new ol.layer.Tile({
  source: new ol.source.TileWMS({
    url: 'http://gis.srh.noaa.gov/arcgis/services/NDFDTemps/' +
    'MapServer/WMSServer',
    params: {
      LAYERS: 16,
      FORMAT: 'image/png',
      TRANSPARENT: true
    },
    attributions: [
      new ol.Attribution({
        html: 'Data provided by the ' +
        '<a href="http://noaa.gov">NOAA</a>.'
      })
    ]
  }),
  opacity: 0.50
}));
```

For the `url` property of the source, we provide the URL of the WMS server from NOAA (`http://www.noaa.gov`).

The `params` property expects an object of key/value pairs. The content of which is appended to the aforementioned URL as query string parameters, for example, `http://gis.srh.noaa.gov/arcgis/services/NDFDTemps/MapServer/WMSServer?LAYERS=16`.

As mentioned earlier, this object requires, at minimum, the `LAYERS` property with a value. We request for the layer by the name of 16. Along with this parameter, we also explicitly ask for the tile images to be in the `.PNG` format (`FORMAT: 'image/png'`) and that the background of the tiles be transparent (`TRANSPARENT: true`), rather than white, which would undesirably block out the background map layer.

 The default values for format and transparency are already image/ PNG and false, respectively. This means you don't need to pass them in as parameters, OpenLayers will do it for you. We've shown you this for learning purposes but it isn't strictly necessary.

There are also other parameters OpenLayers fills in for you if not specified, such as service (WMS), version (1.3.0), request (GetMap) and so on.

For the attributions property we have created a new attribution instance to cover our usage of the WMS service, which simply contains a string of HTML linking back to the NOAA website.

Lastly, we set the `opacity` property of the layer to 50% (`0.50`), which suitably overlays the OpenStreetMap layer underneath.

```
map.addLayer(new ol.layer.Tile({
   source: new ol.source.TileWMS({
      url: 'http://ogc.bgs.ac.uk/cgi-bin/' +
      'BGS_Bedrock_and_Superficial_Geology/wms',
       params: {
          LAYERS: 'BGS_EN_Bedrock_and_Superficial_Geology'
      },
       attributions: [
          new ol.Attribution({
             html: 'Contains <a href="http://bgs.ac.uk">' +
                    'British Geological Survey</a> ' +
                    'materials &copy; NERC 2015'
          })
       ]
   }),
   opacity: 0.85
})));
```

 Check the WMS standard to know which parameters you can use within the `params` property.

The use of layers is mandatory, so you always need to specify this value.

This layer from the British Geological Survey (`http://bgs.ac.uk`) follows the same structure as the previous WMS layer. Similarly, we provided a source URL and a layers parameter for the HTTP request. The layer name is a string rather than a number this time, delimited by underscores. The naming convention is at the discretion of the WMS service itself.

As well as before, an attribution instance has been added to the layer, which contains a string of HTML linking back to the BGS website, covering our usage of the WMS service.

The `opacity` property of this layer is a little less transparent than the last one, at 85% (`0.85`).

```
document.getElementById('js-layers')
   .addEventListener('change', function() {
      var values = this.value.split(',');
      var view = map.getView();
```

```
      view.setCenter([
        parseFloat(values[0]),
        parseFloat(values[1])
      ]);
      view.setZoom(values[2]);
    });
```

Finally, we added a change-event listener and handler to the select menu containing both the WMS layers. If you recall from the HTML, an option's value contains a comma-delimited string. For example, the Bedrock WMS layer option looks like this:

```
<option value="-408479,7213209,6">Bedrock (UK)</option>
```

This translates to *x* coordinate, *y* coordinate, and zoom level.

With this in mind when the `change` event fires, we store the value of the newly-selected option in a variable named `values`. The `split` JavaScript method creates a three item array from the string. The array now contains the *xy* coordinates and the zoom level, respectively.

We store a reference to the view into a variable, namely `view`, as it's accessed more than once within the event handler.

The map view is then centered to the new location with the `setCenter` method. We've made sure to convert the string values into float types for OpenLayers, via the `parseFloat` JavaScript method. The zoom level is then set via the `setZoom` method.

Continuing with the Bedrock example, it will recenter at `-408479, 7213209` with zoom level 6.

Integrating with custom WMS services plays an essential role in many web mapping applications. Learning how we did it in this recipe should give you a good idea of how to integrate with any other WMS services that you might use.

There's more...

It's worth mentioning that WMS services do not necessarily cover a global extent, and will more likely cover only subset extents of the world. Case in point, the NOAA WMS layer covers only the USA, and the BGS WMS layer only covers the UK.

During this topic, we only looked at the request type of `GetMap`, but there's also a request type called `GetCapabilities`. Using the `GetCapabilities` request parameter on the same URL endpoint returns what capabilities (such as extent) a WMS server supports.

If you don't specify the type of projection, the view default projection will be used. In our case this will be EPSG:3857, which is passed up in a parameter named CRS (it's named SRS for the `GetMap` version requests less than 1.3.0). If you want to retrieve WMS tiles in different projections, you need to ensure the WMS server supports that particular format.

WMS servers return images no matter whether there is information in the bounding box being requested or not. Taking this recipe as an example, if the viewable extent of the map is only the UK, blank images will get returned for WMS layer requests made for the USA (via the NOAA tile requests). You can prevent these unnecessary HTTP requests by setting the visibility of any layers to false that do not cover the extent of the area being viewed.

There are some useful methods of the `ol.source.TileWMS` class that are worth being aware of, such as `updateParams`, which can be used to set parameters for the WMS request, and `getUrls`, which returns the URLs used for the WMS source.

See also

▶ The *Using Bing imagery* recipe
▶ The *Using OpenStreetMap* imagery recipe
▶ The *Changing layer opacity* recipe
▶ The *Buffering the layer data to improve map navigation* recipe

Changing the zoom effect

The panning and zoom effects are very important actions that are related to the user navigation experience. In *Chapter 1, Web Mapping Basics*, the *Moving around the map view* recipe shows you how you can control and animate the way the map can be panned, zoomed, and rotated.

In this recipe, we'll explore animations even further by demonstrating different ways that you can customize transition effects between two zoom levels on the layer.

By default, OpenLayers animates the zoom transitions. In order to customize this ourselves, OpenLayers comes with a series of different animation methods that are available from `ol.animation` object. For this recipe, we'll use the `ol.animation.bounce` and `ol.animation.zoom` methods to customize the zoom effects.

We will have a panel on the right so that you can choose the animation-easing algorithm, the duration and whether or not to use the bounce effect.

Here's a screenshot of what we'll end up with (the source code can be found in `ch02/ch02-zoom-effect`):

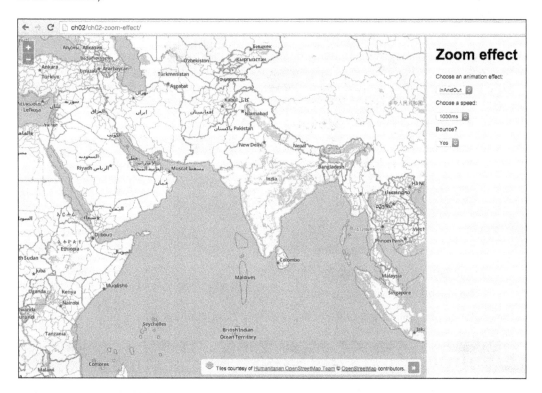

How to do it...

In this section we'll see how to change the zoom effects. Follow the steps outlined:

1. Create an HTML file and include the required OpenLayers dependencies. In particular, create the form elements to dynamically update the effects:

```
<p>Choose an animation effect:</p>
<select id="js-zoom-effect">
  <option value="easeIn">easeIn</option>
  <option value="easeOut">easeOut</option>
  <option value="inAndOut" selected>inAndOut</option>
  <option value="linear">linear</option>
</select>

<p>Choose a speed:</p>
<select id="js-zoom-speed">
  <option value="100">100ms</option>
```

```html
    <option value="250">250ms</option>
    <option value="500">500ms</option>
    <option value="1000" selected>1000ms</option>
</select>

<p>Bounce?</p>
<select id="js-bounce">
    <option value="true">Yes</option>
    <option value="false">No</option>
</select>
```

2. Create your custom JavaScript file and build the `map` instance with the Humanitarian OpenStreetMap layer:

```javascript
var map = new ol.Map({
  view: new ol.View({
    zoom: 5,
    center: [9686000, 1707000]
  }),
  target: 'js-map',
  layers: [
    new ol.layer.Tile({
      source: new ol.source.OSM({
        attributions: [
          new ol.Attribution({
            html: 'Tiles courtesy of ' +
            '<a href="http://hot.openstreetmap.org">' +
            'Humanitarian OpenStreetMap Team</a>'
          }),
          ol.source.OSM.ATTRIBUTION
        ],
        url: 'http://{a-c}.tile.openstreetmap.fr/' +
            'hot/{z}/{x}/{y}.png'
      })
    })
  ]
});
```

3. Cache the form DOM elements into variables, as follows:

```javascript
var easingSelect = document.getElementById('js-zoom-effect');
var durationSelect = document.getElementById('js-zoom-speed');
var bounceSelect = document.getElementById('js-bounce');
```

4. Add an event listener to the map view for zoom changes and create the animation effects based off the current form input values:

```
map.getView().on('change:resolution', function(event) {
  if (bounceSelect.value === 'true') {
    map.beforeRender(ol.animation.bounce({
      resolution: map.getView().getResolution() * 1.5,
      duration: parseInt(durationSelect.value, 10)
    }));
  } else {
    map.beforeRender(ol.animation.zoom({
      resolution: event.oldValue,
      duration: parseInt(durationSelect.value, 10),
      easing: ol.easing[easingSelect.value]
    }));
  }
});
```

How it works...

The HTML form elements provide a live reflection of the animation configuration. Each form element has an ID attribute that we use to select and cache the DOM elements within JavaScript, as we'll potentially access the values of these elements many times.

Our JavaScript sets up the map and associative properties, including the OpenStreetMap Humanitarian layer. This should all look familiar to you, so without further ado, we'll examine the logic behind the zoom transitions:

```
map.getView().on('change:resolution', function(event) {
```

We subscribe to any resolution (zoom) changes on the map view and register an anonymous function as the event handler.

```
if (bounceSelect.value === 'true') {
  map.beforeRender(ol.animation.bounce({
    resolution: map.getView().getResolution() * 1.5,
    duration: parseInt(durationSelect.value, 10)
  }));
}
```

We run a conditional check to see whether or not the value for the bounce select menu is 'true' or 'false'. If it's true, then we register a customized ol.animation.bounce method to be added onto the beforeRender queue. We pass in a desired resolution of 1.5 times the original resolution, to give it a suitable bounce effect. The duration amount is derived from the durationSelect menu value. We run the duration value through the JavaScript parseInt method to ensure it's in the right type for OpenLayers. The duration is in milliseconds.

> To describe the bounce effect by analogy, is to imagine a tennis ball hitting the ground from some height. As it impacts the surface, it jumps back up until it finally loses momentum and comes to rest on the surface. For example, when you zoom into the map, it's as though you become the descending ball, so you bounce your way to the final resolution. When you alter the easing value (the algorithm used), such as easeOut, it changes the spacing between the animation frames resulting in a different motion of events.

As we can see, the map instance has a beforeRender method that expects a function of type ol.PreRenderFunction. The ol.animation methods return a function of this expected type. This function type performs incremental manipulation of the view before rendering the final state of the view, which is perfect for animations.

The ol.PreRenderFunction method accepts two parameters: the map instance, and the frame state. The latter is a shared object in OpenLayers that represents the current render frame state. It provides information such as the current state of the view (center position, resolution, and so on) and current timestamp. These are metrics that animation algorithms (made up mostly of mathematical calculations to apply easing techniques) utilize to perform their visual effects. Within the function, you return true to run this function for the next frame; otherwise, you return false to dispose of it (in other words, your animation is complete).

The ol.animation.bounce variation of this function type performs incremental manipulations that produce a zooming request that 'bounces' into position.

```
  } else {
    map.beforeRender(ol.animation.zoom({
      resolution: event.oldValue,
      duration: parseInt(durationSelect.value, 10),
      easing: ol.easing[easingSelect.value]
    }));
  }
```

If the bounce effect has been disabled, then we add a standard zoom animation with the ol.animation.zoom method to the beforeRender map method.

For the starting point of the animation, the resolution is set to the old resolution value, which is available from the event object (`event.oldValue`). The duration is once again plucked straight from the duration select menu and passed into the JavaScript `parseInt` method for type conversion.

We can customize the easing algorithm that is used for the zoom animation effect. The `easing` property expects an appropriate easing function. OpenLayers comes with a selection of effects to choose from, the majority of which we made available from the easing select menu.

For example, one of the OpenLayers easing methods is `ol.easing.easeIn`. To dynamically use one of these easing functions from a value in the select menu, we perform an object lookup via array notation. So, to continue with this example, if you select the `easeIn` option from the select menu, `ol.easing[easingSelect.value]` becomes `ol.easing['easeIn']`.

There's more...

Although OpenLayers offers some easing methods out of the box, you can just as well extend the list and provide any easing algorithms yourself. You may have used some easing algorithms from other libraries that you'd like to port into OpenLayers.

The `ol.animation` methods all have a `start` property. This means that you can delay the start of the animation. The default start time is immediately.

See also

- ▸ The *Adding WMS layer* recipe
- ▸ The *Changing layer opacity* recipe
- ▸ The *Moving around the map view* recipe

Changing layer opacity

When you are working with many layers, both raster and vector layers, you will probably find situations where a layer that is on top of another layer obscures the one below it. This is more common when working with raster WMS layers without the transparent property set to true or tiled layers, such as OpenStreetMaps, and Bing Maps.

In this recipe, we'll create a slider that updates the layer opacity of the topmost layer, revealing a layer underneath as the opacity is lowered. The source code can be found in `ch02/ch02-layer-opacity/`. Here's a screenshot showing the layer opacity at 60%:

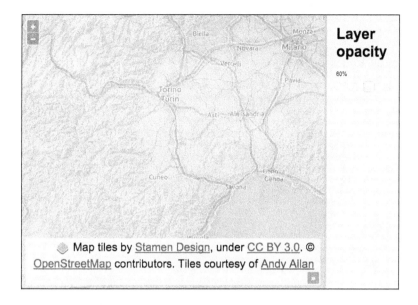

Map tiles by Stamen Design, under CC BY 3.0. © OpenStreetMap contributors. Tiles courtesy of Andy Allan

How to do it...

We used jQuery UI to create the slider widget. Here are the steps to create this recipe:

1. Create an HTML file adding the required OpenLayers dependencies, as well as jQuery UI and dependencies. In particular, here's the markup for the map and opacity panels:

```
<div id="js-map" class="map"></div>
<div class="pane">
  <h1>Layer opacity</h1>
  <p id="js-opacity">100%</p>
  <div id="js-slider"></div>
</div>
```

2. Next, create a `map` instance with the Stamen watercolor tile layer and the landscape WMS layer from Andy Allan:

```
var map = new ol.Map({
  view: new ol.View({
    zoom: 8,
    center: [860000, 5558000]
  }),
  target: 'js-map',
  layers: [
    new ol.layer.Tile({
      source: new ol.source.Stamen({
```

```
                layer: 'watercolor'
            })
        }),
        new ol.layer.Tile({
            source: new ol.source.OSM({
                attributions: [
                    new ol.Attribution({
                        html: 'Tiles courtesy of ' +
                        '<a href="http://www.thunderforest.com">' +
                        'Andy Allan</a>'
                    }),
                    ol.source.OSM.ATTRIBUTION
                ],
                url: 'http://{a-c}.tile.thunderforest.com/' +
                    'landscape/{z}/{x}/{y}.png'
            })
        })
    ]
});
```

3. Cache the DOM element that reflects the opacity percentage:

    ```
    var $opacity = $('#js-opacity');
    ```

4. Finally, create the jQuery UI slider widget and update the layer opacity and
    percentage display on the slide:

    ```
    $('#js-slider').slider({
      min: 0,
      max: 100,
      value: 100,
      slide: function(event, ui) {
        $opacity.text(ui.value + '%');
        map.getLayers().item(1).setOpacity(ui.value / 100);
      }
    });
    ```

How it works...

For the purpose of this recipe, let's focus in on the instantiation of the jQuery UI slider and
how the map layer opacity is subsequently updated:

```
$('#js-slider').slider({
  min: 0,
  max: 100,
  value: 100,
```

Using jQuery, we target the DOM element that we want to convert into the slider widget. On the returned jQuery object, we attach the jQuery UI slider method with some configuration properties, which will create the slider widget as desired. The properties set an initial value of `100` to match the initial state of the map layer opacity, as well as a min and max value.

```
slide: function(event, ui) {
  $opacity.text(ui.value + '%');
  map.getLayers().item(1).setOpacity(ui.value / 100);
}
```

The `slide` property enables us to attach an event handler, which is called whenever the slider position updates. When this event fires, we have access to the `event` object and also the `ui` object from the jQuery UI. The `ui` object contains the new value from the slide action, and we update the text value of the DOM element to inform the user of the new opacity percentage.

We then fetch all the layers from the map using the map `getLayers` method, returning an `ol.Collection` object. This object provides us with some useful methods, such as `item`, which takes the index of an array item. We use this to get the second layer of the map.

The item method returns the second layer from the collection. This layer (an instance of `ol.layer.Base`), also contains many methods, one of which is `setOpacity`. We take the latest slider value (between 0 and 100) and convert it into the expected format for the `setOpacity` method (it must be between 0 and 1). This is achieved by dividing the value from the slider by 100. If the slider value is 60%, then *60 / 100 = 0.6*. This change takes immediate effect, and you'll see the layer transparency update accordingly.

Layer opacity changes will fire an event called `change:opacity`. This is one of many layer events that you can subscribe to.

See also

- ▶ The *Changing the zoom effect* recipe
- ▶ The *Adding WMS layer* recipe
- ▶ The *Buffering the layer data to improve map navigation* recipe

Buffering the layer data to improve map navigation

Map navigation is an important factor to take into account for a good user experience. When we pan and zoom the map, you'll often notice blank areas during transitions (because the content is loading), and after a few moments, the tile images appear.

On gridded layers (the focus of this recipe) and WMS layers working in single image mode, we can improve this at the cost of increasing the number of requests or increasing the computation time at the server side.

The idea behind improving map navigation is simple; load the tiles beyond the map view so that they are loaded before the user pans the map view in this direction or changes resolution, thus improving the navigation experience for users.

For this recipe we will create two side by side maps with tiled layers, one with (the top map) and one without (the bottom map) tile buffering enabled. You'll be able to see the differences when navigating around the two maps. The source code for this recipe can be found in `ch02/ch02-layer-preloading/`.

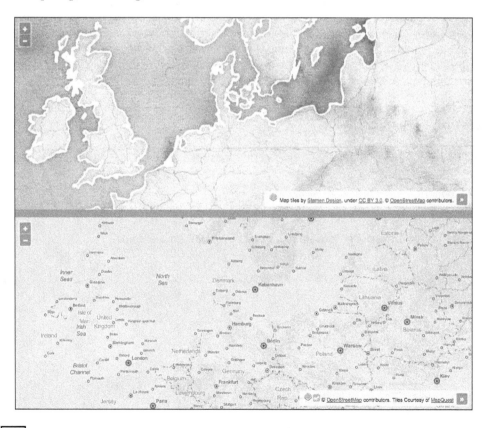

How to do it...

Let's produce this recipe using the steps outlined as follows:

1. Create an HTML file and include the OpenLayers dependencies. In particular, we create two `div` elements to hold both maps with a central divide:

```
<div id="js-map-preload"></div>
<hr/>
<div id="js-map-no-preload"></div>
```

2. Create a `view` instance that has to be shared by both maps:

```
var view = new ol.View({
  zoom: 5,
  center: [1252000, 7240000]
});
```

3. Create the map with preloading enabled, as follows:

```
new ol.Map({
  view: view,
  target: 'js-map-preload',
  layers: [
    new ol.layer.Tile({
      source: new ol.source.Stamen({
        layer: 'watercolor'
      }),
      preload: Infinity
    })
  ]
});
```

4. Create the comparison map, with no preloading techniques:

```
new ol.Map({
  view: view,
  target: 'js-map-no-preload',
  layers: [
    new ol.layer.Tile({
      source: new ol.source.MapQuest({
        layer: 'osm'
      })
    })
  ]
});
```

How it works...

The HTML and CSS split the page in two, with a clear horizontal divide. We won't go into any more details for this, but please do check out the source code for this recipe.

The view created is used for both map instances. This means that when one map updates the view, the changes will be mirrored by the other map instance. It's this easy to have two maps imitate each other.

```
layers: [
  new ol.layer.Tile({
    source: new ol.source.Stamen({
      layer: 'watercolor'
    }),
    preload: Infinity
  })
]
```

This first map instance uses the watercolor layer source from Stamen. For the `ol.layer.Tile` configuration, we set the `preload` property to `Infinity`. The `preload` property instructs OpenLayers to load in tiles of lower resolutions (for the current extent) up to the specified level.

In theory, to the same effect, the value of `preload` could be set to the quantity of lower resolution levels from the currently visible layer. However, rather than figuring this out manually, we put in place `Infinity`, for convenience so that all lower resolution levels will be taken into account. In this scenario, we could have arbitrarily chosen a preload value of 100 for the same outcome.

To further understand this, let's explain what the preload setting actually does. Firstly, let's visualize this explanation somewhat: go and remind yourself what the top map looks like from the recipe screenshot at the beginning of this topic. Given the tile images that you see before you that make up the top map, be aware that the following map tile (at a lower resolution) has been additionally preloaded behind the scenes, but it isn't currently visible:

This is not the only preloaded tile at a lower resolution either—there are others of lower resolutions that cover the viewable extent.

 For a deeper dive, run this recipe in the browser and inspect the network requests for this layer (using the browser development tools). You'll observe that the extent of the viewport has lower resolution tiles preloaded all the way to the lowest available resolution for this layer. It has done this because we specified a preload value of `Infinity`. If we had specified a preload value of, say 2, then OpenLayers would have restricted preloading to just 2 lower resolutions beyond the currently visible resolution.

Due to the implemented preloading mechanism, blank areas are greatly reduced (if not eliminated, depending on network latency, and so on). On the contrary, when navigating around the MapQuest tile layer (with no preloading), you should be able to observe blank areas appearing much more frequently than the preloaded Stamen layer.

 The method that decides whether or not to continue loading lower resolution tiles is called `manageTilePyramid`, which is a method of `ol.renderer.Layer`.

OpenLayers doesn't preload higher resolution tiles, as it doesn't really *need* to. This is because when you zoom in, the currently visible tiles are automatically increased in size (creating an illusion of getting closer towards the point of interest) so that no blank areas are revealed. When the new tiles are loaded and available from the requests, the old tiles are removed from the map to reveal the new tiles underneath.

There's more...

To enable custom layer buffering in single image mode with WMS layers (through the use of `ol.layer.Image`), you can adjust the ratio property of `ol.source.ImageWMS`. By adjusting the ratio, we can control the image size that is returned from the server. A ratio value of 1 means that an image with the exact dimensions of the map view is requested. By default, the ratio value is set to 1.5, which means we are requesting an image with the map view dimensions plus a half. You could decide to increase this ratio amount as desired.

Just because you can utilize preloading, it doesn't necessarily mean it's always the most preferable solution. Consider mobile phone users with limited amounts of data allowance on lower bandwidth connections. You may actually end up negatively impacting their user experience. Loading more tiles inevitably means more image requests to the server and more data to download to the device.

The same applies to a WMS layer in single image mode; the greater the bounding box you request, the greater the computation time on the server and the larger the image size for download. With this in mind, increasing the `preload` or ratio values too much is not always the best solution.

Consider how your users will likely navigate the map and explore the data. If your data is probably better explored in its extension, then a preload of one, or two, or a larger ratio could be a good idea.

 The `ol.layer.Tile` class also has `setPreload` and `getPreload` methods, which you may find useful.

See also

- ► The *Setting the tile size in WMS layers* recipe
- ► The *Adding WMS layer* recipe

Creating an image layer

Sometimes a tiled layer, such as Bing Maps, OpenStreetMap, or from WMS services, is not what you need. You may have access to a georeferenced image or know of a server that can return an image for arbitrary extents and resolutions.

In these cases, OpenLayers offers the `ol.layer.Image` class that allows us to create a layer that is based on an image. For this recipe, we hook up to a WMS service that returns a single image on request for a given bounding box. The source code can be found in `ch02/ch02-image-layer/`.

This recipe will use the `ol.source.ImageWMS` source class to connect to the WMS server. However, if you have a static georeferenced image, then you should use `ol.source.ImageStatic`, which works in much the same way.

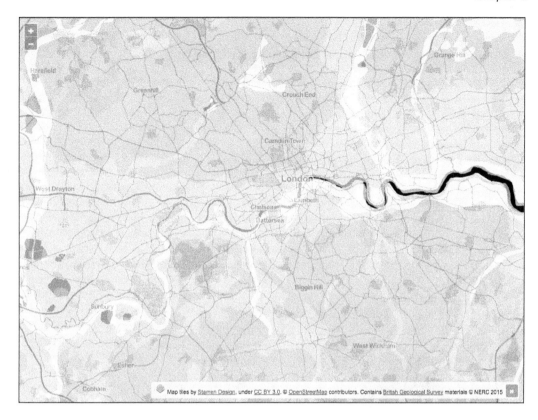

How to do it...

To create an image layer, perform the following steps:

1. Create an HTML file with the OpenLayers dependencies and a `div` for the map container.

2. Within your custom JavaScript file, create an `extent`, which will be used to center the map and restrict the `extent` variable for our image layer:

```
var extent = [-93941, 6650480, 64589, 6766970];
```

3. Initialize the map with a tiled raster layer from Stamen, as follows:

```
var map = new ol.Map({
  view: new ol.View({
    zoom: 10,
    center: ol.extent.getCenter(extent)
  }),
  target: 'js-map',
```

```
      layers: [
        new ol.layer.Tile({
          source: new ol.source.Stamen({
            layer: 'toner'
          })
        })
      ]
    });
```

4. Create the WMS image layer and add it to the map:

```
map.addLayer(new ol.layer.Image({
  source: new ol.source.ImageWMS({
    url: 'http://ogc.bgs.ac.uk/cgi-bin/' +
        'BGS_Bedrock_and_Superficial_Geology/wms',
    params: {
        LAYERS: 'BGS_EN_Bedrock_and_Superficial_Geology'
    },
    attributions: [
      new ol.Attribution({
        html: 'Contains <a href="http://bgs.ac.uk">' +
              'British Geological Survey</a> ' +
              'materials &copy; NERC 2015'
      })
    ]
  }),
  opacity: 0.7,
  extent: extent
}));
```

How it works...

We decided to make use of a WMS service from the British Geological Survey, which can be utilized to return a single image for specified extents of Great Britain. For the background mapping, we chose to use the Stamen provider with a layer style called toner that will provide context for the WMS image.

```
var extent = [-93941, 6650480, 64589, 6766970];
```

We store an arbitrary extent into a variable, namely `extent`. This extent (using the EPSG:3857 projection) covers the city of London and surrounding areas.

```
var map = new ol.Map({
  view: new ol.View({
    zoom: 10,
```

```
        center: ol.extent.getCenter(extent)
    })
});
```

When we create the map instance, the center value of the view is calculated from our custom extent. The `ol.extent` object provides many helper methods when working with extents, one of which is `getCenter`. This method expects an `ol.Coordinate` method (an array of coordinates), which we provide, it and returns the center coordinates for us:

```
map.addLayer(new ol.layer.Image({
    source: new ol.source.ImageWMS({
        url: 'http://ogc.bgs.ac.uk/cgi-bin/' +
            'BGS_Bedrock_and_Superficial_Geology/wms',
        params: {
            LAYERS: 'BGS_EN_Bedrock_and_Superficial_Geology'
        },
        attributions: [
            new ol.Attribution({
                html: 'Contains <a href="http://bgs.ac.uk">' +
                    'British Geological Survey</a> ' +
                    'materials &copy; NERC 2015'
            })
        ]
    }),
    opacity: 0.7,
    extent: extent
}));
```

We create the image layer using the `ol.layer.Image` class. Using this class will request and return a single image, rather than multiple tile images. On the layer, we set the `opacity` property to 70% and restrict the extent of the layer by passing in our custom extent to the extent property.

The source property is an instance of `ol.source.ImageWMS`, which is similar to `ol.source.TileWMS` in its available properties. We provide the necessary details to successfully retrieve an image from this WMS service, such as the URL, the parameters of the request to include the specific layer that we're interested in, and the attribution to cover our usage.

OpenLayers will accompany our `LAYERS` parameter by sending some other parameters along with the request as default, such as *FORMAT*, *VERSION*, *TRANSPARENT*, and so on.

As we have restricted the extent of this layer, when you zoom to lower resolutions, this restriction becomes apparent, as demonstrated in the following screenshot:

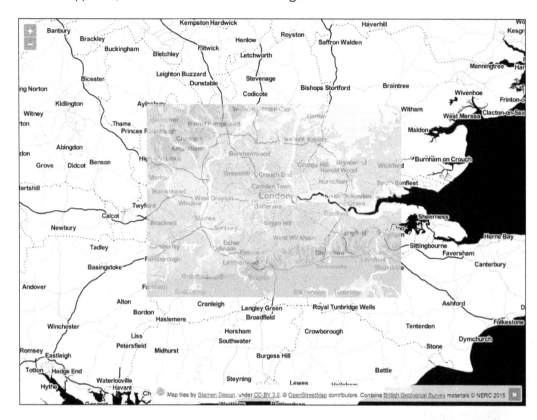

When examining the returned image in the browser development tools, it weighed over half a megabyte with dimensions (in pixels) of *1556 × 1143*. Suffice to say that the time to download and render this image on the map was not instantaneous.

When compared against tile requests that begin building up the map view incrementally, the user may feel a perceived loss of responsiveness with single image layers. It's up to you how to combat this—perhaps a loading bar or spinner as a visual cue of the current progress. *Chapter 4, Working with Events*, has a topic on *implementing a work-in-progress indicator for map layers*.

See also

▸ The *Adding WMS layer* recipe

▸ The *Buffering the layer data to improve map navigation* recipe

Setting the tile size in WMS layers

Setting a custom tile size for a WMS layer in OpenLayers 3 is a bit more involved than with OpenLayers 2. It requires the use of the `ol.tilegrid.TileGrid` class. This class provides some flexible control over the grid pattern that is used for sources accessing tiled image servers.

Of course, controlling the tile size of the WMS request can affect the performance. By default, the tile size is *256 x 256* pixels, but we can set this to something different. Bigger tile sizes mean fewer requests to the server but more computation time to generate a bigger image and a larger download size per image. On the contrary, smaller tile sizes mean more server requests and less time to compute smaller images. If you use the default tile sizes, then it's more likely the images will have already been cached, so it may increase performance.

In any case, it's good to know how we can make these adjustments. The source code can be found in `ch02/ch02-tile-size/`. Here's what we'll end up with:

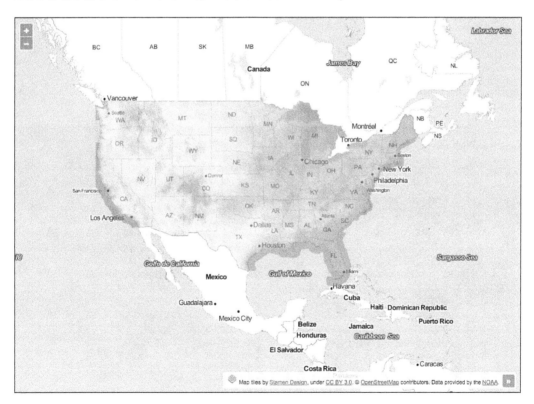

How to do it...

To set the tile size for our WMS layer requests, perform the following steps:

1. Create an HTML file with OpenLayers dependencies and a `div` for the map container.

2. Create a custom JavaScript file and initialize the map with a background layer from the Stamen collection:

```
var map = new ol.Map({
  view: new ol.View({
    zoom: 0,
    maxZoom: 8,
    center: [-10439500, 4256000]
  }),
  target: 'js-map',
  layers: [
    new ol.layer.Tile({
      source: new ol.source.Stamen({
        layer: 'toner-lite'
      })
    })
  ]
});
```

3. Cache `view` into a variable for reuse and build up the resolutions for our customized WMS layer:

```
var view = map.getView();

var resolutions = [view.getResolution()];
for (var i = 1; i < 8; i++) {
  resolutions.push(resolutions[0] / Math.pow(2, i));
}
```

4. Adjust the zoom level for the `view` and create the custom tile grid layer:

```
view.setZoom(4);

var tileGrid = new ol.tilegrid.TileGrid({
  extent: view.getProjection().getExtent(),
  resolutions: resolutions,
  tileSize: [512, 512]
});
```

5. Finally, create the tile layer, apply the custom tile grid to the layer source, and add the layer to the map:

```
map.addLayer(new ol.layer.Tile({
  source: new ol.source.TileWMS({
    url: 'http://gis.srh.noaa.gov/arcgis/services/' +
         'NDFDTemps/MapServer/WMSServer',
    params: {
      LAYERS: 16
    },
    attributions: [
      new ol.Attribution({
        html: 'Data provided by the ' +
              '<a href="http://noaa.gov">NOAA</a>.'
      })
    ],
    tileGrid: tileGrid
  }),
  opacity: 0.50
}));
```

How it works...

We've used a WMS layer from NOAA that provides temperature data across the USA. To provide some context for this data the background mapping is from the Stamen source provider using a layer called toner-lite. For the remainder of this section, let's focus on the code that primarily influences the custom tile size:

```
var resolutions = [view.getResolution()];
for (var i = 1; i < 8; i++) {
  resolutions.push(resolutions[0] / Math.pow(2, i));
}
```

We build up a custom list of resolutions for the WMS layer. The array is stored inside of the variable named `resolutions`. We've preloaded this array at index 0 with the initial resolution of the view via the `getResolution` method on the view instance. As we instantiated the view with a zoom level of 0, this initial view resolution is equal to the minimum resolution available.

We use a `for` loop in order to populate our custom list of resolutions. New resolutions are added into the array from index 1 (`var i = 1`), as index 0 already contains the minimum resolution. We've arbitrarily decided to add an additional seven resolutions only (`i < 8`). The imagery returned from the WMS service doesn't add much value beyond this resolution, so restricting it to a zoom level of 8 felt appropriate.

As we iterate through the `for` loop, we calculate what the next resolution should be. To break this logic down, let's come up with a contrived example: say the minimum resolution began at 20. To get the next resolution, we divide this by the zoom factor of 2 (which is the default zoom factor for `ol.View`). This results in 10. To get the next resolution level, we again divide 10 by 2, resulting in 5, and so on (for another 5 more times).

A concise way to accomplish this result is through exponentiation. The starting (minimum) resolution becomes the constant value during calculation, which is divided by the result of 2 (the zoom factor) multiplied by the iteration value. To demonstrate this, we'll continue with our example from earlier: *20 / (2 x 1) = 10*, then *20 / (2 x 2) = 5*, and so on.

The minimum resolution is always at index 0 (`resolutions[0]`) of the array, so as we iterate through the loop we use the JavaScript `Math.pow` method (does exponentiation) to calculate the next resolution (explained previously), then we push it onto the resolutions array.

```
var tileGrid = new ol.tilegrid.TileGrid({
    extent: view.getProjection().getExtent(),
    resolutions: resolutions,
    tileSize: [512, 512]
});
```

We store our instance of `ol.tilegrid.TileGrid` into a variable, namely `tileGrid`. The first property that we set is the `extent`.

In order to get an appropriate extent, we first retrieve the projection object being used by the view with the `getProjection` method. This method returns the projection object of type `ol.proj.Projection`. The default projection the view initializes with is EPSG:3857. As default, OpenLayers includes the projection objects for EPSG:3857 and EPSG:4326.

The `ol.proj.Projection` object contains some useful utility methods when working with projections, one of which is `getExtent`. This method returns the full extent of the projection that we use for our custom grid layer.

 We could have restricted the extent of this layer to the USA, as the data is only available for this region anyway. It would be a slight optimization, as it would avoid unnecessary tile requests for areas that are out of bounds.

The `resolutions` property is provided with our custom array of resolutions created from earlier.

The `tileSize` property expects an `ol.Size` type array, which is simply a pair of numbers representing a size: width, then height. We chose to double the default tile size from *256 x 256* to *512 x 512* pixels.

This completes our custom grid configuration, which we later add to the `ol.source.TileWMS` settings via the `tileGrid` property.

There's more...

The `ol.tilegrid.TileGrid` class allows you to set a custom set of resolutions (as we've seen) but also match different tile sizes against particular resolutions. Instead of using the `tileSize` property, you use the plural `tileSizes` property and pass in an array of tile sizes. The total number of items in the `tileSizes` array should match the length of the resolutions array. For example, the first resolution in the `resolutions` array would use the first tile size dimensions in the `tileSizes` array.

See also

- ▸ The *Creating an Image layer* recipe
- ▸ The *Buffering the layer data to improve map navigation* recipe

3
Working with Vector Layers

In this chapter, we will cover the following topics:

- Adding a GML layer
- Adding a KML layer
- Creating features programmatically
- Exporting features as GeoJSON
- Reading and creating features from a WKT
- Using point features as markers
- Removing or cloning features using overlays
- Zooming to the extent of a layer
- Adding text labels to geometry points
- Adding features from a WFS server
- Using the cluster strategy
- Reading features directly using AJAX
- Creating a heat map

Introduction

This chapter talks about vector layers. In addition to raster imagery, vector information is the other important type of data that we can work with in a GIS system. Throughout the coming recipes, we'll summarize the most common and important concepts that you may need to work with in OpenLayers.

 We will make some AJAX requests during this chapter. If you're following along with this book's source code, then be sure to download and install Node.js (`https://nodejs.org`) and follow the `README.md` instructions.

In GIS, a real-world phenomenon is represented by the concept of a feature. This can be a place, such as a city or a village; it can be a road or a railway, it can be a region, a lake, the border of a country, or something entirely arbitrary.

Features can have a set of attributes, such as population, length, and so on. These can be represented visually through the use of points, lines, polygons, and so on, using some visual style: color, radius, width, and so on.

As you can see, there are many concepts to take into account when working with vector information. Fortunately, OpenLayers provides an extensive range of feature-related classes to work with. We will learn more about these in this chapter.

The base class for vector layers is `ol.layer.Vector`, which defines the common properties and methods. Most of these are inherited from `ol.layer.Base`. The vector layer's properties and methods share close similarities with the `ol.layer.Tile` class, which we've explored in detail in *Chapter 2, Adding Raster Layers*.

The vector layer class requires a source of `ol.source.Vector`, in the same way as the raster layers do. The vector source expects a set of features, which can come in numerous formats (GeoJSON, GML, or an OpenLayers-specific type of `ol.geom`, and so on). These features are converted to the `ol.Feature` types when added to the layer.

Each feature can contain custom attribute properties, and it will typically have a single geometry. Features can also be individually styled, or they can inherit styles through cascading methods. We'll explore many of the methods that the `ol.Feature` class has to offer.

In addition to representation onscreen, we need to take into account the data source. OpenLayers offers classes to read/write features from/to many sources or protocols in different formats, such as GML, KML, GeoJSON, WKT, and so on.

Additionally, the vector layer can utilize different feature loading strategies, such as load all features onto the map in one go, load features based on the current extent, and so on.

Without further ado, let's discover and embrace the capabilities of vector layers and features.

Adding a GML layer

The **Geography Markup Language** (**GML**) is an XML grammar that is used to express geographic features. It is an OGC standard and is very widely accepted by the GIS community.

In this recipe (the source code is in `ch03/ch03-gml-layer/`), we will show you how to create a vector layer from a GML file which can be seen in the following screenshot:

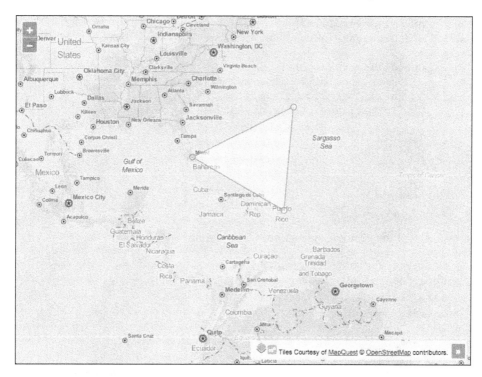

 You can find the necessary files in the GML format attached to the source code of this book on the Packt Publishing website.

How to do it...

In order to import features in GML format into the map, follow these instructions:

1. Create an HTML file with the required OpenLayers dependencies and prepare the `div` element to hold the map:

   ```
   <div id="js-map"></div>
   ```

2. Create the JavaScript file to initialize the map with a base layer, then add the vector layer pointing to the GML source, as follows:

```
var map = new ol.Map({
  view: new ol.View({
    zoom: 4,
    center: [-7494000, 2240000]
  }),
  target: 'js-map',
  layers: [
    new ol.layer.Tile({
      source: new ol.source.MapQuest({layer: 'osm'})
    }),
    new ol.layer.Vector({
      source: new ol.source.Vector({
        url: 'bermuda-triangle.gml',
        format: new ol.format.GML2()
      })
    })
  ]
});
```

How it works...

Let's take a look at the vector layer instantiation in detail:

```
new ol.layer.Vector({
  source: new ol.source.Vector({
    url: 'bermuda-triangle.gml',
    format: new ol.format.GML2()
  })
})
```

Just as raster layers require a source, as seen in *Chapter 2, Adding Raster Layers*, so do vector layers. Vector layers use the `ol.source.Vector` class in order to present features.

We provide an HTTP endpoint as a string to the `url` property. OpenLayers will make an AJAX request on our behalf for this URL, which contains the GML file.

We inform OpenLayers what the format of the source is by setting the format property to `GML2`. The GML source is at version 2.1.2, which `ol.format.GML2` can read and process. For GML 3.1.1, use the `ol.format.GML` or `ol.format.GML3` constructors.

In this example, the vector layer source request will load all of the features from the source on to the map and make no further AJAX requests, implicitly using the `ol.loadingstrategy.all` strategy. However, there is a property of `ol.source.Vector` called `strategy`, which can be used to specify an alternative feature loading strategy, such as loading features only for the extent of the view (`ol.loadingstrategy.bbox`).

On receiving the GML source, OpenLayers reads the GML-formatted features and converts each feature into a format that can be used on the map (ol.Feature).

OpenLayers offers many other formats to read/write data, but in this recipe, we made use of the ol.format.GML2 instance because our data source is a GML version 2 file.

See also

▶ The *Adding a KML layer* recipe

▶ The *Creating features programmatically* recipe

Adding a KML layer

The arrival of Google Maps led to an explosion in the world of GIS and web mapping. Google introduced not only an API but also certain file formats.

The **Keyhole Markup Language** (**KML**) has become one of the most extensively-used formats, and it has become an OGC standard. For some more details on the KML standard, refer to https://en.wikipedia.org/wiki/Keyhole_Markup_Language. The following screenshot shows how to create vector layers from a KML file:

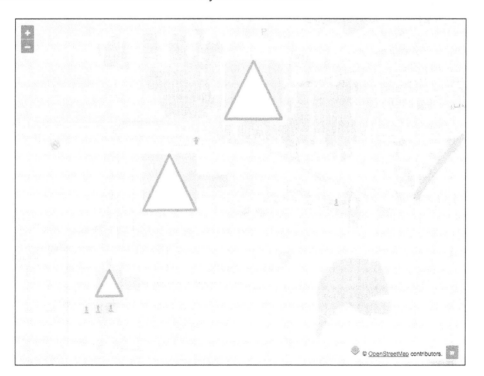

This recipe (found in `ch03/ch03-kml-layer/`) will show you how easy it is to add features from a KML file. You can find the necessary files in the KML format attached to the source code of this book and available on the Packt Publishing website.

How to do it...

In order to import features from KML format into the map, follow these instructions:

1. Create an HTML file that includes the OpenLayers dependencies and insert a `div` to contain the map:

   ```
   <div id="js-map"></div>
   ```

2. Create the JavaScript file and initialize the map with a base layer and then add the vector layer pointing to the KML source, as follows:

   ```javascript
   var map = new ol.Map({
     view: new ol.View({
       zoom: 16,
       center: [3465642, 3500474]
     }),
     target: 'js-map',
     layers: [
       new ol.layer.Tile({
         source: new ol.source.OSM(),
         opacity: 0.4
       }),
       new ol.layer.Vector({
         source: new ol.source.Vector({
           url: 'egypt-pyramids.kml',
           format: new ol.format.KML()
         })
       })
     ]
   });
   ```

How it works...

The instantiation of the vector layer follows the same structure as seen in the previous GML layer recipe. The only noticeable change is the difference in `url` and `format`:

```
new ol.layer.Vector({
  source: new ol.source.Vector({
    url: 'egypt-pyramids.kml',
    format: new ol.format.KML()
  })
})
```

OpenLayers makes an AJAX request for the KML file from the string passed to the `url` property. The format (`ol.format.KML`) corresponds to the KML file request so that OpenLayers knows how to process the response. The `ol.format.KML` class provides some properties that can be customized on instantiation. One of which is `extractStyles`. This property informs OpenLayers whether or not to extract feature styling information from the KML file (such as color and line width) and use it to render on the map. This defaults to true.

There's more...

Like GML, the KML format offers tons of options and possibilities at the cost of complexity. Google has some useful documentation to help developers structure their KML files at `https://developers.google.com/kml/documentation`

In the KML format, placemarks can have a description attached to them, and if you load a KML file in Google Maps, the placemark's description is shown as a balloon (or a popup) when you click on it. With OpenLayers, this kind of behavior requires some manual intervention to achieve similar results.

See also

- ▶ The *Adding a GML layer* recipe
- ▶ The *Creating features programmatically* recipe
- ▶ The *Removing or cloning features using overlays* recipe

Creating features programmatically

Loading data from an external source is not the only way to work with vector layers. Imagine a web-mapping application where the user can create new features on the fly, such as landing zones, perimeters, areas of interest, and so on, and add them to a vector layer with some style. This scenario requires the ability to create and add the features programmatically.

In this recipe, we will take a look at some ways to create a selection of features programmatically. The source code can be found in `ch03/ch03-creating-features/`. The following screenshot shows some features that are created programmatically:

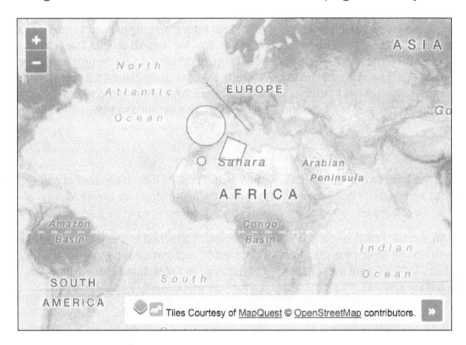

How to do it...

Here, we'll create some features programmatically, without any file importing. Follow these instructions to find out how this is done:

1. Start by creating a new HTML file with the required OpenLayers dependencies. In particular, add the `div` element to hold the map:

   ```
   <div id="js-map"></div>
   ```

2. Create an empty JavaScript file and instantiate a `map` with a background raster layer:

```
var map = new ol.Map({
  view: new ol.View({
    zoom: 3,
    center: [-2719935, 3385243]
  }),
  target: 'js-map',
  layers: [
    new ol.layer.Tile({
      source: new ol.source.MapQuest({layer: 'osm'})
    })
  ]
});
```

3. Create the `point` and `circle` features, as follows:

```
var point = new ol.Feature({
  geometry: new ol.geom.Point([-606604, 3228700])
});

var circle = new ol.Feature(
  new ol.geom.Circle([-391357, 4774562], 9e5)
);
```

4. Create the `line` and `polygon` features:

```
var line = new ol.Feature(
  new ol.geom.LineString([
    [-371789, 6711782], [1624133, 4539747]
  ])
);
var polygon = new ol.Feature(
  new ol.geom.Polygon([[
    [606604, 4285365], [1506726, 3933143],
    [1252344, 3248267], [195678, 3248267]
  ]])
);
```

5. Create the vector layer and add `features` to this layer:

```
map.addLayer(new ol.layer.Vector({
  source: new ol.source.Vector({
    features: [point, circle, line, polygon]
  })
}));
```

How it works...

Although we've created some random features for this recipe, features in mapping applications would normally represent some phenomenon of the real world with an appropriate geometry and style associated with it.

Let's go over the programmatic feature creation and how it is added to a vector layer:

```
var point = new ol.Feature({
  geometry: new ol.geom.Point([-606604, 3228700])
});
```

Features are instances of `ol.Feature`. This constructor contains many useful methods, such as `clone`, `setGeometry`, `getStyle`, and others. When creating an instance of `ol.Feature`, we must either pass in a geometry of type `ol.geom.Geometry`, or an object containing properties. We demonstrate both variations throughout this recipe.

For the `point` feature, we pass in a configuration object. The only property that we supply is `geometry`. There are other properties available, such as `style`, and the use of custom properties to set the `feature` attributes ourselves, which come with getters and setters.

The `geometry` instance belongs to `ol.geom.Point`. The `ol.geom` class provides a variety of other feature types that we don't get to see in this recipe, such as `MultiLineString` and `MultiPoint`. The point `geometry` type simply requires an `ol.Coordinate` type array (*xy* coordinates).

```
var circle = new ol.Feature(
  new ol.geom.Circle([-391357, 4774562], 9e5)
);
```

The `circle` feature follows almost the same structure as the `point` feature. This time, however, we don't pass in a configuration object to `ol.Feature`, but instead, we directly instantiate an `ol.geom.Geometry` type of `Circle`. The constructor takes an array of coordinates and a second parameter for the radius. 9e5 or 9e+5 is exponential notation for 900,000.

The `circle` geometry also has useful methods, such as `getCenter`, and `setRadius`.

```
var line = new ol.Feature(
  new ol.geom.LineString([
    [-371789, 6711782], [1624133, 4539747]
  ])
);
```

Remember to express the coordinates in the appropriate projection, the one used by the view, or translate the coordinates yourself. We will cover working with feature styles in *Chapter 6, Styling Features*. For now, all features will be rendered with the default OpenLayers styling.

The only noticeable difference with the `LineString` feature is that `ol.geom.LineString` expects an array of coordinate arrays. For more advanced line strings, use the `ol.geom.MultiLineString` geometry type (more information can be found in the OpenLayers API documentation at `http://openlayers.org/en/v3.13.0/apidoc/`).

The `LineString` feature also has useful methods, such as `getLength`.

```
var polygon = new ol.Feature(
  new ol.geom.Polygon([[
    [606604, 4285365], [1506726, 3933143],
    [1252344, 3248267], [195678, 3248267]
  ]])
);
```

The final feature, a `Polygon` geometry type, differs slightly from the `LineString` feature in that it expects an `ol.Coordinate` type array within an array within another wrapping array. This is because the constructor (`ol.geom.Polygon`) expects an array of rings, with each ring being represented as an array of coordinates. Ideally, each ring should be closed.

The polygon feature also has useful methods, such as `getArea`, and `getLinearRing`.

```
map.addLayer(new ol.layer.Vector({
  source: new ol.source.Vector({
    features: [point, circle, line, polygon]
  })
}));
```

 The OGC's *Simple Feature Access* specification (`http://www.opengeospatial.org/standards/sfa`) contains an in-depth description of the standard. It also contains a UML class diagram where you can see all the geometry classes and hierarchy.

Finally, we create the vector layer with a vector source instance and add all four features to an array and pass it to the `features` property.

All the features that we've created are subclasses of `ol.geom.SimpleGeometry`. This class provides useful base methods, such as `getExtent` and `getFirstCoordinate`.

All features have a `getType` method that can be used to identify the type of feature, for example, 'Point', or 'LineString'.

Sometimes, the `polygon` features may represent a region with a hole in it. To create a hollow part of a polygon, we use the `LinearRing` geometry. The outcome is best explained with the following screenshot:

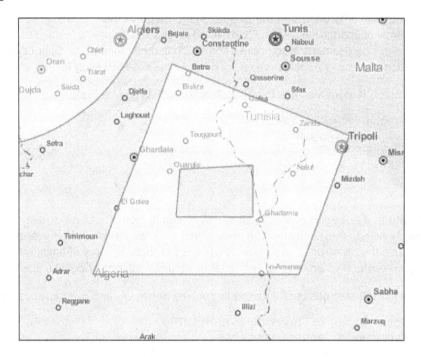

You can see that the polygon has a section cut out of it. To achieve this geometry, we must create the polygon in a slightly different way. Here are the steps:

1. Create the `polygon` geometry, as follows:

```
var polygon = new ol.geom.Polygon([[
    [606604, 4285365], [1506726, 3933143],
    [1252344, 3248267], [195678, 3248267]
]]);
```

2. Create and add the linear ring to the `polygon` geometry:

```
polygon.appendLinearRing(
  new ol.geom.LinearRing([
    [645740, 3766816], [1017529, 3786384],
    [1017529, 3532002], [626172, 3532002]
  ])
);
```

3. Create the completed feature, as follows:

```
var polygonFeature = new ol.Feature(polygon);
```

4. Finish off by adding the polygon feature to the vector layer:

```
vectorLayer.getSource().addFeature(polygonFeature);
```

We won't break this logic down any further, as it's quite self-explanatory now that we're comfortable with geometry creation.

 The `ol.geom.LinearRing` feature can only be used in conjunction with a `polygon` geometry, and not as a standalone feature.

See also

▶ The *Adding markers to the map* recipe

▶ The *Reading and creating features from a WKT* recipe

▶ The *Styling features based on geometry type* recipe in *Chapter 6, Styling Features*

Exporting features as GeoJSON

In the earlier recipes, we saw how to read in data from different formats, such as GML and KML, but what about exporting data from a map? A user of your mapping application may want to get a copy of the vector layer data to use it somewhere else. Or perhaps, you're saving the state of a map and need to send the layer content to a server for persistent storage so that the same geometry can be retrieved later.

In this recipe, we will export the contents of a vector layer to the GeoJSON format. The source code can be found in `ch03/ch03-export-geojson`. Here's what we'll end up with:

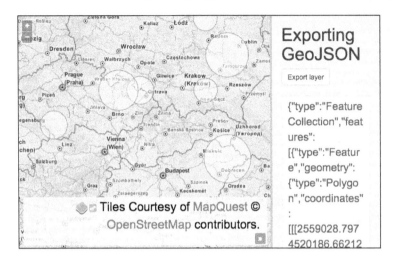

How to do it...

We are going to enable the use of an `export` button that will output the vector layer features as GeoJSON in a text box. Follow these steps to achieve this goal:

1. Create the HTML file with OpenLayers dependencies. In particular, create the following:

    ```html
    <div id="js-map"></div>
    <div>
      <h1>Exporting GeoJSON</h1>
      <form>
        <button type="submit">Export layer</button>
        <textarea id="js-textarea"></textarea>
      </form>
    </div>
    ```

2. Create a JavaScript file, and initialize the `map`, `view`, and background raster layers:

    ```javascript
    var map = new ol.Map({
      view: new ol.View({
        zoom: 5,
        center: [2103547, 6538117]
      }),
      target: 'js-map',
      layers: [
        new ol.layer.Tile({
    ```

```
      source: new ol.source.MapQuest({layer: 'osm'})
    })
  ]
});
```

3. Create a method for randomly picking an integer from a range of integers, as follows:

```
var getRandomInt = function(min, max) {
  return Math.floor(Math.random() * (max - min + 1)) + min;
};
```

4. Build an array of randomly generated circular features, as follows:

```
var features = [], numberOfFeatures = 0;

while(numberOfFeatures < 10) {
  var circle = new ol.geom.Circle(
    ol.proj.fromLonLat(
      [getRandomInt(14, 23), getRandomInt(48, 54)]
    ), getRandomInt(4, 15) * 10000
  );
  var polygonCircle = ol.geom.Polygon.fromCircle(circle);
  features.push(new ol.Feature(polygonCircle));
  numberOfFeatures++;
}
```

5. Create the vector layer, add `features` to the vector source, and add this to `map`:

```
var vectorLayer = new ol.layer.Vector({
    source: new ol.source.Vector({
        features: features
    })
});
map.addLayer(vectorLayer);
```

6. Add a listener to the `export` button and export `features` as GeoJSON to the text box:

```
document.forms[0].addEventListener('submit', function(event) {
    event.preventDefault();
    var format = new ol.format.GeoJSON();
    var features = vectorLayer.getSource().getFeatures();
    var geoJson = format.writeFeatures(features);
    document.getElementById('js-textarea').value = geoJson;
});
```

How it works...

The JavaScript contains a method (`getRandomInt`) that picks an integer between a range at random. For more information on the inner workings of this method, visit `http://stackoverflow.com/questions/1527803`.

Let's focus on the new components that are utilized throughout this recipe:

```
var circle = new ol.geom.Circle(
  ol.proj.fromLonLat(
    [getRandomInt(14, 23), getRandomInt(48, 54)]
  ),
  getRandomInt(4, 15) * 10000
);
```

Within the `while` loop (that performs 10 iterations), we created a `circle` geometry each time. In order to programmatically create a set of differently sized circles, we've supplied a range of numbers representing longitude and latitude values that are randomly selected by `getRandomInt`. These ranges form an inaccurate bounding box around Poland, Europe.

The view uses the `EPSG:3857` projection, so we use `ol.proj.fromLonLat` to convert the longitude and latitude values to this projection (which is the default if it is not specified as the second parameter).

We also create a randomly generated radius, which then gets multiplied by `10,000` so that it's clearly visible at the starting resolution.

```
var polygonCircle = ol.geom.Polygon.fromCircle(circle);
```

We convert the circle geometry to a regular polygon feature, which produces an approximated circle. This part may not be apparent, but GeoJSON (at the time of writing) doesn't support circle geometries yet, so we must convert it to a regular polygon so that it can be serialized and exported later on.

```
features.push(new ol.Feature(polygonCircle));
```

 You can increase the circular accuracy of `ol.geom.Polygon.fromCircle` by passing a higher number of sides as the second parameter. The default is 32.

The polygon circle is then converted into an `ol.Feature` instance so that OpenLayers can use it on the layer source, as follows.

```
document.forms[0].addEventListener('submit', function(event) {
    event.preventDefault();
    var format = new ol.format.GeoJSON();
```

```
    var features = vectorLayer.getSource().getFeatures();
    var geoJson = format.writeFeatures(features);
    document.getElementById('js-textarea').value = geoJson;
});
```

We add a `submit` event listener to the first and only form on the page, which prevents the default form submission.

We create a new instance of the GeoJSON format and store it in the `format` variable. The vector features are retrieved from the layer source via the helpful `getSource` method from the vector layer and through the `getFeatures` method from the vector source.

The GeoJSON is finally serialized using the `writeFeatures` method from the GeoJSON format provider, which expects an array of OpenLayers features. The GeoJSON string is then displayed inside the `textarea` element.

Displaying it in the textbox is one idea. You may decide to perform other actions with this data, such as posting it via AJAX to a server to save it, and so on.

See also...

- ▶ The *Adding a GML layer* recipe
- ▶ The *Creating features programmatically* recipe
- ▶ The *Reading features directly using AJAX* recipe

Reading and creating features from a WKT

As we're already discovering, OpenLayers comes with a great set of format helpers, which are used to read/write from/to different file data formats. GeoJSON, GML, and KML are some of the many available formats that we already explored.

If you read the *Adding a GML layer* recipe in this chapter, you will know that a vector layer can read the features stored in a file, specify the format of the data source, and place the contained features in the map.

For this recipe, we will programmatically create a polygon in the WKT format and then export the feature as WKT from the vector layer. You can read more about the WKT GIS format on Wikipedia (`http://en.wikipedia.org/wiki/Well-known_text`). The source code can be found in `ch03/ch03-wkt-format/`. Here's what we'll end up with:

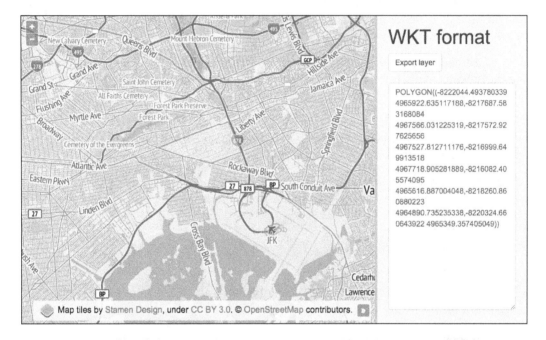

How to do it...

1. Create a new HTML file with OpenLayers dependencies. In particular, add the HTML to create the map and side panel, as follows:

```
<div id="js-map"></div>
<div>
  <h1>WKT format</h1>
  <form>
    <button type="submit">Export layer</button>
    <textarea id="js-textarea"></textarea>
  </form>
</div>
```

2. Create a custom JavaScript file and build a polygon geometry using WKT:

```
var wkt = [
  'POLYGON ((',
  '-8222044.493780339 4965922.635117188,',
  '-8217687.583168084 4967566.031225319,',
```

```
  '-8217572.927625656 4967527.812711176,',
  '-8216999.649913518 4967718.905281889,',
  '-8216082.405574095 4965616.887004048,',
  '-8218260.860880223 4964890.735235338,',
  '-8220324.660643922 4965349.357405049',
  ')))'
];
```

3. Convert the array to a string, as follows:

```
var feature = new ol.format.WKT().readFeature(wkt.join(''));
```

4. Create the `map` instance with a background raster layer and a vector layer, which we will add the `feature` to, as follows:

```
var map = new ol.Map({
  view: new ol.View({
    zoom: 12,
    center: [-8224433, 4965464]
  }),
  target: 'js-map',
  layers: [
    new ol.layer.Tile({
      source: new ol.source.Stamen({layer: 'terrain'})
    }),
    new ol.layer.Vector({
      source: new ol.source.Vector({
        features: [feature]
      })
    })
  ]
});
```

5. Listen to form submissions and export the vector layer features as WKT:

```
document.forms[0].addEventListener('submit', function(event) {
  event.preventDefault();
  var wktFormat = new ol.format.WKT();
  var features = map.getLayers().item(1)
                    .getSource().getFeatures();
  var wkt = wktFormat.writeFeatures(features);

  document.getElementById('js-textarea').value = wkt;
});
```

How it works...

The map creation process will look familiar to the ones in the previous recipes. For the background raster layer, we used the terrain layer from Stamen, which, at the time of writing, only covers the extent of the USA. Let's continue by concentrating on the WKT OpenLayers code and functionality.

We created an array, namely `wkt`, that builds a polygon geometry. You can create many other geometry types from WKT, such as points, line strings, and so on. The parts of the WKT have been populated using an array because it's somewhat easier to read than a concatenated string over multiple lines.

```
var feature = new ol.format.WKT().readFeature(wkt.join(''));
```

The `readFeature` method expects the WKT to be a string. You'll see this as when we pass our array (`wkt`) to the WKT format method, `readFeature`, the JavaScript array method, `join`, converts our array of items into a single string by joining them together with an empty space.

As expected, we must instantiate a new instance of the WKT format (`new ol.format.WKT()`), which returns the format object. We chain on the reading feature method that we discussed earlier.

```
document.forms[0].addEventListener('submit', function(event) {
    event.preventDefault();
    var wktFormat = new ol.format.WKT();
    var features = map.getLayers().item(1)
                    .getSource().getFeatures();
    var wkt = wktFormat.writeFeatures(features);

    document.getElementById('js-textarea').value = wkt;
});
```

As part of the WKT format export, we attach a handler for the form `submit` event and prevent the default action.

We create a new WKT format object and store it in the `wktFormat` variable. We then retrieve the polygon feature from the vector layer. To do this, we return an `ol.Collection` object from the map via `map.getLayers()`. This collection has a useful method called `item`, which is used to select the array index of the layer. We know that our map has just two layers, of these, the second one is the vector layer, at index 1.

We continue to chain on another function called `getSource`, which retrieves the vector layer source. Then finally, we fetch all the features with the `getFeatures` method available from the vector source object.

Using the WKT format object (`wktFormat`), we serialize the OpenLayers features in the WKT format via the `writeFeatures` method. The content of the textbox is updated to include the exported WKT.

See also

▸ The *Adding a GML layer* recipe

▸ The *Creating features programmatically* recipe

▸ The *Reading features directly using AJAX* recipe

Using point features as markers

A marker can be understood as a **point of interest** (**POI**) where we place an icon to identify it, and this icon has some information associated with it, such as a monument, a parking area, a bridge, and so on.

In this recipe, we will learn how to associate a custom marker icon with a point geometry type. The source code can be found in `ch03/ch03-markers/`. Here's what we'll end up with:

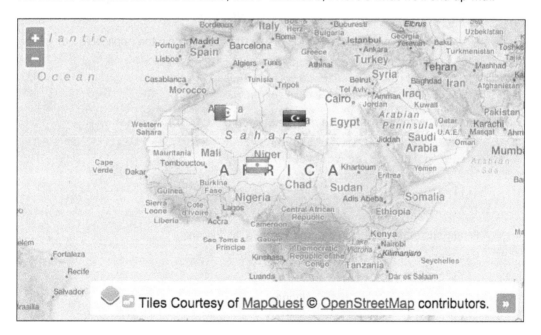

How to do it...

Use the following steps to learn how to attach an icon, in this case a flag, to a geometry point on the map:

1. Create the HTML file with the OpenLayers dependencies and a `div` to contain the map.

2. Create a custom JavaScript file; within this file, create a function to generate and return a custom feature style:

    ```
    var createIconStyle = function(country) {
      return new ol.style.Style({
        image: new ol.style.Icon({
          src: country + '.png'
        })
      })
    };
    ```

3. Create three geometry point features:

    ```
    var algeria = new ol.Feature(new ol.geom.Point([146759,3297187]));
    var libya = new ol.Feature(new ol.geom.Point([1927436,3160212]));
    var niger = new ol.Feature(new ol.geom.Point([968610,1986139]));
    ```

4. Assign the custom styles to each feature so that they contain the applicable icon image:

    ```
    algeria.setStyle(createIconStyle('algeria'));
    libya.setStyle(createIconStyle('libya'));
    niger.setStyle(createIconStyle('niger'));
    ```

5. Create a vector layer and add the `features` to the vector `source`:

    ```
    var vectorLayer = new ol.layer.Vector({
      source: new ol.source.Vector({
        features: [algeria, libya, niger]
      })
    });
    ```

6. Finally, instantiate `map`, `view`, and `layers`, as follows:

    ```
    var map = new ol.Map({
      view: new ol.View({
        zoom: 3,
        center: [1995923, -4167958]
      }),
      target: 'js-map',
      layers: [
        new ol.layer.Tile({
          source: new ol.source.MapQuest({layer: 'osm'})
    ```

```
        }),
        vectorLayer
    ]
  });
```

How it works...

We picked three geometry points that reside in three different countries across Africa. Each POI is provided with an icon that represents its respective country's flag.

To achieve this result, we have to use classes from the `ol.style` OpenLayers object. Let's take a closer look at this code:

```
return new ol.style.Style({
   image: new ol.style.Icon({
      src: country + '.png'
   })
})
```

Within our `createIconStyle` function, we instantiate a new instance of `ol.style.Style`. This returns the wrapper object that we need in order to create rendering styles for our vector features. It provides methods such as `getImage`, `getFill`, and `setZIndex`.

The `image` property expects a type of `ol.style.Image`, which is the base class for `ol.style.Icon` that we utilize here. The `ol.style.Style` class has other properties available, such as `fill`, `stroke`, and `text`. The `ol.style.Image` base class provides methods, such as `getOpacity`, `getScale`, and `setRotation`.

We dynamically set the value of the `src` property of our `ol.style.Icon` instance to a URL, which is built from the passed in country name. All images are in the `.PNG` format, so `.png` is always concatenated on to the end.

We've implicitly accepted a lot of the OpenLayers property defaults for `ol.style.Icon`, such as `opacity` as 1, `anchor` as [0.5, 0.5], which centers the icon position in the middle of the flag icon (which can be customized accordingly to suit the icon type), and the `anchorXUnits` type of '*fraction*', rather than '*pixels*'. There are many more customizable properties that I encourage you to check out.

```
algeria.setStyle(createIconStyle('algeria'));
```

After we've created an instance of `ol.Feature` for each country, we must set the vector feature style for each individual feature, as they're all using unique images. The `ol.Feature` class provides the `setStyle` method that takes an instance (or an array of instances) of `ol.style.Style`, which is what's returned from our custom `createIconStyle` function.

The further parts of this recipe set up the vector layer and map, both of which we're comfortable with and will need no explanation.

There's more...

The markers can, of course, be mutated after they've initially been added to a vector layer. For example, we may wish to programmatically adjust a property, such as the opacity of one of the flag icons.

Let's extend this recipe by setting the opacity of the first flag to 50%:

```
var vectorLayer = map.getLayers().item(1);
var feature = vectorLayer.getSource().getFeatures()[0];
feature.getStyle().getImage().setOpacity(0.5);
vectorLayer.changed();
```

We store a reference to the vector layer (the second layer on the map) in a variable named `vectorLayer`. We then go searching for the feature that we'd like to manipulate by accessing the vector layer source, grabbing all features from this source, and plucking just the first feature from the array. The result is stored in the `feature` variable.

We retrieve the style object from the feature (`getStyle`) and narrow our interest down to the image style object that contains our flag icon (`getImage`). We set the opacity to 50%.

However, this won't show any visible changes to the flag yet, as the vector layer needs to re-render itself for the changes to take effect. It's blissfully unaware of our modifications, so we give it a friendly nudge by manually calling the `changed` method on the vector layer, which subsequently increments the internal revision counter and dispatches a change event. OpenLayers responds by re-rendering the vector layer, and we can finally see that the first flag (Algeria) is now semi-opaque.

See also

- ▸ The *Creating features programmatically* recipe
- ▸ The *Adding text labels to geometry points* recipe
- ▸ The *Using the cluster strategy* recipe

Removing or cloning features using overlays

A common characteristic of web mapping applications is their ability to display information or perform actions that are related to the features on the map. By features, we mean any real phenomenon or aspect that we can visually represent with points, lines, polygons, and so on.

We can select a feature, retrieve its associated information, and choose to display it anywhere in our application layout. A common way to do this is using *overlays*.

In this recipe, we'll make it possible to clone and remove a feature from an overlay bubble that is displayed when clicking on a feature attached to the map. The source code can be found in `ch03/ch03-removing-cloning-feature-overlay`. This will look like the following screenshot:

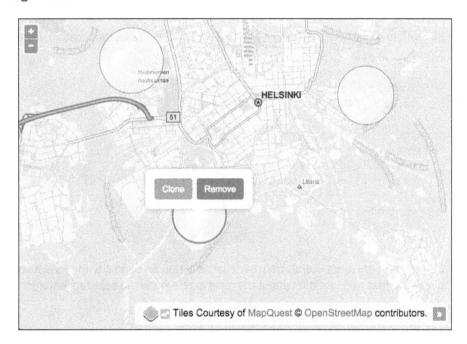

How to do it...

We will perform some feature manipulation from map overlays using the following instructions:

1. Create an HTML file with OpenLayers dependencies, a `div` element to hold the map, and also the overlay and content, as follows:

```
<div id="js-map"></div>
<div id="js-overlay">
  <button id="js-clone">Clone</button>
  <button id="js-remove">Remove</button>
</div>
```

2. Create a custom JavaScript file and instantiate a new vector layer with three circle features, as follows:

```
var vectorLayer = new ol.layer.Vector({
  source: new ol.source.Vector({
    features: [
      new ol.Feature(new ol.geom.Circle([2780119, 8437147], 900)),
```

```
            new ol.Feature(new ol.geom.Circle([2774826, 8433459], 850)),
            new ol.Feature(new ol.geom.Circle([2772686, 8438217], 999))
        ]
    })
});
```

3. Instantiate a map instance with `view` and `layers`, including our custom vector layer:

```
var map = new ol.Map({
  view: new ol.View({
    zoom: 13,
    center: [2775906, 8433717]
  }),
  target: 'js-map',
  layers: [
    new ol.layer.Tile({
      source: new ol.source.MapQuest({layer: 'osm'})
    }),
    vectorLayer
  ]
});
```

4. Create an OpenLayers overlay from our custom HTML and add it to the `map`. Also, define a variable that we'll use throughout the code to reference the selected feature:

```
var overlay = new ol.Overlay({
  element: document.getElementById('js-overlay')
});
map.addOverlay(overlay);
var selectedFeature;
```

5. Create an OpenLayers interaction to allow the selection of features:

```
var select = new ol.interaction.Select({
    condition: ol.events.condition.click,
    layers: [vectorLayer]
});
map.addInteraction(select);
```

6. Subscribe to the `select` event on the interaction and toggle the `overlay` accordingly:

```
select.on('select', function(event) {
  selectedFeature = event.selected[0];
  if (selectedFeature) {
    overlay.setPosition(selectedFeature.getGeometry().getCenter())
  } else {
    overlay.setPosition(undefined);
  }
});
```

7. For the `clone` button, attach a `click` event handler and clone the circle:

```
document.getElementById('js-clone')
  .addEventListener('click', function() {
    var circle = selectedFeature.clone();
    var circleGeometry = circle.getGeometry();
    var circleCenter = circleGeometry.getCenter();

    circleGeometry.setCenter([
        circleCenter[0] + circleGeometry.getRadius() * 2,
        circleCenter[1]
    ]);
    vectorLayer.getSource().addFeature(circle);
    overlay.setPosition(undefined);
    select.getFeatures().clear();
});
```

8. Finally, for the `remove` button, attach a `click` event handler and remove the feature:

```
document.getElementById('js-remove')
  .addEventListener('click', function() {
    vectorLayer.getSource().removeFeature(selectedFeature);
    overlay.setPosition(undefined);
    select.getFeatures().clear();
});
```

How it works...

We've omitted showing the CSS that styles the overlay as seen in the screenshot so that we can focus on the OpenLayers code. The complete code can be found within the accompanying source code for this book.

The map uses a raster base layer from MapQuest and the vector layer contains three arbitrary circle geometries of varying size. We will spend the rest of this section looking at the newly introduced concepts:

```
var overlay = new ol.Overlay({
  element: document.getElementById('js-overlay')
});
map.addOverlay(overlay);
```

OpenLayers provides a mechanism in order to display overlays or popups over a map at designated coordinates. This differs from controls, such as the zoom buttons, which are statically located on the viewport.

The `ol.Overlay` constructor is used to create our custom `overlay` bubble. We provide minimal configuration by passing in the DOM element that is used for the overlay content. OpenLayers wraps this content in an absolutely positioned `div` over the map. We finish off by assigning this overlay to the map with the `addOverlay` map method.

The overlay can be configured with other properties, such as `autoPan` and `position`. Map instances also contain a method to remove overlays, namely `removeOverlay`.

```
var select = new ol.interaction.Select({
  condition: ol.events.condition.click,
  layers: [vectorLayer]
});
map.addInteraction(select);
```

In order to make features (un)selectable, we use the OpenLayers interaction method called `ol.interaction.Select`. Some interactions are already enabled on the map by default, such as `ol.interaction.MouseWheelZoom`, among many others.

The interaction type expects a condition that is used to trigger the event. We used the `click` event here, which has a type of `ol.MapBrowserEvent`. The `ol.events.condition` object provides many other events, such as the `ol.events.condition.singleClick` event, which is the default for the `select` interaction. We avoided the default `singleClick` event because it has a delay of 250 ms (to ensure that it's not a double-click) in favor of the snapper `click` event that fires without any delay.

We restricted the layer coverage to just the vector layer containing the circles via the `layers` property. We finish by adding the interaction to the map via the `addInteraction` map method.

Using the `select` interaction has the benefit of automatically styling selected features differently, so that it's apparent they've been selected. You can customize the styling that's rendered on the map through the `style` property.

```
select.on('select', function(event) {
  selectedFeature = event.selected[0];
  if (selectedFeature) {
    overlay.setPosition(selectedFeature.getGeometry().getCenter());
  } else {
    overlay.setPosition(undefined);
  }
});
```

Although the select interaction has been added to the map, we can't respond to the actions without first subscribing to some of its published events. We forge a subscription by using the `on` method to create an event handler for the `select` event.

When this event gets published, the event object contains the selected features (if there are any) inside the selected array. If applicable, it also contains any previously unselected features inside the deselected array. We store the first selected feature (as we're only expecting one to be selected at a time for this recipe) in the `selectedFeature` variable.

If a feature has been selected, then the overlay is positioned in the center of the circle geometry using the `setPosition` method. If there is no feature selected, then we ensure that the overlay is not visible. This is accomplished by passing `undefined` to `setPosition`.

```
var circle = selectedFeature.clone();
var circleGeometry = circle.getGeometry();
var circleCenter = circleGeometry.getCenter();

circleGeometry.setCenter([
  circleCenter[0] + circleGeometry.getRadius() * 2,
  circleCenter[1]
]);
vectorLayer.getSource().addFeature(circle);
overlay.setPosition(undefined);
select.getFeatures().clear();
```

There's a fair amount going on inside the click handler for the `clone` button. You'll see that we use many methods that are available from the `ol.Feature` instance.

We begin by cloning the selected circle with the `clone` method. With our copy of the circle, we cache the geometry (`getGeometry`) and center coordinates (`getCenter`) to variables that we reference later on.

The new circle geometry is centered at a different location via the `setCenter` method. The method expects an array of type `ol.Coordinate`. When we populate this array, we modify the x coordinate (`circleCenter[0]`) so that it's a full diameter width (of the original circle) away from the circle that we're cloning. The y coordinate remains untouched, resulting in the new circle horizontally adjacent to the original.

This new circle is then added to the vector layer source. To do this, we access the vector layer source through the `getSource` method from the vector layer, and then we chain on the `addFeature` vector source method passing in our circle. Once this feature has been added to the vector source, we close the overlay by setting the position to `undefined`.

The `select` interaction temporarily adds a copy of the circle feature, which provides the 'selected' style. To remove this feature from the map, we retrieve the selected features (`getFeatures`) from the select interaction, which returns an `ol.Collection` of features. We remove all these features from the collection using the `clear` method.

```
vectorLayer.getSource().removeFeature(selectedFeature);
overlay.setPosition(undefined);
select.getFeatures().clear();
```

Within the less complicated `click` event handler for the remove button, we gain access to the vector layer source (`getSource`) and remove the currently selected feature (stored in `selectedFeature` during the `select` event handler). As seen in the clone handler, we reset the overlay position in order to hide it from the map, and we also clear any temporary features that were held in the `select` interaction collection.

We covered some important ground here by introducing map interactions and some of the powerful benefits that they can provide to a mapping application. We'll get to explore other map interactions as this book progresses.

See also

▶ The *Using point features as markers* recipe

Zooming to the extent of a layer

When a group of features coexist on a vector map layer, such as circles and polygons, they make up a shared extent, which is also known as a *bounding box*. This rectangular extent accommodates all the geometries. It can be useful to acquire the extent of such a group of features so that we can reposition the map at optimal resolution for the point of interest, which is exactly what we will do in this recipe.

We will place some features on the map at low resolution, but initially, we will configure the map resolution to start much higher. The group of features will appear small to begin with, but we'll provide a button that conveniently pans and zooms the user much closer to the group of features, based on their combined extent.

The source code can be found in `ch03/ch03-zoom-to-extent/`. We'll end up with something that looks like the following screenshot:

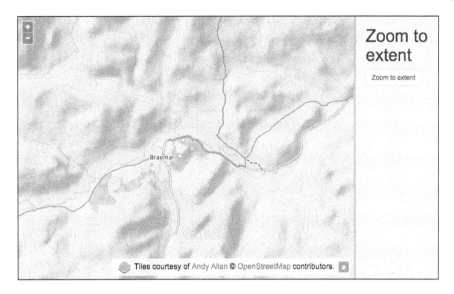

How to do it...

Discover how you can zoom to the extent of some features on a layer using the following instructions:

1. Create an HTML file with OpenLayers dependencies, a `div` element to hold the map, and also the panel to house the button:

```
<div id="js-map"></div>
<div>
  <button id="js-zoom">Zoom to extent</button>
</div>
```

2. Create a custom JavaScript file and create a raster layer for the background mapping:

```
var rasterLayer = new ol.layer.Tile({
  source: new ol.source.OSM({
    attributions: [
      new ol.Attribution({
        html: 'Tiles courtesy of ' +
        '<a href="http://www.thunderforest.com">Andy Allan</a>'
      }),
      ol.source.OSM.ATTRIBUTION
    ],
    url: 'http://{a-c}.tile.thunderforest.com/cycle/' +
        '{z}/{x}/{y}.png'
  })
});
```

3. Create a vector layer with some geometries, as follows:

```
var vectorLayer = new ol.layer.Vector({
  source: new ol.source.Vector({
    features: [
      new ol.Feature(new ol.geom.Circle([-376645, 7762876], 200)),
      new ol.Feature(new ol.geom.Circle([-375955, 7762195], 200)),
      new ol.Feature(new ol.geom.Circle([-376953, 7761632], 200))
    ]
  })
});
```

4. Instantiate a new `map`:

```
var map = new ol.Map({
  view: new ol.View({
    zoom: 11,
    center: [-372592, 7763536]
  }),
  target: 'js-map',
  layers: [rasterLayer, vectorLayer]
});
```

5. Finally, add the button `click` handler and logic to recenter the map, as follows:

```
document.getElementById('js-zoom')
  .addEventListener('click', function() {
    map.beforeRender(
      ol.animation.pan({
        source: map.getView().getCenter(),
        duration: 150
      }),
      ol.animation.zoom({
        resolution: map.getView().getResolution(),
        duration: 500,
        easing: ol.easing.easeIn
      })
    );
    map.getView().fit(
  vectorLayer.getSource().getExtent(), map.getSize()
  );
});
```

How it works...

Let's concentrate on what happens when the button is clicked, as this is where the OpenLayers code is utilized to relocate the map:

```
map.beforeRender(
  ol.animation.pan({
    source: map.getView().getCenter(),
    duration: 150
  }),
  ol.animation.zoom({
    resolution: map.getView().getResolution(),
    duration: 500,
    easing: ol.easing.easeIn
  })
);
```

Within the click handler, we start off by adding two animation pre-render functions (`ol.animation.pan` and `ol.animation.zoom`). We are momentarily going to be relocating the map view center position and zoom level based on the extent of the features, and we wish to perform this change through graceful transitions. The details of these types of transition behaviors and how they work have previously been covered in the *Moving around the map view* recipe in *Chapter 1, Web Mapping Basics*.

```
map.getView().fit(
    vectorLayer.getSource().getExtent(), map.getSize()
);
```

The map view (retrieved via the `getView` map method) contains a method called `fit`. The purpose of `fit` is to accommodate the given geometry or extent into a customized area (normally the same size of map viewport, but it doesn't have to be).

The `fit` method expects the first parameter to be one of two types, of which, we're interested in the type `ol.Extent`. This type is just an array of coordinates that make up the bounding box of our features. The vector source has a method called `getExtent` that enables us to retrieve this information. We pass in the resulting `ol.Extent` array as the first parameter.

The second parameter of `fit` expects a type of `ol.Size`, which is simply an array containing the width and height of the box in pixels. We want the extent of the features to fit as best they can into the viewport of the map, so we use the `getSize` map method, which returns the size in the desired format.

The `fit` method optionally takes a third parameter—an object of configurable properties, such as `minResolution`, which can be used to determine the minimum resolution that you'd like to see the extent of the features at when this function is called.

The `fit` method will automatically adjust the map view at the most optimal resolution that's available so that all features are in sight.

Adding text labels to geometry points

Points of interest in the real world can be represented through a variety of shapes, such as circles and lines, but the geometry alone may not be informative enough for various purposes. For example, you may have some polygons representing zones, but you want to label these zones as zone A, zone B, and zone C. Or perhaps, you need to display the number of people at a location, represented with a circle and a label containing the count.

For this recipe, we will assign the name of a person to a geometry point. The features will be placed at some houses. You can use your imagination as to why this may be useful! The source code can be found in `ch03/ch03-geometry-labels/`. Here's a screenshot of what we'll end up with:

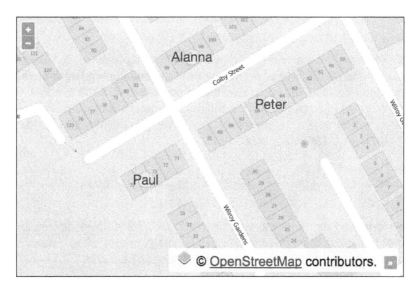

How to do it...

We will learn how to add useful text labels to geometry points using the following steps:

1. Create an HTML file with OpenLayers dependencies and a `div` element to hold the map.

2. Create a custom JavaScript file and instantiate the `map`, `view`, and raster layer:

    ```
    var map = new ol.Map({
      view: new ol.View({
        zoom: 19,
        center: [-161669, 6609321]
      }),
    ```

```
  target: 'js-map',
  layers: [
    new ol.layer.Tile({
      source: new ol.source.OSM()
    })
  ]
});
```

3. Create a function that'll be used to generate point features with a text label:

```
var createPoint = function(coords, resident) {
  var feature = new ol.Feature(new ol.geom.Point(coords));
  feature.set('resident', resident);
  return feature;
};
```

4. Create the function that'll be used to style the point features:

```
var getStyle = function(feature) {
  return [
    new ol.style.Style({
      text: new ol.style.Text({
        text: feature.get('resident'),
        fill: new ol.style.Fill({
          color: '#333'
        }),
        stroke: new ol.style.Stroke({
          color: [255, 255, 255, 0.8],
          width: 2
        }),
        font: '26px "Helvetica Neue", Arial'
      }),
      image: new ol.style.Circle({
        fill: new ol.style.Fill({
          color: [255, 255, 255, 0.3]
        }),
        stroke: new ol.style.Stroke({
          color: [51, 153, 204, 0.4],
          width: 1.5
        }),
        radius: 15
      })
    })
  ];
};
```

5. Add the vector layer to the map with our generated point features and styling function:

```
map.addLayer(
  new ol.layer.Vector({
    source: new ol.source.Vector({
      features: [
        createPoint([-161705, 6609398], 'Alanna'),
        createPoint([-161659, 6609371], 'Peter'),
        createPoint([-161732, 6609328], 'Paul')
      ]
    }),
    style: getStyle
  })
);
```

How it works...

The main two aspects of this recipe are how to set a custom property against a feature, and how to render this label on to the map. Let's break it down, as follows:

```
var createPoint = function(coords, resident) {
  var feature = new ol.Feature(new ol.geom.Point(coords));
  feature.set('resident', resident);
  return feature;
};
```

For convenience, we create the point features from this reusable function. Our function takes an array of coordinates (`coords`) and the name of the resident (`resident`). This creates the point geometry feature based on the passed in coordinates, then assigns the name of the resident to a custom property of the feature itself, namely `resident`. The `set` method is inherited from the `ol.Object` class.

Next up is our `getStyle` function, which is in the format that OpenLayers requires (`ol.style.StyleFunction`). When it's called by OpenLayers, it is passed the instance of `ol.Feature` and the view's resolution, respectively. Our function will completely determine how this feature gets styled. In order to meet the OpenLayers function contract, our method must return an array with one or more `ol.style.Style` instances.

```
text: new ol.style.Text({
  text: feature.get('resident'),
  fill: new ol.style.Fill({
    color: '#333'
  }),
  stroke: new ol.style.Stroke({
    color: [255, 255, 255, 0.8],
```

```
      width: 2
    }),
    font: '26px "Helvetica Neue", Arial'
  }),
```

Inline of the returned array, we create one new instance of `ol.style.Style`, omitted in the previous code for brevity. Within the configuration object, we supply a value for the `text` property, which is an instance of `ol.style.Text`. The configuration object for this constructor also has a `text` property. As OpenLayers passes in the feature for us, the `feature` variable will be in scope when `getStyle` is called, so we simply retrieve the `resident` value from the feature itself via the `get` method of `ol.Object`.

We also provide fill with color, stroke with color, width, and font with size and family. There are many other properties and style types available, such as the `lineDash` property for strokes and the style type `ol.style.RegularShape`.

You'll notice that color can be defined in various ways. For the `fill` property, we provided the color as a string in shorthand Hex format. For `stroke`, we passed in an array of type `ol.Color` in the RGBA (Red, Green, Blue, Alpha) format.

```
  image: new ol.style.Circle({
    fill: new ol.style.Fill({
      color: [255, 255, 255, 0.3]
    }),
    stroke: new ol.style.Stroke({
      color: [51, 153, 204, 0.4],
      width: 1.5
    }),
    radius: 15
  })
```

The second and last property of the `ol.style.Style` instance is `image`. This is what's used to render a circle behind the text label. We set the `fill` and `stroke` colors using the RGBA array technique and also provide a stroke width and circle radius.

```
  new ol.layer.Vector({
      source: new ol.source.Vector({
        features: [
          createPoint([-161705, 6609398], 'Alanna'),
          createPoint([-161659, 6609371], 'Peter'),
          createPoint([-161732, 6609328], 'Paul')
        ]
      }),
      style: getStyle
    })
```

When the vector layer is created, we call our custom `createPoint` function three times to return the geometry points inline of the `features` array.

Our custom `getStyle` method is assigned to the `style` property of the vector layer. It will be called by OpenLayers when a feature from this layer needs styling with the `feature` and `resolution` arguments, as previously mentioned.

We explore styling much further in *Chapter 6, Styling Features*.

Adding features from a WFS server

The **Web Feature Service** (**WFS**) is an OGC standard that provides independent platform calls to request geographical features to a server. In practice, this means that a client makes an HTTP request to a server that implements the WFS standard and gets a set of features in varying formats, typically GML (Geographic Markup Language, `http://en.wikipedia. org/wiki/Geography_Markup_Language`).

> If you want to learn more about this, there is a complete specification on the OGC site, `http://www.opengeospatial.org/standards/ wfs`. From the OpenLayers point of view, the WFS is nothing more than another data source that we can read to fill a vector layer.

Before continuing, there is an important point to take into account. Most of the requests made by OpenLayers when data is loaded, such as GML, KML, or GeoJSON files, are made asynchronously through AJAX requests.

Any JavaScript call is limited by the security model imposed by the browser, which avoids cross-domain requests. This means that you can only make requests to the same server that the web page originally came from.

There are different ways to bypass this limitation. Such techniques include JSONP (`https://en.wikipedia.org/wiki/JSONP`) and adjusting CORS permissions (`https://en.wikipedia.org/wiki/Cross-origin_resource_sharing`), or the use of a proxy on the server-side.

> You can read a clearer explanation of proxy implementations at `http://developer.yahoo.com/javascript/howto-proxy.html`.

The idea of a proxy is simple; instead of making a request directly to a cross domain, we make a request to a script on the same domain, which is responsible for forwarding the cross-domain request for us and returning the results. A script on the server is not limited by the cross-domain requests that browser vendors impose.

For this recipe (found in `ch03/ch03-wfs-layer/`), we will be using a proxy server written in Node.js in order to forward the request and return the response (refer to the `server.js` file in the root of the book's source code). We'll end up with a rendered WFS layer looking similar to the following screenshot:

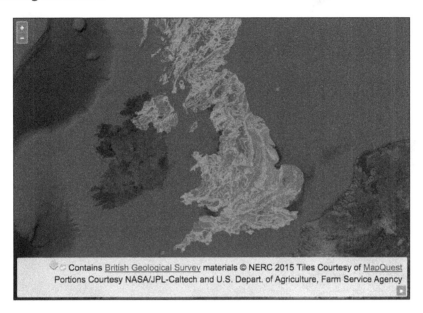

Contains British Geological Survey materials © NERC 2015 Tiles Courtesy of MapQuest
Portions Courtesy NASA/JPL-Caltech and U.S. Depart. of Agriculture, Farm Service Agency

How to do it...

Connect to an external WFS server and render the features on the map by following these instructions:

1. Create an HTML file including the OpenLayers dependencies, and add a `div` element to hold the map.

2. Create a custom JavaScript file and initiate `map`:

```javascript
var map = new ol.Map({
  view: new ol.View({
    zoom: 6,
    center: [-415817, 6790054]
  }),
  target: 'js-map',
  layers: [
    new ol.layer.Tile({
      source: new ol.source.MapQuest({layer: 'sat'})
    })
  ]
});
```

3. Create the vector source that will be responsible for the WFS requests:

```
var vectorSource = new ol.source.Vector({
  format: new ol.format.WFS(),
  url: function(extent, resolution, projection) {
    return [
      '/proxy?proxyHost=ogc.bgs.ac.uk',
      'proxyPath=/digmap625k_gsml32_cgi_gs/wfs?',
      'service=WFS',
      'version=1.1.0',
      'request=GetFeature',
      'typename=test:uk_625k_mapped_feature',
      'srsname=' + projection.getCode(),
      'bbox=' + extent.join(',') + ',' + projection.getCode(),
      'outputformat=gml3'
    ].join('&');
  },
  strategy: ol.loadingstrategy.tile(ol.tilegrid.createXYZ()),
  attributions: [
    new ol.Attribution({
      html: 'Contains <a href="http://bgs.ac.uk/">British
Geological Survey</a> ' +
        'materials &copy; NERC 2015'
    })
  ]
});
```

4. Set up a vector layer, add the vector source to it, and add the layer to the map:

```
var vectorLayer = new ol.layer.Vector({
  source: vectorSource,
  opacity: 0.4
});
map.addLayer(vectorLayer);
```

How it works...

There's always some amount of upfront work involved when creating WFS layers, as you'll need to interpret the capabilities of the service that you're trying to retrieve information from and then shape the HTTP requests accordingly.

To help us find out about the WFS service, the server normally provides an XML document outlining the capabilities of the service. As an example, the capabilities document for the WFS service that we access in this recipe can be found here at `http://ogc.bgs.ac.uk/ digmap625k_gsml32_cgi_gs/wfs?service=WFS&request=GetCapabilities`.

```
var vectorSource = new ol.source.Vector({
  format: new ol.format.WFS(),
```

When this vector source retrieves content from the WFS service, we inform OpenLayers what the expected format of the response will be in order to successfully parse the data and add it to the map. The format of the data will be in the WFS format, and the features will be presented in GML3 (which we specify as part of the URL string, namely output format).

You can pass an optional configuration object to the WFS format constructor, which has some properties worth mentioning, as follows:

▸ **gmlFormat**: The default GML format for `ol.format.WFS` is `ol.format.GML3`, but you can specify `ol.format.GML2` if you need to

▸ **featureType**: This is the feature type; you've got an opportunity to be selective here

▸ **featureNS**: This is the namespace URI used for features

Let's move on to the next property of the vector source configuration:

```
url: function(extent, resolution, projection) {
    return [
        '/proxy?proxyHost=ogc.bgs.ac.uk',
        'proxyPath=/digmap625k_gsml32_cgi_gs/wfs?',
        'service=WFS',
        'version=1.1.0',
        'request=GetFeature',
        'typename=test:uk_625k_mapped_feature',
        'srsname=' + projection.getCode(),
        'bbox=' + extent.join(',') + ',' + projection.getCode(),
        'outputformat=gml3'
    ].join('&');
},
```

We manually construct the URL that will make up the AJAX request through a function assigned to the `url` property. This function must conform to the function type of `ol.FeatureUrlFunction`, which, as you see, takes `extent` (type `ol.Extent`), the map's `resolution` (type number) and the map's `projection` (type `ol.proj.Projection`). We can use these available arguments to dynamically build out the URL. Our function must return the URL as a string.

We are using a proxy mechanism to complete the request for us. The proxy implementation requires that we pass the host name as the `proxyHost` parameter, and the path name as the `proxyPath` parameter. If it helps, so far, we have the following endpoint: `ogc.bgs.ac.uk/digmap625k_gsml32_cgi_gs/wfs?`. We append further criteria to this string as query key/value pairs.

Some of the key/value pairs are static values that match up with the capabilities offered by the WFS service. These will begin to look more familiar to you once you've worked with a few different web services, such as version 1.1.0, and requests, such as `GetFeature`. The `typename` key specifies what type of feature set we're interested in. This will inevitably vary between providers.

We dynamically set the `srsname` key (spatial reference), which is retrieved from the map's current projection (for example, `EPSG:3857`). The `bbox` is dynamically determined from a combination of the view extent (which is originally an array converted into a comma-delimited string via the JavaScript `join` method) and the map's projection (`projection.getCode()`).

This function must return the URL as a string, so we convert the array into a string once again using the `join` method, which inserts an ampersand between each item in the array, conforming to the standard query string structure, that is, `service=WFS&version=1.0.0`.

```
strategy: ol.loadingstrategy.tile(ol.tilegrid.createXYZ()),
```

We have chosen to use a nondefault data loading strategy of tile (`ol.loadingstrategy.all` being the default). This makes requests and loads in features based on the tile grid with the XYZ tiling scheme. To find out more about the XYZ tiling scheme, refer to `http://wiki.openstreetmap.org/wiki/Slippy_map_tilenames`. There's also a good resource that explains the difference between XYZ and **Tile Map Service** (**TMS**) tiling schemes, found here at `https://gist.github.com/tmcw/4954720`.

This WFS service only covers the UK, so we could optimally restrict the extent of the tile grid to the bounds of the UK so that wasteful requests are avoided. The `ol.tilegrid.createXYZ` class can be optionally given a configuration object, of which the `extent` property can be assigned an `ol.Extent` array that will confine the bounds of the requests. We can also specify minimum and maximum zoom levels and the tile size.

There's more...

You may find that map servers that support WMS and WFS protocols can serve the same information both in raster and vector formats.

Imagine a set of regions stored in PostgreSQL/PostGIS and a map server, such as GeoServer, with a layer of countries configured to be served both as raster images via WMS requests or in the vector GML format using WFS requests.

See also

> ▸ The *Adding WMS layers* recipe from *Chapter 2, Adding Raster Layers*
> ▸ The *Removing or cloning features using overlays* recipe
> ▸ The *Using point features as markers* recipe
> ▸ The *Reading features directly using AJAX* recipe

Using the cluster strategy

Imagine a scenario where we want to show all the gas stations in every city around the world. What will happen when the user navigates within the map and sets a zoom level to look at the whole world? We're presented with an overwhelming dominance of points, overlapping each other all at the same place, providing little visual value to the user.

A solution to this problem is to cluster the features on each zoom level. OpenLayers makes this very easy to implement.

This recipe (source code in ch03/ch03-clustering) shows how easy it is to apply clustering on a vector layer, which is responsible for grouping the features to avoid a situation similar to the one discussed earlier that can be seen in the following screenshot:

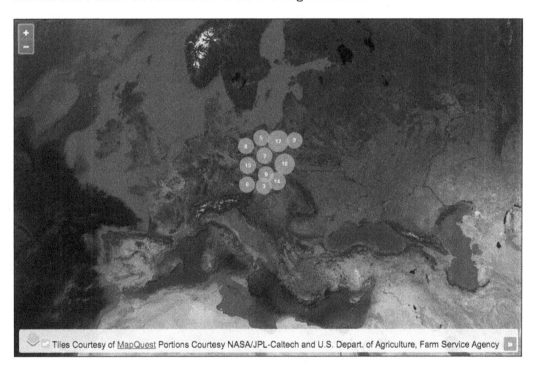

Tiles Courtesy of MapQuest Portions Courtesy NASA/JPL-Caltech and U.S. Depart. of Agriculture, Farm Service Agency

How to do it...

Utilize the great clustering capability of OpenLayers using the following instructions:

1. Create an HTML file with OpenLayers dependencies and a `div` element to hold the map.

2. Initialize the `map`, as follows:

```
var map = new ol.Map({
  view: new ol.View({
    zoom: 4,
    center: [2152466, 5850795]
  }),
  target: 'js-map',
  layers: [
    new ol.layer.Tile({
      source: new ol.source.MapQuest({layer: 'sat'})
    })
  ]
});
```

3. Randomly generate a bunch of points that are restricted to a particular extent:

```
var getRandomInt = function(min, max) {
  return Math.floor(Math.random() * (max - min + 1)) + min;
};

var features = [];
var numberOfFeatures = 0;

while(numberOfFeatures < 100) {
  var point = new ol.geom.Point([
    getRandomInt(1545862, 2568284),
    getRandomInt(6102732, 7154505)
  ]);

  features.push(new ol.Feature(point));
  numberOfFeatures++;
}
```

4. Set up the styling function used to render the clusters:

```
var getStyle = function(feature) {
  var length = feature.get('features').length;
  return [
    new ol.style.Style({
```

```
        image: new ol.style.Circle({
          radius: Math.min(
            Math.max(length * 1.2, 15), 20
          ),
          fill: new ol.style.Fill({
            color: [0, 204, 0, 0.6]
          })
        }),
        text: new ol.style.Text({
          text: length.toString(),
          fill: new ol.style.Fill({
            color: 'white'
          }),
          stroke: new ol.style.Stroke({
            color: [0, 51, 0, 1],
            width: 1
          }),
          font: '10px "Helvetica Neue", Arial'
        })
      })
    ];
  };
```

5. Create the vector layer, add the cluster source, then add the layer to the map:

```
var vectorLayer = new ol.layer.Vector({
  source: new ol.source.Cluster({
    distance: 25,
    source: new ol.source.Vector({
      features: features
    })
  }),
  style: getStyle
});
map.addLayer(vectorLayer);
```

How it works...

We randomly placed 100 geometry points within an arbitrary extent across Europe. We previously used this technique in the *Exporting features as GeoJSON* recipe, where we explained in detail how this works. If you need a reminder, head over to that recipe, as we'll move on and focus our attention on how the clustering is achieved.

Our `getStyle` method is called by OpenLayers when the cluster needs rendering. It's attached to the `style` property of the vector layer. We want to add a text label to display the number of points beneath the cluster and give the cluster some nondefault styling. We saw very similar styling with accompanying explanations in the *Adding text label to geometry point* recipe, so we will only take a look over some parts of the styling used for this recipe:

```
image: new ol.style.Circle({
  radius: Math.min(
    Math.max(length * 1.2, 15), 20
  ),
```

Circles will be drawn on the map to represent clusters of points. The more points a cluster contains, the larger the radius of the circle will be. Features that are part of a clustered source are applied a custom property, namely `features`. This contains an array of all the features within that cluster. We retrieve this value using the `ol.Feature get` method, `feature.get('features').length`, and store it in a variable, namely `length`.

We multiply the length of the features by `1.2`, but we pick the maximum number of either the result of the multiplication or `15` using the JavaScript `Math.max` method. We don't want any clusters smaller than a radius of `15`.

On the contrary, we don't want any cluster bigger than a radius of `20`, so `Math.min` is used to wrap the result of the maximum radius and limit the radius if required.

```
text: new ol.style.Text({
  text: length.toString(),
```

The text of the cluster is simply derived from the number of features within the cluster array. The number must be converted to a string type for OpenLayers. The `toString` method is a native JavaScript method for type coercion.

The rest of the `ol.style.Style` object simply assigns colors, widths, and fonts wherever applicable.

```
var vectorLayer = new ol.layer.Vector({
  source: new ol.source.Cluster({
    distance: 25,
    source: new ol.source.Vector({
      features: features
    })
  })
```

We create a vector layer as normal, but `source` is an instance of `ol.source.Cluster` (which extends the `ol.source.Vector` class).

The `distance` property of the cluster source enforces the minimum distance (in pixels) between clusters. The default is 20.

The `source` property of the cluster source is an instance of `ol.source.Vector`, where we pass in the 100 generated features from earlier.

Every time the zoom level changes, the cluster strategy computes the distance among all features and adds all the features that conform to some parameters of the same cluster.

See also

▶ The *Creating features programmatically* recipe

▶ The *Adding features from a WFS server* recipe

Reading features directly using AJAX

The goal of this recipe is to show us how we can work directly with AJAX requests and load content from different data sources on the same vector layer.

OpenLayers allows us to read data from different origins and sources. We've seen that we can connect to a variety of services (such as WMS and WFS) and/or customize the request according to our needs (such as providing a URL directly pointing to a GML file).

We've seen that providing a URL and format type to the vector source is convenient and works for many cases. OpenLayers makes the AJAX request for us and automatically formats the response. However, there are times when we need even more control over the AJAX request and response, and this is where the `loader` function comes into play.

We have chosen to use jQuery to perform the AJAX requests. The requests will pull in two separate geometry files of different formats and add them both to the same vector layer. The source code for this recipe can be found in `ch03/ch03-reading-features-from-ajax/`. Here's the resulting geometry that we'll collate and render on the map:

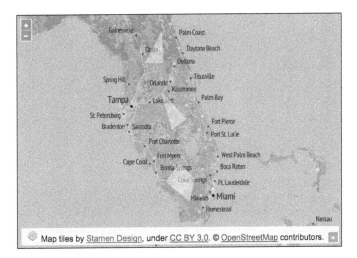

How to do it...

Create your custom AJAX loader using the following instructions:

1. Create an HTML file and add the OpenLayers dependencies and the jQuery library. Add a `div` element to hold the map.

2. Next, initialize the `map`, add a raster layer, and center the viewport:

```
var map = new ol.Map({
  view: new ol.View({
    zoom: 7,
    center: [-9039137, 3169996]
  }),
  target: 'js-map',
  layers: [
    new ol.layer.Tile({
      source: new ol.source.Stamen({layer: 'terrain'})
    })
  ]
});
```

3. Now, create a vector layer with a source that's responsible for making the multiple AJAX requests to fetch the two geometry files. Parse and then add the returned data to the vector source features list:

```
var vectorLayer = new ol.layer.Vector({
  source: new ol.source.Vector({
    loader: function() {
      $.ajax({
        type: 'GET',
        url: 'points.wkt',
        context: this
      }).done(function(data) {
        var format = new ol.format.WKT({splitCollection: true});
        this.addFeatures(format.readFeatures(data));
      });

      $.ajax({
        type: 'GET',
        url: 'polygons.json',
        context: this
      }).done(function(data) {
        var format = new ol.format.GeoJSON();
        this.addFeatures(format.readFeatures(data));
      });
```

```
        }
     })
  });
```

4. Add the vector layer to the `map`:

```
map.addLayer(vectorLayer);
```

How it works...

Let's get straight to it and break down the important parts of this recipe:

```
source: new ol.source.Vector({
   loader: function() {
```

We use the `loader` property of the vector source to provide a custom function of type `ol.FeatureLoader`. Similar to the `url` property (which takes a function type of `ol.FeatureUrlFunction`), the `loader` function is also passed `extent`, `resolution`, and `projection`, respectively. We've omitted these as we don't make any use of them for our requests.

```
$.ajax({
   type: 'GET',
   url: 'points.wkt',
   context: this
```

With the help of jQuery, we set up an HTTP `GET` request, pointing towards a local geometry file, packed with points in the WKT format.

Within the `loader` function, the `this` keyword in JavaScript points to the vector source. We intend to use this reference when we add the returned features to the source from within the AJAX promise (done). jQuery offers a useful property called `context` that enables us to specify what the value of `this` references in the callbacks or promises. This saves us writing temporary variables or referencing the vector source in another way.

```
}).done(function(data) {
   var format = new ol.format.WKT({splitCollection: true});
   this.addFeatures(format.readFeatures(data));
});
```

Once the AJAX request has responded with success, our `done` promise is fired. The data parameter contains the content of the WKT file.

When the WKT format object is created, we pass a configuration object with the `splitCollection` property set to `true`. By default, OpenLayers will wrap the WKT geometries into a geometry collection, but we'd prefer each point to be classified as an individual feature in the feature collection. This is really just minor semantics for our example.

The features are processed (`format.readFeatures`) and added to the vector source (`this.addFeatures`), this is the equivalent of `vectorLayer.getSource()` here.

```
$.ajax({
  type: 'GET',
    url: 'polygons.json',
    context: this
  }).done(function(data) {
    var format = new ol.format.GeoJSON();
    this.addFeatures(format.readFeatures(data));
  });
```

This request is the same as the previous request, although this time around, we fetch a file containing data in the GeoJSON format. The features are added to the same vector layer.

When using the `loader` function, we are responsible for loading and adding the features to the layer ourselves.

There's more...

With the `loader` function, you have an opportunity to filter the list of features before adding them to a layer. This can be extremely useful if, for example, you're only interested in a subset of the feature list. You may filter based on geometry type, size, arbitrary properties, and so on.

See also

- ▸ The *Adding a GML layer* recipe
- ▸ The *Adding features from a WFS server* recipe
- ▸ The *Adding a KML layer* recipe

Creating a heat map

When you consider heat maps, you may literally think of an application that is used to visualize heat distribution across the planet, which is definitely an appropriate use case. You can, however, adapt the heat map effect to convey other properties, such as the relative quantity of any data type within areas. The more intense the *'heat'*, the more dense the information underneath.

For example, imagine a map that reflects how many users are currently online, playing your favorite game. We can specify locations with a `weight` attribute, which is indicative of the amount of players online for that geographic location. This is the scenario we'll go with for this recipe and can be seen in the following screenshot:

The source code can be found in `ch03/ch03-heat-map`.

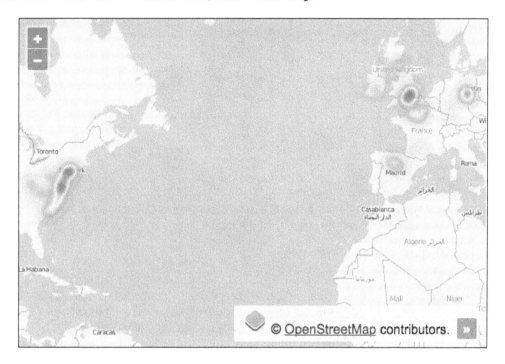

How to do it...

Here's how to build a heat map of some fictional online users:

1. Create an HTML file and add the OpenLayers dependencies and also a `div` element to hold the map.

2. Next, initialize the `map`, add a raster layer, and set up `view`:

```
var map = new ol.Map({
  view: new ol.View({
    zoom: 3,
    center: [-4187526, 4481044]
  }),
  target: 'js-map',
  layers: [
    new ol.layer.Tile({
      source: new ol.source.OSM()
    })
  ]
});
```

3. Finish off by creating a heat map layer with a source reaching out to a GeoJSON file of geometry points. Add this layer to the map:

```
map.addLayer(new ol.layer.Heatmap({
    source: new ol.source.Vector({
        url: 'users-online.json',
        format: new ol.format.GeoJSON({
            defaultDataProjection: 'EPSG:3857'
        })
    })
}));
```

How it works...

You'll notice that creating a heat map with the default settings in OpenLayers is very straightforward. Let's look over the creation of the heat layer:

```
map.addLayer(new ol.layer.Heatmap({
    source: new ol.source.Vector({
```

The heat map layer, `ol.layer.Heatmap`, extends the `ol.layer.Vector` class. This extension offers many styling properties for the heat effect that we haven't modified for this example, such as `gradient` (where you can explicitly choose the color palette used for the heat intensity increments) and the self-explanatory blur and shadow properties. I encourage you to familiarize yourself with the other available properties for the heat layer.

```
    url: 'users-online.json',
    format: new ol.format.GeoJSON({
        defaultDataProjection: 'EPSG:3857'
    })
```

The vector source points to an external GeoJSON file (`users-online.json`) and parses it through the GeoJSON formatter. OpenLayers takes care of the AJAX request for us.

The GeoJSON file contains a series of geometry points. Importantly, every point feature has a `weight` attribute. For example, here's one of the points taken directly from the GeoJSON file:

```
{
    "type": "Feature",
    "geometry": {
        "type": "Point",
        "coordinates": [-342437, 7435794]
    },
    "properties": {
        "weight": 0.6
    }
}
```

When OpenLayers reads this feature for heat layers, it looks for a feature property called `weight`. The `weight` attribute (which must be between _0_ and _1_) reflects the intensity at this location. In other words, _1_ infers a high amount of users online and _0.1_ infers a low amount of users online.

The feature attribute doesn't have to be named `weight`, though. You can name it something arbitrary and inform OpenLayers what the attribute is called via the `weight` property of `ol.layer.Heatmap`.

Within the GeoJSON formatter (`ol.format.GeoJSON`), we inform OpenLayers (via the `defaultDataProjection` property) that the coordinates within the file belong to the `EPSG:3857` projection so that they render correctly on the map.

This recipe concludes our exploration of vector layers. We've learned how to create layers with appropriate strategies for the data, how to integrate with external geometry sources in a variety of different formats, how to package up layer data for export, how to interact with features on these layers, and also some basic feature manipulation and styling.

See also

- ▸ The _Adding a GML layer_ recipe
- ▸ The _Using the cluster strategy_ recipe
- ▸ The _Modifying layer appearance_ recipe from _Chapter 7, Beyond the Basics_.

4
Working with Events

In this chapter, we will cover the following topics:

- ▶ Creating a side-by-side map comparator
- ▶ Implementing a work-in-progress indicator for map layers
- ▶ Listening for the vector layer features' events
- ▶ Listening for mouse or touch events
- ▶ Using the keyboard to pan or zoom

Introduction

This chapter is focused on events, which is an important concept in any JavaScript application. Although this chapter is brief, the concepts explained here are very important to understand when working with OpenLayers and mapping applications in general.

Events are fundamental in JavaScript. They are the impulses that allow us to produce a reaction. As programmers of a mapping application, we are interested in reacting when the map zoom changes, when a layer is loaded, or when a feature is added to a layer. Every class, which is susceptible to emit events, is responsible for managing its listeners (those interested in being notified when an event is fired) and also to emit events under certain circumstances.

For example, we can register a function handler that listens for the `change:resolution` event on the OpenLayers map `view` instance. Every time the `view` instance changes its zoom level, it has the responsibility to trigger the `change:resolution` event, so all its listeners will be notified by the new event.

To help in all this process, OpenLayers has an event class called `ol.ObjectEvent` that extends the event class (`goog.events.Event`) from the Google Closure library, which takes care of registering listeners and simplifying the action of firing an event to all of them. In summary, this class allows listeners to perform the following:

- Define an event
- Register listeners
- Trigger events to notify all listeners

Some classes, such as `ol.Map`, extend the base `ol.ObjectEvent` class to customized subclasses that are better suited for the specific set of available events. The `ol.Map` class has an event class called `ol.MapEvent` that provides some base properties and events. For example, it contains an event called `moveend`, which needless to say, fires when the map is moved.

The `ol.MapEvent` class gets further extended by a class called `ol.MapBrowserEvent`, providing extra methods and events: `click` and `pointerdrag`, to name a few. The event object, which is reflective of the action against the map, has additional information, such as the coordinates of the map event and the pixel position of the browser event.

Besides the `ol.Map` class, many other classes, such as `ol.layer.Vector`, also emit an abundance of event types (of `ol.ObjectEvent`). When layer properties, such as `extent`, `opacity`, and `source` change, there's an opportunity to register a subscription (handler or listener) to these events that get published.

As a programmer, you'll need to look at the OpenLayers API documentation, which is accessible from the OpenLayers website (`http://openlayers.org`), or you can also refer to the source code to find out about the available events that you can register on each class. The source code is also hosted on GitHub (`https://github.com/openlayers/ol3`).

Creating a side-by-side map comparator

We are going to create a map comparator. The goal is to have two maps side-by-side from different providers and synchronize the same position and zoom level. The source code can be found in `ch04/ch04-map-comparator`. Here's a screenshot of our two synchronized maps, side-by-side:

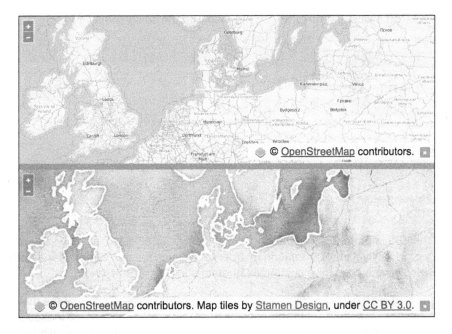

How to do it...

To have two maps work in synchronization, perform the following steps:

1. Create an HTML file with OpenLayers library dependencies. In particular, the markup for the two maps and separator should look like the following:

```
<div id="js-map1"></div>
<hr/>
<div id="js-map2"></div>
```

2. Create a custom JavaScript file and set up the shared `view`:

```
var view = new ol.View({
  zoom: 5,
  center: [1252000, 7240000]
});
```

3. Instantiate the first map with the shared `view`, as follows:

```
var map1 = new ol.Map({
  view: view,
  target: 'js-map1',
  layers: [
    new ol.layer.Tile({source: new ol.source.OSM()})
  ]
});
```

4. Finish off by instantiating the second map with the same shared `view`:

```
var map2 = new ol.Map({
  view: view,
  target: 'js-map2',
  layers: [
    new ol.layer.Tile({
      source: new ol.source.Stamen({layer: 'watercolor'})
    })
  ]
});
```

How it works...

Although the CSS importantly presents the two maps side-by-side, we're going to skip over the details of the styling implementation in order to focus on the JavaScript. Please view the accompanying source code for a complete understanding behind the layout.

You can see that, with minimal effort, we can mirror the zoom and position of the map by simply sharing the view. We caught wind of how easy this was to do when we looked at the *Buffering the layer data to improve the map navigation* recipe in *Chapter 2, Adding Raster Layers,* where the solution also had two maps in synchronization.

OpenLayers 3 has externalized the view from any given map instance. This loose coupling design decision makes techniques like this possible. The OpenLayers `view` object is referenced by both map instances; so, when one map moves, the underlying object updates. This means that the new values also get presented within the other map instance.

As a learning exercise, we can demonstrate how to manually subscribe to the zoom, and position change events from one map instance and reflect the changes onto the other map instance. In this example, the views would not be shared:

```
map1.getView().on(['change:resolution', 'change:center'], syncMap);

function syncMap(event) {
  if (event.type === 'change:resolution') {
    map2.getView().setZoom(event.currentTarget.getZoom());
  } else {
    map2.getView().setCenter(event.currentTarget.getCenter());
  }
};
```

For the first map instance, we get hold of the view (`getView`), subscribe to the `change:resolution` and `change:center` events, and provide a handler function, namely `syncMap`. The `change:center` event is published when the map position has moved, and the `change:resolution` event is published when the map zoom level has changed.

When these events get published, our handler is called and passed an `event` object. This object contains the type of event (`event.type`). This is important as our handler captures multiple types of events. So, using this information, we're able to determine what action to perform based on the type of event.

The `event` object also contains a reference to the view that has been modified, namely `event.currentTarget`. We use this reference to the view to either retrieve the new zoom value (`getZoom`) or the new center coordinates (`getCenter`). We reflect these new values on the second map instance using either the `setZoom` or `setCenter` methods from the `view` object (of the second map instance).

This code has been simplified for brevity, as you'd also need to register for the same event types from the second map instance so that the first map instance can also be updated.

As well as listening to events, we can also cease listening to the notifications if we wish to do so.

The `ol.Observable` class has the `un` method, as well as the `on` method. The `un` method allows us to unsubscribe our listener functions from the published events that we previously subscribed to.

If we continue with our manual subscription example, to unsubscribe from future changes in the zoom level, we can perform the following:

```
map1.getView().un('change:resolution', syncMap);
```

Similar to the `on` method, the `un` method allows you to unregister multiple listeners, so we could have passed an array of event types like we did for `on`, had we wanted to do this.

Our `syncMap` event handler will no longer be passed the zoom level event type.

There's also a method of `ol.Observable`, which is called `once`, that provides the ability to subscribe to an event, listen to just one published event of that type, and then automatically unsubscribe from future notifications.

There may be circumstances where this could prove very useful.

See also

- ▶ The *Using Bing imagery* recipe in *Chapter 2, Adding Raster Layers*
- ▶ The *Implementing a work-in-progress indicator for map layers* recipe
- ▶ The *Listening for vector layer features events* recipe

Implementing a work-in-progress indicator for map layers

In the art of creating great applications, one of the most important things to take into account is the user experience. A good application does what it must do, but it does this by making the user feel comfortable.

When working with remote servers, a lot of time is spent waiting for data retrieval. For example, when working with a tile service, every time we change the zoom level or pan the map, the user has to wait for some time until the data is obtained from the server and the tiles start rendering.

It would be great to show some feedback to the user with a spinner icon, a progress bar, or other familiar visual cues that inform the user that the application is working but needs some time.

This recipe shows us how we can give some feedback to the user by displaying when the application is loading content from an external service, making use of some layer events.

The source code can be found in `ch04/ch04-map-loading-progress`. For convenience, you can also view this recipe at `https://jsfiddle.net/pjlangley/qd6z4p8b/`.

Tiles Courtesy of MapQuest Portions Courtesy NASA/JPL-Caltech and U.S. Depart. of Agriculture, Farm Service Agency

How to do it...

In order to create a map loading progress bar, perform the following steps:

1. Create an HTML file with OpenLayers dependencies. In particular, we have the following markup:

```
<div id="js-map"></div>
<div class="progress">
  <div id="js-progress-bar"></div>
</div>
```

2. Create a custom JavaScript file and set up the raster source and some other global variables that we'll use throughout the code:

```
var rasterSource = new ol.source.MapQuest({layer: 'sat'});
var progressBar = document.getElementById('js-progress-bar');
var tilesLoaded = 0;
var tilesPending = 0;
```

3. Subscribe to some tile events on the source and update the progress bar accordingly when the tiles have finished loading:

```
rasterSource.on(['tileloadend', 'tileloaderror'], function() {
  ++tilesLoaded;
  var percentage = Math.round(tilesLoaded / tilesPending * 100);
  progressBar.style.width = percentage + '%';

  if (percentage >= 100) {
    setTimeout(function() {
      progressBar.parentNode.style.opacity = 0;
      progressBar.style.width = 0;
      tilesLoaded = 0;
      tilesPending = 0;
    }, 600);
  }
});
```

4. Subscribe to one other source event and update the progress bar visibility and the quantity of tiles still pending:

```
rasterSource.on('tileloadstart', function() {
  progressBar.parentNode.style.opacity = 1;
  ++tilesPending;
});
```

5. Finally, instantiate a new map instance and attach the tile source:

```
new ol.Map({
  view: new ol.View({
    zoom: 5,
    center: [-6291073, -1027313]
  }),
  target: 'js-map',
  layers: [
    new ol.layer.Tile({
      source: rasterSource
    })
  ]
});
```

How it works...

We placed a progress bar in the top-right corner of the map. We used the CSS framework Bootstrap to help with some of the styling. The CSS for this won't be covered in detail, so please view the source code for more on how it's achieved. The progress bar reflects the percentage of loaded tiles against those still in flight.

We're going to focus on the event subscriptions and how they influence the progress-loading bar. The rest of this code should look familiar from previous recipes:

```
rasterSource.on(['tileloadend', 'tileloaderror'], function() {
  ++tilesLoaded;
  var percentage = Math.round(tilesLoaded / tilesPending * 100);
  progressBar.style.width = percentage + '%';
```

Using the on method (which sources inherit from ol.Observable), we subscribe to two source event types (of type ol.source.TileEvent). The tileloadend event is published when a tile has been successfully loaded on the map. The tileloaderror event is published when a tile load has failed. It's important that we still capture the failed event type; otherwise, we'd lose track of the pending versus loaded state.

Our handler firstly increments the tilesLoaded count (which is originally set to 0). The percentage is calculated by dividing number of the loaded tiles by the total amount of tiles still pending, and then this is multiplied by 100 so that it can be used as a percentage for the progress bar width. For example, let's say two tiles have loaded, but eight are still pending. *2 / 8 = 0.25. 0.25 * 100 = 25.*

When the width of the progress bar is set, we concatenate the percentage string onto the end of the number so that it can be used as a valid CSS value. The progress bar displays at 25% complete.

```
if (percentage >= 100) {
  setTimeout(function() {
    progressBar.parentNode.style.opacity = 0;
    progressBar.style.width = 0;
    tilesLoaded = 0;
    tilesPending = 0;
  }, 600);
}
```

Within the same handler, we check to see whether the percentage of loaded tiles has reached 100% or more. A user can trigger extra tile loading by further panning or zooming before a previous loading session has completed. Checking for greater than 100% covers us in this scenario.

Within the conditional block, we know that all the tiles have loaded. We reset the progress bar so that it's hidden, has a new starting width of 0, and the tile tracking variables are put back to their original starting value of 0. We wrap this reset within a `setTimeout` JavaScript method because the progress bar width animates into the new position. So, this gives the animation a chance to complete to 100% before hiding it from the map:

```
rasterSource.on('tileloadstart', function() {
  progressBar.parentNode.style.opacity = 1;
  ++tilesPending;
});
```

On the contrary, we subscribe to the event that's published when a tile load is initiated. Our handler ensures the progress bar is visible (as there's at least one tile to load) and increments the amount of tiles pending.

See also

▸ The *Adding WMS layer* recipe in *Chapter 2, Adding Raster Layers*
▸ The *Adding features from a WFS server* recipe in *Chapter 3, Working with Vector Layers*
▸ The *Creating a side-by-side map comparator* recipe
▸ The *Listening for vector layer features' events* recipe

Listening for the vector layer features' events

When working with vector layers, it is common to find a situation where you need to respond to something that's occurred on the layer, such as when a new feature is added, modified, deleted, and so on. Fortunately, these types of events are available from the vector source, and we can easily subscribe to them.

The goal of this recipe is to show you how simple it is to listen for events on a vector source and perform some actions with this information.

We are going to load an external GeoJSON file of geometry points, and we will style the fill color and radius depending on the feature attributes. We will also track how many features are on the vector source layer and allow the user to delete a feature by clicking on it, subsequently updating the feature count. The source code can be found in `ch04/ch04-vector-feature-events`, and here's what we'll end up with:

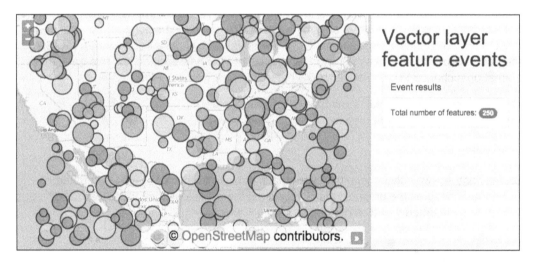

How to do it...

In order to understand how vector layer feature events work, code this recipe yourself by using the following instructions:

1. Create an HTML file and add the OpenLayers dependencies. In particular, add a `div` element to hold the `map` instance and the markup for the side panel and content:

```
<div id="js-map"></div>
<div class="pane">
  <h1>Vector layer feature events</h1>
```

```
      <div class="panel panel-default">
        <h3 class="panel-title">Event results</h3>
          Total number of features:
          <span id="js-feature-count">0</span>
      </div>
    </div>
```

2. Initialize the `map` instance with a base layer and `view`:

```
var map = new ol.Map({
  view: new ol.View({
    zoom: 4,
    center: [-10703629, 2984101]
  }),
  target: 'js-map',
  layers: [
    new ol.layer.Tile({source: new ol.source.OSM()})
  ]
});
```

3. Create a vector layer and read in the GeoJSON file:

```
var vectorLayer = new ol.layer.Vector({
  source: new ol.source.Vector({
    url: 'points.geojson',
    format: new ol.format.GeoJSON({
      defaultDataProjection: 'EPSG:3857'
    })
  })
});
```

4. Create the map select interaction so that features can be selected for removal. Also cache the DOM element that displays the total feature count:

```
var select = new ol.interaction.Select({
  condition: ol.events.condition.click,
  layers: [vectorLayer]
});
map.addInteraction(select);

select.on('select', function(event) {
  if (event.selected[0]) {
    vectorLayer.getSource().removeFeature(event.selected[0]);
    select.getFeatures().clear();
  }
});
var featureCount = document.getElementById('js-feature-count');
```

5. Subscribe to the add feature event and style the feature based on the feature's attributes. Update the feature count display, too:

```
vectorLayer.getSource().on('addfeature', function(event) {
    event.feature.setStyle(new ol.style.Style({
        image: new ol.style.Circle({
            fill: new ol.style.Fill({
                color: event.feature.get('colour')
            }),
            stroke: new ol.style.Stroke({
                color: [0, 13, 51, 0.8],
                width: 2
            }),
            radius: event.feature.get('size')
        })
    }));
    featureCount.innerHTML =
        vectorLayer.getSource().getFeatures().length;
});
```

6. Subscribe to the remove feature event and update the feature count. Finish off by adding the vector layer to the map:

```
vectorLayer.getSource().on('removefeature', function() {
    featureCount.innerHTML =
        vectorLayer.getSource().getFeatures().length;
});
map.addLayer(vectorLayer);
```

How it works...

We've used the CSS framework Bootstrap to help with the side-panel styling. Please view the book's source code for full details of the implementation. Let's move on to the OpenLayers code:

```
select.on('select', function(event) {
    if (event.selected[0]) {
        vectorLayer.getSource().removeFeature(event.selected[0]);
        select.getFeatures().clear();
    }
});
```

We've previously used the select interaction in *Chapter 3, Working with Vector Layers*, in the *Removing or cloning features using overlays* recipe, so we won't go into details here. When a feature is selected (clicked or tapped), it is immediately removed from the vector source (`removeFeature`) and the selection is cleared down. This action will result in a vector layer feature event being published, namely `removefeature`, which we subscribe to. We will cover this handler later on.

```
vectorLayer.getSource().on('addfeature', function(event) {
  event.feature.setStyle(new ol.style.Style({
    image: new ol.style.Circle({
      fill: new ol.style.Fill({
        color: event.feature.get('colour')
      }),
      stroke: new ol.style.Stroke({
        color: [0, 13, 51, 0.8],
        width: 2
      }),
      radius: event.feature.get('size')
    })
  }));
  featureCount.innerHTML =
    vectorLayer.getSource().getFeatures().length;
});
```

We used the `on` method of the vector source to subscribe to the `addfeature` event. Once the vector source retrieves and parses the GeoJSON file, it'll add each feature on to the map, one at a time. This provides us a with a window of opportunity to manipulate the feature before it's added to the layer.

Each geometry point from the file has two custom attributes, namely `color` and `size`. We use this embedded information to style the feature accordingly.

The event object contains a reference to the feature (`event.feature`) that's about to be added to the layer. The feature, of type `ol.Feature`, has a `setStyle` method, which is used to individually style each feature as desired. The fill color of the image is derived from the feature's `colour` attribute (`event.feature.get('colour')`), and the radius is determined from the feature's `size` attribute (`event.feature.get('size')`).

The last bit of work that we do inside the handler is to update the new feature count. This is achieved using the `getFeatures` method of the vector source, which returns an array of all the features. We can get the new length (`getFeatures().length`) and use this number to replace the HTML content with the JavaScript method `innerHTML` on the DOM element.

```
vectorLayer.getSource().on('removefeature', function() {
  featureCount.innerHTML =
    vectorLayer.getSource().getFeatures().length;
});
```

Thankfully, there's not as much work to do when the `removefeature` event is published. All we need to do is update the DOM element with the new feature count, just like before.

There's more...

Vector source events are under a namespace of `ol.source.VectorEvent`. Apart from the two events that we looked over during this recipe, there are others such as `changefeature` and `clear`. These are published when a feature is updated (such as setting a new style) and when all features are cleared from a vector source, respectively.

A vector layer (not vector source) also publishes events, such as `change:extent`, `change:opacity`, and `change:minResolution`. Some of these may become useful when working with vector layers. I encourage you to look over the documentation and/or OpenLayers source code to discover what events are available that could enhance the user's experience.

See also

▸ The *Styling features based on geometry type using symbolizers* recipe from Chapter 6, *Styling Features*

▸ The *Adding a GML layer* recipe in Chapter 3, *Working with Vector Layers*

▸ The *Creating a side-by-side map comparator* recipe

Listening for mouse or touch events

So far, in this chapter, we've looked at how to respond to events that OpenLayers itself publishes, such as tile load events and vector feature events, such as feature added. However, what about user-driven gestures and interactions with the map? This recipe takes a look at some of these types of events.

We'll demonstrate the click or tap and map panning events. When the user clicks on or touches the map, the geometry and pixel coordinates will be displayed in the sidebar. When the map is panned, the new visible extent of the map will be displayed in the sidebar as well.

The source code can be found in `ch04/ch04-mouse-touch-events`, and here's a screenshot of what this will look like:

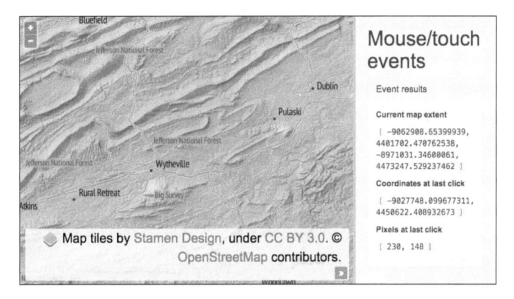

How to do it...

To set up and subscribe to some user-driven events, follow these steps:

1. Create an HTML file and include the OpenLayers dependencies. In particular, include the `div` element for the map and the markup for the side panel and content:

```
<div id="js-map" class="map"></div>
<div class="pane">
  <h1>Mouse/touch events</h1>
  <div class="panel panel-default">
    <h3 class="panel-title">Event results</h3>
    <div class="panel-body">
      <p class="event-heading">Current map extent</p>
      <p>
        <code>[</code>
        <samp id ="js-extent">n/a</samp>
        <code>]</code>
      </p>

      <p class="event-heading">Coordinates at last click</p>
      <p>
        <code>[</code>
        <samp id="js-coords">n/a</samp>
```

```
      <code>]</code>
    </p>

    <p class="event-heading">Pixels at last click</p>
    <p>
      <code>[</code>
      <samp id="js-pixels">n/a</samp>
      <code>]</code>
    </p>
   </div>
  </div>
</div>
```

2. Cache some DOM elements to be used for display, as follows:

```
var coords = document.getElementById('js-coords');
var pixels = document.getElementById('js-pixels');
var extent = document.getElementById('js-extent');
```

3. Set up the map with a `view` and raster layer:

```
new ol.Map({
  view: new ol.View({
    zoom: 10,
    center: [-9016970, 4437475]
  }),
  target: 'js-map',
  layers: [
    new ol.layer.Tile({source: new ol.source.Stamen(
      {layer: 'terrain'}
    )})
  ]
})
```

4. Subscribe to some map events and update the sidebar elements accordingly:

```
.on(['click', 'moveend'], function(event) {
  if (event.type === 'click') {
    coords.innerHTML = event.coordinate.join(',<br>');

    var pixelsAtCoords =
      event.map.getPixelFromCoordinate(event.coordinate);
    pixels.innerHTML = [
      pixelsAtCoords[0].toFixed(0),
      pixelsAtCoords[1].toFixed(0)
    ].join(', ');
  } else {
```

```
        extent.innerHTML = event.map.getView().calculateExtent(
          event.map.getSize()
        ).join(',<br>');
    }
  });
```

How it works...

We've used the CSS framework Bootstrap to style the sidebar content. Some of the HTML has been omitted for brevity, so please view the book source code for the complete implementation.

Referring to the following code section, note that after we instantiate the map, we immediately chain the on method. The map instantiation returns the map instance (of ol.Map), which enables us to carry on without storing a reference to the map in another variable.

```
.on(['click', 'moveend'], function(event) {
  if (event.type === 'click') {
    coords.innerHTML = event.coordinate.join(',<br>');

    var pixelsAtCoords =
      event.map.getPixelFromCoordinate(event.coordinate);
    pixels.innerHTML = [
      pixelsAtCoords[0].toFixed(0),
      pixelsAtCoords[1].toFixed(0)
    ].join(', ');
```

We have supplied an array of events as the first parameter to the on method, namely the click and moveend events. Due to this combined event handler, we must differentiate between the event types when the handler is called, which is why we conditionally check the event.type property before performing the relevant logic.

The event object contains the coordinates of where the map was clicked or touched within event.coordinate. This is an array of *x* and *y* coordinates that we convert into a string, which is separated by a comma and an HTML break tag using the helpful JavaScript join method. This formats the coordinates as desired, which are then added to the DOM via the JavaScript innerHTML method.

As well as the geometry coordinates, we also want the pixel coordinates of the event. The event object stores a reference to the map (event.map), for which the map object has a method that'll return the pixel coordinates from the geometry coordinates, which is called getPixelFromCoordinate. This method expects an array of type ol.Coordinates, so we pass in the event coordinates (event.coordinate) and store the ol.Pixel type array into a variable, namely pixelsAtCoords.

It's worth mentioning that the event object already provides the pixel coordinates within `event.pixel`. The pixel values are conveniently returned without any decimal places. In any case, this was a good learning exercise to expose another OpenLayers API method.

We finish by updating the DOM element that displays the pixel coordinates. To save manual string concatenation, we have built up a temporary array containing the pixel coordinates without any decimal places (using the `toFixed` JavaScript method). We also fused together the array items with a comma and space delimiter using the JavaScript `join` method once again.

```
    } else {
        extent.innerHTML = event.map.getView().calculateExtent(
          event.map.getSize()
        ).join(',<br>');
    }
```

Within the same handler, if it's not a `click` event, then it must be a `moveend` event. This event is published when the user has finished panning the map. In order to retrieve the new extent of the visible map, we grab a reference for the view (`event.map.getView`) and utilize the `calculateExtent` view method. This method expects the size, in pixels, of the area of interest. For us, this is the whole map in sight, which is retained from the map method, `getSize`.

The returned extent array is converted into a string, delimited by a comma and HTML break element, and added to the applicable DOM element for display.

There's more...

There are plenty more map events that are up for grabs, such as the self-explanatory events `pointerdrag` and `pointermove`. To capture double-clicks or taps, you can use `dblclick`, and there are also events for when the map's view is changed (`change:view`) and when the map's size changes (`change:size`). This is useful for responsive design techniques.

I recommend that you take a look at the OpenLayers documentation in your own time to familiarize yourself with what's on offer.

See also

- The *Creating features programmatically* recipe in *Chapter 3, Working with Vector Layers*
- The *Zooming to extent of layer* recipe in *Chapter 3, Working with Vector Layers*
- The *Creating a side-by-side map comparator* recipe
- The *Listening for vector layer features' events* recipe

Using the keyboard to pan or zoom

Users of your mapping application may feel more comfortable navigating around the map with the use of a keyboard. This may also fulfill some accessibility requirements of the app. For whatever reason, we'll demonstrate how to add and customize keyboard control for a map.

The source code of this recipe can be found in `ch04/ch04-keyboard-pan-zoom/`.

How to do it...

To enable the arrow keys to pan and the plus and minus keys to zoom, follow these steps:

1. Create an HTML file and include the OpenLayers dependencies and a `div` element for the map.

2. Create a custom JavaScript file and set up both keyboard interactions, as follows:

```
var keyboardPan = new ol.interaction.KeyboardPan({
  duration: 90,
  pixelDelta: 256
});

var keyboardZoom = new ol.interaction.KeyboardZoom({
  duration: 90
});
```

3. Instantiate and configure the map, making sure to add the keyboard interactions:

```
new ol.Map({
  view: new ol.View({
    zoom: 10,
    center: [-12987415, 3851814]
  }),
  target: 'js-map',
  layers: [
    new ol.layer.Tile({source: new ol.source.Stamen({
      layer: 'terrain'
    })})
  ],
  interactions: ol.interaction.defaults().extend([
    keyboardPan, keyboardZoom
  ]),
  keyboardEventTarget: document
});
```

How it works...

We've enabled full panning and zooming control directly from the keyboard in a small amount of code. Let's dive right in with the details.

```
var keyboardPan = new ol.interaction.KeyboardPan({
  duration: 90,
  pixelDelta: 256
});
```

Both keyboard events are part of the OpenLayers `ol.interaction` object, which houses a whole host of interactions—`DragPan` and `PinchRotate` to name a few. We've customized some properties of the panning interaction, namely `duration` (in milliseconds) and `pixelDelta` (the amount of pixels the map moves in a single pan).

The similar keyboard zoom interaction has been passed a custom `duration` of `90` ms, as well. The keyboard zoom interaction has a delta property that accepts a number representing the quantity of zoom levels to execute per zoom alteration.

There are two specific map configuration properties that we'll look over next:

```
interactions: ol.interaction.defaults().extend([
  keyboardPan, keyboardZoom
]),
keyboardEventTarget: document
```

An instance of an OpenLayers map already comes with a variety of interactions enabled, of which `KeyboardPan` and `KeyboardZoom` are actually included. However, we've decided to customize the settings of these `interactions`, which are easily achieved by extending the array of the default `interactions` with the two modified keyboard ones.

By default, the keyboard events responsible for panning and zooming are only processed by OpenLayers if the map element (the `div` element containing the map) has focus. This means that the DOM element must have a `tabindex` property with a numeric value. This is easy enough to do, but, as our map is fullscreen, we have specified that the event target for keyboard events is the whole web page (document) via the `map` property, `keyboardEventTarget`. So, as long as the browser window has focus, keyboard interaction will work without the need to manually focus on the map DOM element by tabbing around.

Both keyboard interactions have a `getActive` method that can be called to determine whether or not the interaction is currently enabled.

See also

▶   The *Creating features programmatically* recipe in *Chapter 3, Working with Vector Layers*

▶   The *Working with geolocation* recipe in *Chapter 5, Adding Control*

▶   The *Creating a side-by-side map comparator* recipe

▶   The *Listening for vector layer features' events* recipe

5

Adding Controls

In this chapter, we will cover the following topics:

- ▸ Adding and removing controls
- ▸ Working with geolocation
- ▸ Placing controls outside the map
- ▸ Drawing features across multiple vector layers
- ▸ Modifying features
- ▸ Measuring distances and areas
- ▸ Getting feature information from a data source
- ▸ Getting information from a WMS server

Introduction

Controls allow us to navigate around the map, play with layers, zoom in or out, and perform actions, such as editing features, measuring distances, and so on. In essence, controls allow us to interact.

OpenLayers comes with controls that are visually represented on the map through DOM elements and can be styled with CSS. Such controls, such as `Attribution`, `FullScreen`, and `Zoom`, fall under this category. These types of controls are subclasses of `ol.control.Control`.

There are also other kinds of controls that are invisible to the user, but they provide just as important interactions. Controls, such as `KeyboardPan`, `Select`, and `PinchZoom`, are of this type. These types of controls are part of the `ol.interaction` object.

There are also other helper methods that one could consider a type of control, such as the `ol.Geolocation` class that provides HTML5 geolocation capabilities.

Controls can be activated or deactivated as desired. Many controls or interactions are already included on a map by default to cover common interactions that a user may be accustomed to from usage across other mapping applications. Custom controls can be created too, which we will cover in the *Creating a custom control* recipe, in *Chapter 7, Beyond the Basics*.

Controls listen for events, such as a click or tap. This event management is accomplished through the help of the Google Closure library. For example, the `goog.events.listen` subscriber method is used to register for a click event (`goog.events.EventType.CLICK`) on a DOM element, such as the `Zoom` button.

Let's take a look at some recipes that will help us understand the controls better.

Adding and removing controls

OpenLayers offers a great number of controls, which are commonly used on mapping applications.

This recipe shows us how to use all of the available controls that have a visual representation. The list includes the `OverviewMap`, `ScaleLine`, and `ZoomSlider` controls, as well as many more.

We will initialize the map with all controls attached but provide a side panel that contains a button for each control so that the user can toggle the controls as they wish. The source code can be found in `ch05/ch05-adding-removing-controls`. Here's a screenshot of what we'll end up with:

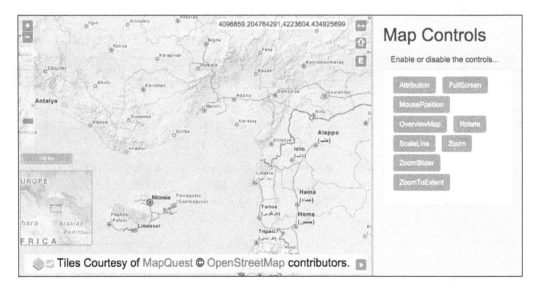

How to do it...

Follow these instructions to create your own map with a whole load of OpenLayers controls, which you can toggle on and off as you please:

1. Create an HTML file and add the OpenLayers dependencies and a `div` element to hold the map. In particular, add the list of buttons representing each control:

```
<ul id="js-buttons">
<li><button class="btn btn-success">Attribution</button></li>
<li><button class="btn btn-success">FullScreen</button></li>
<li><button class="btn btn-success">MousePosition</button></li>
<li><button class="btn btn-success">OverviewMap</button></li>
<li><button class="btn btn-success">Rotate</button></li>
<li><button class="btn btn-success">ScaleLine</button></li>
<li><button class="btn btn-success">Zoom</button></li>
<li><button class="btn btn-success">ZoomSlider</button></li>
<li><button class="btn btn-success">ZoomToExtent</button></li>
</ul>
```

2. Next, we create a custom JavaScript file, and we begin by creating an array of all the OpenLayers controls:

```
var controls = [
  new ol.control.Attribution({collapsed: false}),
  new ol.control.FullScreen(),
  new ol.control.MousePosition(),
  new ol.control.OverviewMap({
    collapsed: false, collapsible: false
  }),
  new ol.control.Rotate({autoHide: false}),
  new ol.control.ScaleLine(),
  new ol.control.Zoom(),
  new ol.control.ZoomSlider(),
  new ol.control.ZoomToExtent()
];
```

3. Create the `map` instance with `view`, a raster layer, and `controls`:

```
var map = new ol.Map({
  view: new ol.View({
    zoom: 7,
    center: [3826743, 4325724]
  }),
  target: 'js-map',
  layers: [
```

```
      new ol.layer.Tile({
        source: new ol.source.MapQuest({layer: 'osm'})
      })
    ],
    controls: controls
  });
```

4. Cache a reference to the button list DOM element and create a regular expression to use later on:

```
var buttonList = document.getElementById('js-buttons');
var controlEnabledRegex = /btn-success/;
```

5. Finally, create a click handler to react to the `click` events on the buttons. Add or remove `control`, accordingly:

```
buttonList.addEventListener('click', function(event) {
  var element = event.target;

  if (element.nodeName === 'BUTTON') {
    if (controlEnabledRegex.test(element.className)) {
      map.getControls().forEach(function(control) {
        if (control instanceof ol.control[element.innerHTML]) {
          map.removeControl(control);
        }
      });
      element.className = element.className.replace(
        'btn-success', 'btn-default'
      );
    } else {
      controls.forEach(function(control) {
        if (control instanceof ol.control[element.innerHTML]) {
          map.addControl(control);
        }
      });
      element.className = element.className.replace(
        'btn-default', 'btn-success'
      );
    }
  }
});
```

How it works...

We have used the CSS framework, Bootstrap, for much of the styling, and some of the HTML that scaffolds the application has been omitted for brevity. We have also used some custom styling of our own to position the controls over the map so that they don't overlap or look too cluttered. Please view the accompanying source code for a complete look at the implementation.

The array of `controls` provides a list of all the available OpenLayers controls that have a visual representation. We created an instance of each `control`, some of which we've customized so that they're always on display. We could have done something very similar for the invisible interactions controls (`ol.interaction`) as well, but this would have added minimal learning value. Please take a look at what interactions are available over at the OpenLayers documentation (`http://openlayers.org`).

The map instantiation will look familiar, so let's move right along to the click handler and the logic within:

```
buttonList.addEventListener('click', function(event) {
  var element = event.target;
  if (element.nodeName === 'BUTTON') {
```

For efficiency, we add a click event handler to the entire `ul` DOM element where the buttons reside. Due to this, within the handler, we first check whether the event was sourced from an element of type button, and if so, we proceed, as follows:

```
if (controlEnabledRegex.test(element.className)) {
```

We check to see whether the button that was clicked contains the string, `'btn-success'`, within the `class` attribute. If it does, this means that the control is currently added to the map, but the user wishes to remove it. To achieve this, we have created a regular expression, which is used as part of the `test` JavaScript method, that checks for the applicable string within the DOM element's class name.

For example, the `<button class="btn btn-success">Rotate</button>` button contains a `className` string, `'btn btn-success'`, so this regular expression would successfully match this class name. From this information, we can ascertain that the button and `control` is enabled.

```
map.getControls().forEach(function(control) {
  if (control instanceof ol.control[element.innerHTML]) {
    map.removeControl(control);
  }
});
```

To process the removal of the control from the map, we begin by fetching all of the controls from the map via the `getControls` method. This returns an `ol.Collection` array that we loop over with the `forEach` method.

When we instantiate a new control, that is, `new ol.control.Zoom()`, it is an instance of the `ol.control.Zoom` constructor. Using this knowledge when we loop over all the controls, we take the text of the button (`element.innerHTML`), which, for example, equals `'Zoom'`, and check whether the current iteration of the loop matches this control type. For example, `ol.control[element.innerHTML]` is the equivalent of `ol.control.Zoom` in this case.

When the match is found, this must be the control that the button represents, so it is removed from the map via the `removeControl` method.

```
element.className = element.className.replace(
  'btn-success', 'btn-default'
);
```

In order to keep the HTML in sync with the map controls, we update the button class name from `'btn btn-success'` to `'btn btn-default'` via the JavaScript replace method.

```
} else {
  controls.forEach(function(control) {
    if (control instanceof ol.control[element.innerHTML]) {
      map.addControl(control);
    }
  });
  element.className = element.className.replace(
    'btn-default', 'btn-success'
  );
}
```

On the contrary, if the button is currently disabled (doesn't have the class of `'btn-success'`), the user wishes to enable the control. To achieve this, we loop over the controls array that contains all of the controls, regardless of whether or not they're currently added to the map.

The same logic is applied so that if the button text in conjunction with the control object (`ol.control[element.innerHTML]`) matches the control instance in this iteration, it is added to the map (`addControl`).

The button HTML is, again, kept in sync with the JavaScript by updating the class name string.

See also

▶ The *Placing controls outside the map* recipe
▶ The *Drawing new features across multiple vector layers* recipe

Working with geolocation

With HTML5, one of the many new APIs and concepts introduced in this specification is the possibility of identifying the location of the client that is loading the web page through the Geolocation API (`http://www.w3.org/TR/geolocation-API/`). Of course, in the world of web mapping applications, this opens new and great possibilities.

In this recipe, we are going to show you how easily we can identify the current location of the user and center the map's viewport to it. The source code for this can be found in `ch05/ch05-geolocation`. Here's a screenshot of what we'll produce:

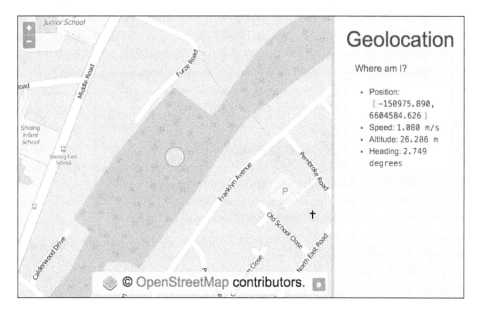

When the user loads the web page, the map's viewport will be moved to the current user's location and a circle will be placed at the center. We will also display other location metrics in the sidebar if available, such as speed and altitude.

To quickly see this recipe in action on your own device, visit a live copy at `https://jsfiddle.net/pjlangley/9yyLovt5/`.

Getting ready

When accessing a map in the browser with geolocation enabled, you may need to manually allow the geolocation request in order for it to work properly. Most browser vendors will conspicuously prompt for your action here. For mobile devices, you may need to check your privacy settings to ensure that location services are available within your mobile browser.

How to do it...

To understand how to work with the Geolocation API in OpenLayers, follow these instructions:

1. First, create the HTML file with OpenLayers dependencies and `div` to hold the map. In particular, here's the markup that makes up the geolocation metrics that'll be populated:

```
<ul>
<li>Position:
<code>[</code>
<samp id="js-position">n/a</samp>
<code>]</code></li>
<li>Speed: <samp id="js-speed">0</samp></li>
<li>Altitude: <samp id="js-altitude">n/a</samp></li>
<li>Heading: <samp id="js-heading">n/a</samp></li>
</ul>
```

2. Create a JavaScript file and cache some DOM elements for reuse, as well as the OpenLayers circle feature:

```
var locationCircle = new ol.Feature();
var positionElem = document.getElementById('js-position');
var speedElem = document.getElementById('js-speed');
var altitudeElem = document.getElementById('js-altitude');
var headingElem = document.getElementById('js-heading');
```

3. Instantiate `map` with `view`, a raster layer, and a vector layer with the circle feature:

```
var map = new ol.Map({
  view: new ol.View({
    zoom: 17,
    center: [10030840, 6731350]
  }),
  target: 'js-map',
  layers: [
    new ol.layer.Tile({
      source: new ol.source.OSM()
    }),
    new ol.layer.Vector({
      source: new ol.source.Vector({
        features: [locationCircle]
      })
    })
  ]
});
```

4. Set up the geolocation options, subscribe to location change events, carry out the necessary logic to reposition the map and circle, and update the sidebar display, as follows:

```
new ol.Geolocation({
  projection: map.getView().getProjection(),
  tracking: true,
  trackingOptions: {
    enableHighAccuracy: true
  }
})
.on('change', function() {
  var position = this.getPosition();
  var speed = this.getSpeed();
  var altitude = this.getAltitude();
  var heading = this.getHeading();

  map.getView().setCenter(position);

  locationCircle.setGeometry(
    new ol.geom.Circle(position, 20)
  );

  positionElem.innerHTML = position.join(',<br>');
  speedElem.innerHTML = speed ? speed.toFixed(3) + ' m/s' : 'n/a';
  altitudeElem.innerHTML =
    altitude ? altitude.toFixed(3) + ' m' : 'n/a';
  headingElem.innerHTML =
    heading ? heading.toFixed(3) + ' degrees' : 'n/a';
});
```

How it works...

With the help of the Bootstrap CSS framework, we've styled the sidebar to present the geolocation information. Please review the source code for the full implementation, as it's been omitted for brevity.

We start the JavaScript by caching references to the DOM elements that'll display the data. This is performant as they'll be frequently accessed throughout the code. The circle feature is also stored into a variable, namely `locationCircle`, as the geometry is frequently updated.

The map instantiation will look familiar to earlier recipes, so let's dig deeper into the OpenLayers code behind the geolocation capabilities:

```
new ol.Geolocation({
    projection: map.getView().getProjection(),
    tracking: true,
    trackingOptions: {
      enableHighAccuracy: true
    }
})
```

OpenLayers has an HTML5 Geolocation API helper class, namely `ol.Geolocation`. This helper class interacts with the JavaScript API on our behalf using the `window.navigator.geolocation.watchPosition` method to set up and subscribe to geolocation changes.

When working with HTML5 technologies, it's a sensible idea to confirm the range of browser support that is available. The website, `http://caniuse.com`, is a useful resource for this type of information.

When instantiating `ol.Geolocation`, we specify some configuration properties. We inform OpenLayers of the projection by passing in the current projection of the view. By setting `tracking` to `true`, we automatically begin tracking the users position (so long as the user has allowed this) as soon as the page loads. In addition to this, we have supplied an object with `enableHighAccuracy` set to `true`. This setting requests for the best possible results from the application. Be mindful that on mobile devices, this could consume more power and bandwidth.

Refer to a list of the other position options available for the Geolocation API at `http://www.w3.org/TR/geolocation-API/#position_options_interface`.

```
.on('change', function() {
    var position = this.getPosition();
    var speed = this.getSpeed();
    var altitude = this.getAltitude();
    var heading = this.getHeading();
```

We chain the `on` method to the end of the geolocation instantiation and subscribe to the generic change event. This is a catch-all event listener that will respond to the latest `position`, `speed`, and `altitude` updates, among many other changes.

The geolocation helper class provides many `get` methods to retrieve the latest values. We store these values in variables, such as `speed`, containing the result of `this.getSpeed()`. In this case, `this` JavaScript keyword references our geolocation instance.

```
map.getView().setCenter(position);
locationCircle.setGeometry(
    new ol.geom.Circle(position, 20)
);
```

With the latest coordinates, we center the map view accordingly and update the geometry of the circle feature on the vector layer with these same coordinates. The `ol.geom.Circle` constructor takes the `ol.Coordinate` array and a radius as arguments. The resulting geometry is used by the feature method, `setGeometry`, in order to update the location of the circle.

```
positionElem.innerHTML = position.join(',<br>');
speedElem.innerHTML = speed ? speed.toFixed(3) + ' m/s' : 'n/a';
altitudeElem.innerHTML =
    altitude ? altitude.toFixed(3) + ' m' : 'n/a';
headingElem.innerHTML =
    heading ? heading.toFixed(3) + ' degrees' : 'n/a';
```

To finish off, we update the sidebar with all the latest readings. The position array of type `ol.Coordinate` is passed through the JavaScript `join` method so that the array entries are presented as strings with a comma and HTML markup, `<br>`, in between.

The `speed`, `altitude`, and `heading` values are fixed at 3 decimal places (`toFixed(3)`) and the units of measurement are appended to the string. If a geolocation type doesn't have a value available, then the `'n/a'` string is used instead. The `innerHTML` JavaScript method populates the DOM element.

As per the Geolocation API specification (`http://www.w3.org/TR/geolocation-API/#coordinates_interface`), `speed` is in meters per second, `altitude` is in meters, and `heading` is in degrees (0-360).

To witness the best results, I suggest viewing this example on a mobile device while on the move. You'll hopefully be able to see all the values update as you move around.

See also

- ▸ The *Adding and removing controls* recipe
- ▸ The *Modifying features* recipe

Placing controls outside the map

By default, all the controls are placed on the map. This way, controls, such as `Zoom`, `Attribution`, or `MousePosition`, are rendered on top of the map and over any layer. This is the default behavior, but OpenLayers is flexible enough to allow us to put controls outside the map. In this recipe (source code in `ch05/ch05-controls-outside-map`), we are going to create a map where the **Zoom to Extent** and **Scale Line** controls are placed outside the map and within the sidebar, as you can see in the following screenshot:

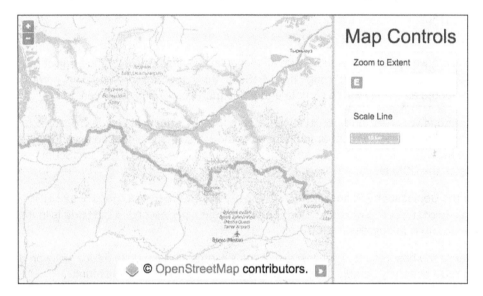

How to do it...

To learn how to customize where the map controls are placed, follow these steps:

1. Create an HTML file and add the OpenLayers dependencies and `div` to hold the map. In particular, create a `div` element for each control within the sidebar markup:

   ```
   <div id="js-zoom-extent"></div>
   <div id="js-scale-line"></div>
   ```

2. Create a custom JavaScript file and instantiate the `map` instance with `view` and a raster tile layer with the Open Street Map source:

   ```
   var map = new ol.Map({
     view: new ol.View({
       zoom: 10,
       center: [4740318, 5344324]
     }),
   ```

```
    target: 'js-map',
    layers: [
      new ol.layer.Tile({source: new ol.source.OSM()})
    ]
});
```

3. Create and add the **Scale Line** control to the sidebar:

```
map.addControl(new ol.control.ScaleLine({
    target: document.getElementById('js-scale-line')
}));
```

4. Create and add the **Zoom to Extent** control to the sidebar:

```
var zoomToExtent = new ol.control.ZoomToExtent({
    extent: [4684596, 5306182, 4796041, 5382466]
});
zoomToExtent.setTarget('js-zoom-extent');
map.addControl(zoomToExtent);
```

How it works...

We've used the Bootstrap CSS framework to style the sidebar content, and much of the HTML has been omitted for brevity. Please take a look at the source code for the complete implementation.

As you can see, adding controls outside of the map is straightforward. We've demonstrated two ways of achieving this. One method is with the target property on the control settings on instantiation, the other way is to use the control's setTarget method. Let's take a closer look at both:

```
map.addControl(new ol.control.ScaleLine({
    target: document.getElementById('js-scale-line')
}));
```

The **Scale Line** control displays rough X-axis distances from the center of view. The target property is used to render the control in a particular area of the web page. The property expects a DOM element, rather than an ID string (which the target property for a map instance would accept). If a target isn't provided, OpenLayers will add the control to the map's overlay container.

```
var zoomToExtent = new ol.control.ZoomToExtent({
    extent: [4684596, 5306182, 4796041, 5382466]
});
```

In order to demonstrate a different method of setting `target`, we need to assign the **Zoom to Extent** control to a variable, namely `zoomToExtent`, so that it can be accessed later. By default, the **Zoom to Extent** control will zoom the map out to the `extent` property of the `view` projection. However, we've chosen an arbitrary `extent` by passing an array of type `ol.Extent` to the `extent` property. The `ol.Extent` array has the following format: [minX, minY, maxX, maxY].

```
zoomToExtent.setTarget('js-zoom-extent');
```

Each control has a `setTarget` method that's inherited from `ol.control.Control` (the base class for controls). We use this method to set the DOM element that the control will render within. Unlike the `target` property, you can alternatively provide an ID string like we've done if you prefer to do so.

When using the `setTarget` method, you must call it before adding the control to the map, or else OpenLayers will render the control to the map's `overlay` container instead.

We purposely haven't adjusted the class names of these controls, as we wanted to inherit the default CSS styles. However, because these controls are naturally positioned within the map's container, they have some CSS rules that use absolute positioning, so be aware that you'll probably need to modify some styling.

The **Scale Line** and **Zoom to Extent** controls have the CSS class names, `.ol-scale-line` and `.ol-zoom-extent`, respectively. Use these CSS hooks to override any styling rules as desired. It's most sensible to do this from within a separate CSS file of your own in order to keep the original styling intact (better for reference, maintainability, and extensibility).

See also

▶ The *Adding and removing controls* recipe

▶ The *Creating a custom control* recipe in *Chapter 7, Beyond the Basics*

Drawing features across multiple vector layers

We've seen various ways to add vector features to a map, such as in the recipes, *Adding a GML layer* from this chapter, and *Creating features programmatically* in *Chapter 3, Working with Vector Layers*. Sometimes, however, we may want to provide the user with drawing capabilities so that they can manually draw almost any shape they like on the map.

For example, you may want the user to mark out a point of interest at a location by drawing a polygon over an area for building planning purposes.

OpenLayers has an abundance of controls (more accurately, interactions) that we can add to the map for exactly this type of purpose.

In this recipe, we will allow the user to draw from a selection of different geometry types (**Point**, **LineString**, **Polygon**, and **Circle**) and add them to a vector layer of their choice. The source code can be found in `ch05/ch05-drawing-features`, and this will look like the following:

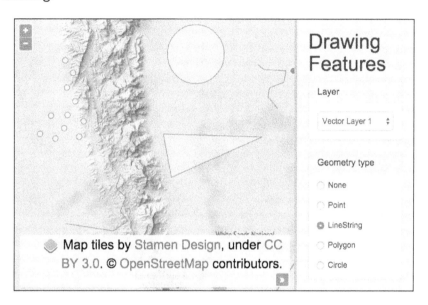

How to do it...

Find out how to draw different vector feature types over multiple vector layers by following these instructions:

1. Create an HTML file with OpenLayers dependencies, jQuery, and `div` to hold the map. In particular, we need a `select` menu with the available vector layers to choose from and the `radio` buttons so that a geometry type can be picked:

```
<select id="js-layer-select">
<option value="vectorLayer1">Vector Layer 1</option>
<option value="vectorLayer2">Vector Layer 2</option>
</select>
<label>
<input type="radio" name="geometries" value="None" checked>
  None
</label>
<label>
<input type="radio" name="geometries" value="Point">
```

```
    Point
  </label>
  <label>
  <input type="radio" name="geometries" value="LineString">
    LineString
  </label>
  <label>
  <input type="radio" name="geometries" value="Polygon">
    Polygon
  </label>
  <label>
  <input type="radio" name="geometries" value="Circle">
    Circle
  </label>
```

2. Create a custom JavaScript file and set up the two vector layers:

```
var vectorLayer1 = new ol.layer.Vector({
  source: new ol.source.Vector()
});
var vectorLayer2 = new ol.layer.Vector({
  source: new ol.source.Vector()
});
```

3. Instantiate map with a view instance and a tile layer and add the vector layers:

```
var map = new ol.Map({
  view: new ol.View({
    zoom: 10, center: [-11863791, 3898899]
  }),
  target: 'js-map',
  layers: [
    new ol.layer.Tile({ source: new ol.source.Stamen({
      layer: 'terrain'
    })}), vectorLayer1, vectorLayer2
  ]
});
```

4. Cache some DOM elements and set up a variable to hold the drawing control:

```
var layerSelect = $('#js-layer-select');
var geomRadios = $('[name=geometries]');
var drawControl;
```

5. Create the function that will update the drawing control accordingly:

```
var updateDrawControl = function() {
  var geometryType = geomRadios.filter(':checked').val();
```

```
    map.removeInteraction(drawControl);

    if (geometryType === 'None') return;

    drawControl = new ol.interaction.Draw({
      type: geometryType,
      source: window[layerSelect.val()].getSource()
    });
    map.addInteraction(drawControl);
  };
```

6. Finally, subscribe to the `change` event on both the `select` menu and the `radio` inputs, and set the `updateDrawControl` function as the handler for both:

```
layerSelect.on('change', updateDrawControl);
geomRadios.on('change', updateDrawControl);
```

How it works...

As we have done in other recipes, the CSS framework, Bootstrap, has been used to style the sidebar content. To see the full HTML and CSS, please view the source code, as it's unfortunately too large to include in this book.

The focus of this section will be on the function that we created, namely `updateDrawControl`, as this is where the core of the logic takes place. It is also where the code may look the least familiar to the other recipes that you've seen up to now.

Let's begin digesting each piece of the function, which is called whenever the vector layer is changed from the `select` menu or when a geometry type is changed from the `radio` inputs:

```
var updateDrawControl = function() {
  var geometryType = geomRadios.filter(':checked').val();
```

We cache the type of geometry that the user has selected from the `radio` input list to a variable, namely `geometryType`. This is achieved with the help of jQuery's method, `filter`, which loops over the collection (the list of `radio` input elements) and determines whether the input is checked (because of the `:checked` condition passed in).

If the `radio` input during iteration is checked, the `filter` method returns the matching DOM element from the collection, from which we retrieve the input value via the `val` method, which is also from jQuery. For example, this may be equal to **'Circle'**, **'LineString'** or any of the other options the user may have chosen.

```
    map.removeInteraction(drawControl);
    if (geometryType === 'None') return;
```

This section of the function first removes any previous instance of the drawing `interaction` (control) from the map. We do this because we must instantiate `interaction` with the latest settings from the combination of the `select` menu (layer) and `radio` inputs (geometry type). Within the confinements of the OpenLayers API, we can't update the geometry type or layer without destroying and then recreating the interaction.

Afterwards, we have a conditional `if` statement to see whether or not the user has selected '**None**' from the geometry types. This means that the user is not interested in drawing and intends to navigate the map instead. With the drawing interaction removed from the map, this is all we need to do in this scenario, so we break out of the function with an early return, job done.

```
drawControl = new ol.interaction.Draw({
    type: geometryType,
    source: window[layerSelect.val()].getSource()
});
map.addInteraction(drawControl);
```

We assign the new instance of the drawing interaction to the variable `drawControl`. This is important as we need a reference of the `interaction` when we remove it from the map (as seen earlier in this function).

The type of geometry that the user wants to draw is set on the `type` property. The `source` property (vector source) needs to be one of our two vector layer sources. The vector layers are global variables, so they are properties of the `window` object. The values for the `select` options are equal to the names of the vector layer variables. This means that when **Vector Layer 1** is selected, the value of `vectorLayer1` is retrieved (remember, the HTML looks like this: `<option value="vectorLayer1">Vector Layer 1</option>`) via the jQuery `val` method. With the array notation lookup on the `window` object, we are able to reference the vector layer. For example, `window[layerSelect.val()]` could be the equivalent of `window[vectorLayer1]`.

We call the `getSource` method from the vector layer and that's what gets provided to the `source` property.

The newly instantiated draw interaction is added to `map`, and so, the user can now craft out the feature over the map.

It's not necessarily obvious how to complete a drawing of a feature, so here's a breakdown:

▸ **Point**: This is when a single-click on the map draws a point.
▸ **LineString/Polygon**: This is when an initial single click adds the starting point and subsequent single clicks draw out new points of the feature. A double-click completes the geometry.

- ▶ **Circle**: This is when a single click on the map sets the center of the circle, then drag the mouse outwards until you're happy with the diameter, then single click again to complete the drawing. For mobile, a second single click at the desired radius completes the circle.

The `ol.interaction.Draw` class has many configurable properties at instantiation that may be of interest, such as `minPoints` and `maxPoints`, to restrict the amount of geometry points that the feature can have. There's also the `features` property, which will be the destination feature collection for the drawn features. We also take a look at the `freehandCondition` property in the recipe, *Drawing in freehand mode*, in *Chapter 7, Beyond the Basics*.

The `ol.interaction.Draw` class also publishes events that you may want to subscribe to, such as the self-explanatory `drawend` and `drawstart` events.

There's more...

As well as the set geometry types out of the box that OpenLayers offers with the draw interaction, there are more advanced techniques that you can use to draw almost any shape that you may require.

The drawing interaction has a property named `geometryFunction` that accepts a function of type `ol.interaction.DrawGeometryFunctionType` function. This function is passed coordinates and the existing geometry as arguments, and it must return a new geometry.

With this method, you can manipulate drawing mechanisms, such as the circle geometry type, and instead draw out a square by dragging the mouse outwards from the point of the click. The `ol.interaction.Draw` class comes with a drawing geometry method that you can easily customize called `ol.interaction.Draw.createRegularPolygon`, which takes a number of sides and an angle as the arguments. To demonstrate drawing out a square (using the same gesture actions as when you draw a circle), you'd use the following:

```
drawControl = new ol.interaction.Draw({
    type: 'Circle',
    source: vectorLayer1.getSource(),
    geometryFunction: ol.interaction.Draw.createRegularPolygon(4)
});
```

This is an advanced topic that unfortunately won't be covered in any more detail throughout this book, but for more information visit the official example from OpenLayers on how to do this at `http://openlayers.org/en/v3.13.1/examples/draw-features.html`.

See also

- ▶ The *Placing controls outside the map* recipe
- ▶ The *Modifying features* recipe

Modifying features

As we saw in the previous recipe, *Drawing features across multiple vector layers*, it's quite straightforward to enable drawing capabilities for the user. However, what if the user needs to edit drawn features? Perhaps they want to move some vertexes around or move the entire feature to a new place. We'll take a look at these types of modifications throughout this recipe.

OpenLayers provides the `ol.interaction.Modify` class to move or add vertexes and the `ol.interaction.Translate` class to move whole features about.

The source code can be found in `ch05/ch05-modifying-features`, and here's a screenshot of what this will look like when it's done:

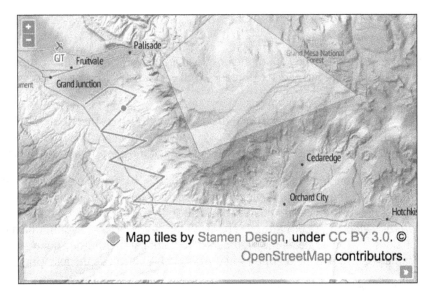

How to do it...

Learn how to modify existing features by following these steps:

1. Create an HTML file with the OpenLayers dependencies and `div` to hold the map.

2. Create a custom JavaScript file and begin by instantiating `map` with `view`, a raster tile layer, and a vector layer that retrieves features from a local GeoJSON file:

```
var map = new ol.Map({
  view: new ol.View({
    zoom: 10, center: [-12035468, 4686812]
  }),
  target: 'js-map',
```

```
    layers: [
      new ol.layer.Tile({ source: new ol.source.Stamen({
        layer: 'terrain'
      })}),
      new ol.layer.Vector({
        editable: true,
        source: new ol.source.Vector({
          url: 'features.geojson',
          format: new ol.format.GeoJSON({
            defaultDataProjection: 'EPSG:3857'
          })
        })
      })
    ]
  });
```

3. Set up the `select` interaction so that particular features can be selected for modification and add it to the map:

```
var select = new ol.interaction.Select({
  filter: function(feature, layer) {
    return layer.get('editable') &&
      /Polygon|LineString/.test(
        feature.getGeometry().getType()
      );
  },
  condition: ol.events.condition.click
});
map.addInteraction(select);
```

4. Finish off by setting up and adding the modify and translate interactions to the map:

```
map.addInteraction(new ol.interaction.Modify({
  features: select.getFeatures()
}));
map.addInteraction(new ol.interaction.Translate({
  features: select.getFeatures()
}));
```

How it works...

As you can see, adding this rich type of capability is made easy with OpenLayers. Once a user has selected a feature from the map, they can edit the feature or move it around. To spice things up a bit, we've added a filter mechanism to the select interaction, which checks a `layer` property and the geometry type before allowing the feature to be selected. Let's take a closer look at what's going on within the JavaScript:

```
new ol.layer.Vector({
    editable: true,
    source: new ol.source.Vector({
      url: 'features.geojson',
      format: new ol.format.GeoJSON({
        defaultDataProjection: 'EPSG:3857'
      })
    })
})
```

Within this instantiation of `map`, we set up a vector layer with a custom property of `editable`, which is used to identify whether or not this layer can be edited. We have also pulled in some GeoJSON that will populate the layer with some premade features.

```
var select = new ol.interaction.Select({
    filter: function(feature, layer) {
      return layer.get('editable') &&
        /Polygon|LineString/.test(
          feature.getGeometry().getType()
        );
    },
    condition: ol.events.condition.click
});
```

The `select` interaction has been configured with a filtering function. The function assigned to the `filter` property must be of type `ol.interaction.SelectFilterFunction`. This type of function is passed the `feature` and the `layer` as arguments, respectively, and it must return either true or false. If true is returned, the feature is eligible for selection and, thus, it is added to the collection. If false is returned, the feature will not be selected and it won't be added to the collection.

Our custom filtering function retrieves the `layer` property of `editable` via the `get` method and checks to see whether it evaluates to true. If so, a second conditional check is performed on the type of geometry.

The geometry object is retrieved from `feature` via the `getGeometry` method. Once we have the geometry, there's a method available to us called `getType`, which returns the geometry type as a string, for example, `Polygon`. This result is passed into the JavaScript `test` method, which runs the result against a regular expression. The `/Polygon|LineString/` regular expression matches a string of either `Polygon` or `LineString` (the geometry type). The pipe (`|`) within this particular regular expression symbolizes an OR logical condition.

If both the layer is set as `editable` and the feature is of one of the accepted types, then the return statement evaluates to true; otherwise, this will be false.

In other words, if a vector layer hasn't been specifically marked as `editable`, then the feature cannot be modified. It also doesn't allow any other geometry types other than the two that were just discussed to be selected, and, subsequently, edited. This demonstrates how you can begin to structure read only or read/write layers, depending on your application requirements.

The `condition` property has been set to `ol.events.condition.click` to avoid the 250 ms delay that you get when accepting the default `ol.events.condition.singleClick` value for this property.

```
map.addInteraction(new ol.interaction.Modify({
  features: select.getFeatures()
}));
map.addInteraction(new ol.interaction.Translate({
  features: select.getFeatures()
}));
```

The modify and translate interactions follow the same setup. The `features` property of each are passed the currently selected features from the `select` interaction via `select.getFeatures()`.

Although we didn't utilize any events within this recipe, the modify interaction publishes the self-explanatory `modifyend` and `modifystart` events. The translate interaction publishes similar events, namely `translateend` and `translatestart`, but it also publishes a `translating` event to subscribe to movement in between.

There's more...

When modifying features in OpenLayers 2, you were also able to effortlessly rotate and resize them. At the time of writing, this functionality hasn't been directly ported across to version 3.

However, there's an interesting function called `applyTransform` from the `ol.geom.SimpleGeometry` base class, which is inherited by most of the geometry types, such as `ol.geom.Polygon`. This function can be used to manually transform each coordinate of the geometry in order to modify the feature in place.

The function is of type `ol.TransformFunction`, which is passed the current array of coordinates and must return the output array of coordinates to be used. There's nothing to stop you performing some creative transforming here to imitate some missing functionality that you've become accustomed to in OpenLayers 2. This is, however, an advanced discussion, and unfortunately, it won't be covered in this book.

See also

- The *Drawing features across multiple vector layers* recipe
- The *Adding and removing controls* recipe
- The *Listening for vector layer features' event* recipe in *Chapter 4, Working with Events*

Measuring distances and areas

The ability to measure distances or areas is an important feature for many GIS applications. For example, a user may wish to draw out a path along some roads to figure out the distance of a journey. Or you may want to draw a polygon around your neighbor's back garden to see how many acres they have!

OpenLayers 2 conveniently came with a measuring control straight out of the box. However, at the time of writing this book, OpenLayers 3 doesn't offer this convenience. However, you'll be pleased to know that this can be cobbled together with the methods that are available to us without much fuss.

The application will contain a sidebar with radio inputs in order to select a measurement type, either area or distance. The user will be able to draw anywhere on the map and see a live update of the measurement in the sidebar as they go. For mobile, the updates will be seen after every new point has been placed on the map.

The source code can be found in `ch05/ch05-measuring`, and this will look like the following screenshot:

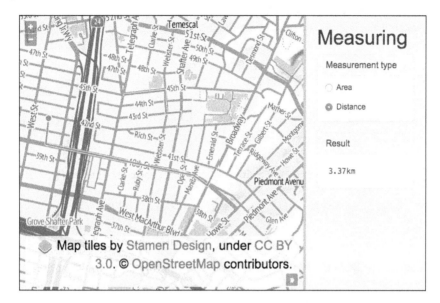

To see a live demonstration of this recipe, visit `https://jsfiddle.net/pjlangley/Ln8wz7ty/`.

How to do it...

To create a measuring tool for distances and areas, use the following instructions:

1. Create an HTML file and add the OpenLayers dependencies, the jQuery library, and `div` to hold the map. In particular, add the following essential markup that we'll be interacting with in the JavaScript:

```
<form>
<label>
<input type="radio" name="measurement" value="Polygon" checked>
    Area
</label>
<label>
<input type="radio" name="measurement" value="LineString">
    Distance
</label>
</form>
<samp id="js-result">n/a</samp>
```

2. Create a custom JavaScript file and store a vector layer with `source` in a variable, and also instantiate `map` with `view` and `layers`:

```
var vectorLayer = new ol.layer.Vector({
  source: new ol.source.Vector()
});

var map = new ol.Map({
  view: new ol.View({
    zoom: 15, center: [-13610530, 4555374]
  }),
  target: 'js-map',
  layers: [
    new ol.layer.Tile({ source: new ol.source.Stamen({
      layer: 'terrain'
    })}), vectorLayer
  ]
});
```

3. Cache some DOM elements and set up a global variable to hold the reference of the measuring tool:

```
var measurementRadios = $('[type=radio]');
var resultElement = $('#js-result');
var measuringTool;
```

4. Implement the method to enable the measuring tool:

```
var enableMeasuringTool = function() {
  map.removeInteraction(measuringTool);

  var geometryType = measurementRadios.filter(':checked').val();
  var html = geometryType === 'Polygon' ? '<sup>2</sup>' : '';

  measuringTool = new ol.interaction.Draw({
    type: geometryType,
    source: vectorLayer.getSource()
  });

  measuringTool.on('drawstart', function(event) {
    vectorLayer.getSource().clear();

    event.feature.on('change', function(event) {
      var measurement = geometryType === 'Polygon'
        ? event.target.getGeometry().getArea()
        : event.target.getGeometry().getLength();
```

```
        var measurementFormatted = measurement > 100
          ? (measurement / 1000).toFixed(2) + 'km'
          : measurement.toFixed(2) + 'm';

        resultElement.html(measurementFormatted + html);
      });
    });
    map.addInteraction(measuringTool);
  };
```

5. Subscribe to the `change` event on the `radio` inputs with a handler to update the measuring control. Finally, enable the measuring tool by default:

```
measurementRadios.on('change', enableMeasuringTool);
enableMeasuringTool();
```

How it works...

We've omitted much of the HTML and all the CSS for brevity. For a complete look at how the styling and structure is achieved, please view the source code, where you'll see our use of the Bootstrap CSS framework.

Let's dive into the core of this recipe where we build the measuring control:

```
var enableMeasuringTool = function() {
  map.removeInteraction(measuringTool);
```

When this method is called, it's sourced from either a change in the `radio` input selection or at page load. We want to ensure that the measuring tool (draw interaction) is set up with the correct configuration, so the old copy (if it exists) is removed from the map first.

```
var geometryType = measurementRadios.filter(':checked').val();
var html = geometryType === 'Polygon' ? '<sup>2</sup>' : '';
```

Next, we store a reference of the geometry type. The `filter` jQuery method is used to identify the checked `radio` input, and the `val` jQuery method extracts the value.

The `html` variable is what we append onto the measurement result in the sidebar. If this is of type `Polygon`, then it's an area measurement and, so, we add 2 to represent squared; otherwise, it's set to an empty string. We've used a ternary operator to conditionally assign a value to a variable, a technique that we used throughout this recipe.

```
  measuringTool = new ol.interaction.Draw({
    type: geometryType,
    source: vectorLayer.getSource()
  });
```

As you can see, our custom measuring tool is simply an instance of the draw interaction behind the scenes. The `type` property is assigned the geometry type, accordingly.

```
measuringTool.on('drawstart', function(event) {
    vectorLayer.getSource().clear();
```

We subscribe to the `drawstart` event that's emitted from the draw interaction. When the user places the first point of their drawing on the map, we clear the vector source of any existing features with the `clear` method.

```
event.feature.on('change', function(event) {
```

When a feature's geometry changes, it publishes a `change` event that we can subscribe to on the `ol.Feature` instance. This means that we can update the sidebar with the latest measurement while the user is still drawing. Potentially, this event can be fired at a high frequency, so you could consider a *throttling* technique here for performance (refer to `https://remysharp.com/2010/07/21/throttling-function-calls` for more details).

```
var measurement = geometryType === 'Polygon'
    ? event.target.getGeometry().getArea()
    : event.target.getGeometry().getLength();
```

Within the geometry change event, we use the event target (an instance of `ol.Feature`) to retrieve the latest geometry. If it's a `Polygon` drawing interaction, then we want to calculate the area. The `ol.geom.Polygon` class has the `getArea` method for this. Alternatively, `ol.geom.LineString` has the `getLength` method to provide the distance. The result is stored in the `measurement` variable.

```
var measurementFormatted = measurement > 100
    ? (measurement / 1000).toFixed(2) + 'km'
    : measurement.toFixed(2) + 'm';
```

As a default, the `measurement` is provided in meters by OpenLayers. In the case where the `measurement` exceeds `100` meters, we convert it to kilometers, as this is probably more useful. There are 1000 meters in a kilometer, so for example, if we have 200 meters, *200 divided by 1000 = 0.2* kilometers. We also round the value to two decimal places with the `toFixed` JavaScript method. The units of measurement is concatenated on to the end of the number.

```
            resultElement.html(measurementFormatted + html);
        });
    });
    map.addInteraction(measuringTool);
```

Finally, the sidebar element which displays the measurement is populated with the formatted version and concatenated with the contents of the `html` variable (which could contain a 2 for area or a blank string for distance) via the jQuery `html` method. The last part of this function adds the completed interaction to the map.

There's more...

The calculations for the measurements are represented in a simple projected plane without the Earth's curvature taken into account. A more involved geodesic calculation can be achieved through OpenLayers, but this is a bit more advanced and won't be covered in this recipe.

This official example from OpenLayers demonstrates how to provide measurements in geodesic metrics at `http://openlayers.org/en/v3.13.1/examples/measure.html`. Microsoft also has an interesting article on the topic at `https://msdn.microsoft.com/en-GB/library/aa940990.aspx`.

See also

- ▸ The *Working with geolocation* recipe
- ▸ The *Drawing features across multiple vector layers* recipe
- ▸ The *Modifying features* recipe

Getting feature information from a data source

When a vector layer is populated with features, it can be very useful to query the data source in order to retrieve feature information. OpenLayers provides some methods from the vector source class (`ol.source.Vector`) that enable us to perform queries, such as finding out what features are within a custom extent (`getFeaturesInExtent`), or returning any features at a particular coordinate (`getFeaturesAtCoordinate`), as well as other useful types of queries.

We are going to create a map with a tile raster layer and a vector layer with features from a custom GeoJSON file. The polygon features will represent campsites within a region, each with some properties that can be extracted for display. We will call the `getFeaturesAtCoordinate` source query method when the map is clicked on and display the applicable feature information within `overlay` if a feature exists at this coordinate.

The source code can be found in `ch05/ch05-feature-info-from-source`, and here's a screenshot of what we'll end up with:

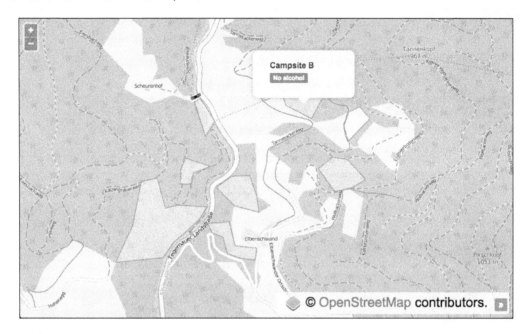

How to do it...

In order to find out how to retrieve feature information from a data source, follow these steps:

1. Create an HTML file with the OpenLayers dependencies and `div` to contain the map. In particular, add the markup for `overlay` and content:

```
<div id="js-overlay" class="overlay">
<ul>
<li><strong id="js-ref"></strong></li>
<li><span id="js-restrictions"></span></li>
</ul>
</div>
```

2. Create a custom JavaScript file and set up a vector source with content from a local GeoJSON file:

```
var vectorSource = new ol.source.Vector({
  url: 'geojson.json',
  format: new ol.format.GeoJSON({
    defaultDataProjection: 'EPSG:3857'
  })
});
```

3. Initialize `map` with a raster tile layer, vector layer, and `view`:

```
var map = new ol.Map({
  view: new ol.View({
    zoom: 15, center: [872800, 6065125]
  }),
  target: 'js-map',
  layers: [
    new ol.layer.Tile({source: new ol.source.OSM()}),
    new ol.layer.Vector({source: vectorSource})
  ]
});
```

4. Cache some DOM elements that are accessed multiple times:

```
var overlayElem = document.getElementById('js-overlay');
var featureRefElem = document.getElementById('js-ref');
var featureRestrictionsElem = document.getElementById(
  'js-restrictions'
);
```

5. Instantiate an instance of `overlay`, add it to `map`, and set the CSS display:

```
var overlay = new ol.Overlay({
  element: overlayElem
});
map.addOverlay(overlay);
overlayElem.style.display = 'block';
```

6. Finish off by subscribing to the `singleclick` map event and display the feature information within `overlay` if appropriate:

```
map.on('singleclick', function(event) {
  overlay.setPosition(undefined);
  var features =
    vectorSource.getFeaturesAtCoordinate(event.coordinate);

  if (features.length > 0) {
    overlay.setPosition(event.coordinate);
    featureRefElem.innerHTML = features[0].get('ref');
    featureRestrictionsElem.innerHTML =
      features[0].get('restrictions');
  }
});
```

How it works...

We have excluded much of the HTML and all CSS from this recipe for brevity, but please take a look at the source code for the complete implementation.

Much of this recipe will be similar to earlier examples in this book, so let's narrow in on the map click event handler and the source query that we utilize:

```
map.on('singleclick', function(event) {
  overlay.setPosition(undefined);
  var features =
    vectorSource.getFeaturesAtCoordinate(event.coordinate);
```

We subscribe to the `singleclick` event published by the `map` object when a user clicks or taps on the map. The `overlay` method is passed an argument of `undefined` so that it's hidden until we know that we wish to display it.

We make use of the `getFeaturesAtCoordinate` source query method to determine whether or not a feature exists at the coordinate of the click event (`event.coordinate`). The result is stored in a variable, namely `features`.

```
if (features.length > 0) {
overlay.setPosition(event.coordinate);
featureRefElem.innerHTML = features[0].get('ref');
featureRestrictionsElem.innerHTML =
  features[0].get('restrictions');
}
```

Although we know that our data contains no overlapping features at any given coordinate, with other data sources this scenario may occur, which is why OpenLayers returns the result of the query as an array of `features`. We check whether the length of the array is greater than zero; if this is the case, we can infer that a feature is present at this particular coordinate.

The `overlay` is positioned at the coordinate via the `setPosition` method, and the `overlay` content is populated with the feature `ref` property and the `restrictions` property, both via the `get` method that `ol.Feature` inherits from `ol.Object`. The text is added to the relevant DOM elements using the JavaScript `innerHTML` method.

We can even use the `getFeaturesAtCoordinate` source query method with a coordinate, where a feature resides but is not currently visible from the viewport extent. It will still return the feature detected at this location.

There's more...

Other powerful data source queries exist, such as `getClosestFeatureToCoordinate` and `getFeaturesInExtent`, which could be very useful when developing mapping applications. I recommend that you visit the OpenLayers documentation (`http://openlayers.org`) to discover other useful methods and find out what these methods can do for you.

See also

 ▶ The *Adding WMS layers* recipe in *Chapter 2, Adding Raster Layers*
 ▶ The *Getting information from a WMS server* recipe
 ▶ The *Adding a GML layer* recipe in *Chapter 3, Working with Vector Layers*
 ▶ The *Listening for vector layer features' event* recipe in *Chapter 4, Adding Controls*

Getting information from a WMS server

We've seen in earlier recipes that we can query external services for map tiles (WMS) and also for features (WFS). In addition to this, WMS servers can implement the `GetFeatureInfo` request. This type of request allows us to, given a point and some layer names that are configured at the WMS server, retrieve information from a feature; that is, we can get feature attributes from a layer, which is rendered as a raster image.

For example, there could be a WMS layer containing parking zones across your region, which can be drawn out as polygons over the map as part of the returned raster tiles. You could listen for a click event on the map and retrieve information from the WMS server in regards to the location that you clicked on. This may return data, such as parking fees, the name of the car park, how many spaces are still available, and so on.

OpenLayers makes this type of feature information request simple with a method called `getGetFeatureInfoUrl`, which is available on the source classes, `ol.source.TileWMS` and `ol.source.ImageWMS`.

We are going to create a map with a base layer and a raster layer containing data from a WMS server. When the user clicks or taps on an area of the map, we will make a feature information request to the WMS server and render the returned information below the map. The source code can be found in ch05/ch05-wms-feature-info, and we'll end up with something that looks like the following screenshot:

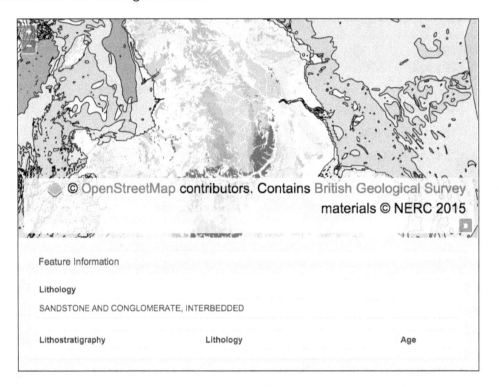

How to do it...

In order to query for feature information from a WMS server, follow these instructions:

1. Let's start by creating the HTML file with the OpenLayers dependencies and also jQuery. In particular, add the HTML for div to contain the feature information response:

   ```
   <div id="js-feature-info"></div>
   ```

2. Create a custom JavaScript file and set up the WMS source instance:

   ```
   var bgsSource = new ol.source.TileWMS({
     url: 'http://ogc.bgs.ac.uk/cgi-bin/' +
         'BGS_Bedrock_and_Superficial_Geology/wms',
     params: {
       LAYERS: 'BGS_EN_Bedrock_and_Superficial_Geology'
   ```

```
    },
    attributions: [
      new ol.Attribution({
        html: 'Contains <a href="http://bgs.ac.uk">' +
          'British Geological Survey</a> ' +
          'materials &copy; NERC 2015'
      })]
  });
```

3. Initialize `map` with a base layer, a WMS raster layer, and `view`:

```
var map = new ol.Map({
  view: new ol.View({
    zoom: 7, center: [-146759, 7060335]
  }),
  target: 'js-map',
  layers: [
    new ol.layer.Tile({source: new ol.source.OSM()}),
    new ol.layer.Tile({source: bgsSource})
  ]
});
```

4. Cache the DOM element to a variable that'll be used to display the returned feature information:

```
var $featureInfo = $('#js-feature-info');
```

5. Subscribe to click events on the map, compose the URL, make the feature information request, and display the returned data on the page:

```
map.on('singleclick', function(event) {
  var url = bgsSource.getGetFeatureInfoUrl(
    event.coordinate,
    map.getView().getResolution(),
    map.getView().getProjection(),
    {INFO_FORMAT: 'text/html'}
  );

  $.ajax({
    type: 'GET',
    url: url
  }).done(function(data) {
    $featureInfo.html(data.match(/<body>([\s\S]+)<\/body>/)[1]);
  });
});
```

How it works...

This recipe contains HTML and CSS that have been excluded for brevity. Please take a look at the accompanying source code for the full implementation.

We've seen how to connect and request map tiles from a WMS server before in the *Adding WMS layer* recipe in *Chapter 2, Adding Raster Layers*, so let's focus on the map click handler, which contains some newly-introduced concepts:

```
map.on('singleclick', function(event) {
  var url = bgsSource.getGetFeatureInfoUrl(
    event.coordinate,
    map.getView().getResolution(),
    map.getView().getProjection(),
    {INFO_FORMAT: 'text/html'}
  );
```

We subscribed to the `singleclick` event on the `map` instance. Within our handler, we determine how the request URL will be structured. The WMS source instance (`bgsSource`) has the `getGetFeatureInfoUrl` method that expects the following four parameters:

- **Coordinate**: This is acquired from the click event object (`event.coordinate`).
- **Resolution**: This is acquired from the map's view via the `getResolution` method.
- **Projection**: This is retrieved from the map's view via the `getProjection` method.
- **Parameters**: This an object of key/value pairs to forge the request parameters. We have specified a supported format (from the WMS server) of `text/html`.

This method will return a string that we can use for the AJAX request coming up next:

```
$.ajax({
    type: 'GET',
    url: url
}).done(function(data) {
    $featureInfo.html(data.match(/<body>([\s\S]+)<\/body>/)[1]);
});
```

 A WMS server implements different request types, such as tile map requests that contain the parameter and value `REQUEST=GetMap`, respectively, as well as other parameters, such as a bounding box, layer name, and so on. It's important to know that the feature information differentiates requests with the following key/value parameter: `REQUEST=GetFeatureInfo`. Have a look at the network requests in any modern browser's development tools for more details.

Once we have the URL, we make the AJAX request using the jQuery `ajax` method. When the WMS server responds to the request, the `done` method is called and contains the response within the `data` argument.

We requested for a response to come back as media type `text/html`, as the content is conveniently structured in HTML tables that we can easily insert into our page without much further intervention. We are, however, only interested in the content of the body element from the response, so we extract only this using a JavaScript regular expression.

For example, here's what could be returned in raw form:

```
<!doctype html>
<head>
<title>Feature Info</title>
</head>
<body>
<table>...</table>
</body>
</html>
```

As per this example, we are only interested in the `table` element (within the body), as this contains all the feature information that we want.

We set up a regular expression to search for the opening and closing body tags and capture any characters in between, across multiple lines, which is what the `[\s\S]`+ part of the regular expression does. There's a great resource from Mozilla if you'd like to become more accustomed with JavaScript regular expressions at `https://developer.mozilla.org/en/docs/Web/JavaScript/Guide/Regular_Expressions`.

The JavaScript method `match` returns an array containing the matched elements. As the regular expression captures the content between the opening and closing body tags (that's what the surrounding parentheses do), we access the second item in the returned array (index of 1). Undesirably, the zero index of the array returned from match contains the text, including the `body` tags.

The content is populated inside the `div` feature information on our page (refer to the recipe screenshot for an example of this output) via the `html` jQuery method.

See also

- The *Getting feature information from data source* recipe
- The *Adding WMS layer* recipe

6

Styling Features

In this chapter we will cover the following topics:

- ▸ Styling layers
- ▸ Styling features based on geometry type
- ▸ Styling based on feature attributes
- ▸ Styling interaction render intents
- ▸ Styling clustered features

Introduction

Once we know how to work with vector layers, such as adding new features or modifying existing ones, the question that we may have in mind is: how do we style them? We have seen examples of feature styling in previous recipes in this book, but this chapter will take a deeper look into what we can do with styles and how styling operates in OpenLayers.

The visual representation of features is one of the most important concepts in GIS applications. It is not only important from the user's experience or the designer's perspective, but it is also important as an information requirement, for example, to identify features that match certain conditions.

The way that we visualize features is not only important to make our application much more attractive, but it is also important to improve the way that we bring information to the user. For example, assuming that a set of points represent some temperatures, if we are interested in the hottest zones, we could represent them with different radius and color values. This way, a lesser radius and a color near to blue would mean that the zone is a cold zone, while a greater radius and a color near to red would mean a hot zone.

OpenLayers offers us a great degree of flexibility when styling features. We can use static styles or dynamic styles that are influenced by feature attributes. Styles can be created through various methods, such as from style functions (`ol.style.StyleFunction`), or by applying new style instances (`ol.style.Style`) directly to a feature or layer.

Let's take a look at all of this in the following recipes.

Styling layers

To demonstrate some of the feature styling options that are available, we'll create a live editor in the side panel to style the features that are already loaded on to the map. To achieve this goal, we'll be using the jQuery UI library to create sliders and the jQuery plugin Spectrum for the color picker widget. The source code can be found in `ch06/ch06-styling-layers`. We'll end up with something that looks similar to the following screenshot:

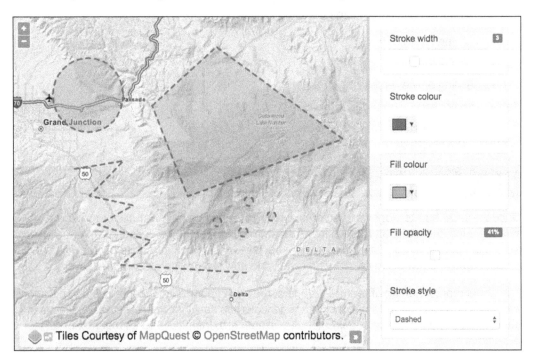

For this recipe, we are going to apply styles at the layer level so that all features within a layer inherit the styling. The current state of all customizable styles will be reflected in the sidebar.

We'll be instantiating many instances of classes that belong to the `ol.style` object, such as `ol.style.Stroke`. Let's take a look at how this is implemented.

Getting ready

The source code has two main sections: one for HTML where all the controls are placed, and a second one for the JavaScript code.

The HTML section contains a lot of markup that gets converted to interactive widgets by the JavaScript, such as the slider and color picker. As mentioned earlier, we've also used the *jQuery, jQuery UI* (`https://jqueryui.com`) and *Spectrum* (`https://bgrins.github.io/spectrum`) libraries. As they're not the goal of this recipe, the HTML won't be listed out in the *How to do it...* section. I encourage you to take a look at the code in the code bundle of this book.

How to do it...

In order to create your own customized layer styling, follow these instructions:

1. After creating the HTML file, including OpenLayers dependencies and other library dependencies (refer to the *Getting ready* section for the HTML code), create a custom JavaScript file and instantiate a new `map` instance, as follows:

```
var map = new ol.Map({
  view: new ol.View({
    zoom: 10, center: [-12036691, 4697972]
  }),
  target: 'js-map',
  layers: [
    new ol.layer.Tile({
      source: new ol.source.MapQuest({layer: 'osm'})
    })
  ]
});
```

2. Create a vector layer for the `source` instance that loads in a GeoJSON file of features:

```
var vectorLayer = new ol.layer.Vector({
  source: new ol.source.Vector({
    url: 'features.geojson',
    format: new ol.format.GeoJSON({
      defaultDataProjection: 'EPSG:3857'
    })
  })
});
```

3. Set up the function that brings the styling together so that it can be used to set the complete vector layer styling, as follows:

```
var setStyles = function () {
  vectorLayer.setStyle(new ol.style.Style({
    stroke: strokeStyle(),
    fill: fillStyle(),
    image: new ol.style.Circle({
      fill: fillStyle(),
      stroke: strokeStyle(),
      radius: 8
    })
  }));
};
```

4. Set up the `stroke-width` and `fill-opacity` sliders with the jQuery UI. The handlers for the `slide` action call our `setStyles` method, and they display the relevant value in the DOM for the user to see, as follows:

```
$('#js-stroke-width').slider({
  min: 1, max: 10, step: 1, value: 1,
  slide: function(event, ui) {
    $('#js-stroke-width-value').text(ui.value);
    setStyles();
  }
});
$('#js-fill-opacity').slider({
  min: 0, max: 100, step: 1, value: 50,
  slide: function(event, ui) {
    $('#js-fill-opacity-value').text(ui.value + '%');
    setStyles();
  }
});
```

5. Convert the markup for the `stroke` and `fill` colors to interactive color pickers with the help of the Spectrum jQuery plugin. When a new color is chosen, call our `setStyles` method:

```
$('#js-stroke-color, #js-fill-color').spectrum({
  color: 'black', change: setStyles
});
```

6. Listen for changes in the stroke line style `select` menu and call our `setStyles` method:

```
$('#js-stroke-style').on('change', setStyles);
```

7. Set up the function that returns the fill style, as follows:

```
var fillStyle = function() {
  var rgb = $('#js-fill-color').spectrum('get').toRgb();
  return new ol.style.Fill({
    color: [
      rgb.r, rgb.g, rgb.b,
      $('#js-fill-opacity').slider('value') / 100
    ]
  });
};
```

8. Set up the function that returns the stroke style, as follows:

```
var strokeStyle = function() {
  return new ol.style.Stroke({
    color: $('#js-stroke-color').spectrum('get').toHexString(),
    width: $('#js-stroke-width').slider('value'),
    lineDash: $('#js-stroke-style').val() === 'solid'
      ? undefined : [8]
  });
};
```

9. Finish off by calling the `setStyles` function and add the vector layer to the `map` instance, as follows:

```
setStyles();
map.addLayer(vectorLayer);
```

How it works...

There's a lot of JavaScript to cover here if we take it line by line. What we're going to do instead is pluck out enough of the key functionality that will allow you to make sense of the overall code yourself:

```
var setStyles = function() {
  vectorLayer.setStyle(new ol.style.Style({
    stroke: strokeStyle(),
    fill: fillStyle(),
    image: new ol.style.Circle({
      fill: fillStyle(),
      stroke: strokeStyle(),
      radius: 8
    })
  }));
};
```

We create a function, namely `setStyles`, that'll be called from multiple places in the code when the user customizes the styling in the side panel. When this method is called, it returns a completed instance of the `ol.style.Style` object and passes it to the vector layer's `setStyle` method. This, in turn, causes the features on the map to be rerendered with the latest styling configuration.

The stroke property of `ol.style.Style` is assigned the value of the stroke style that is generated by the `strokeStyle` method, and the `fill` property is generated by the `fillStyle` method.

The `image` property is an instance of the `ol.style.Circle` styling object, which is the geometry type that point geometries are presented with. We repeat our usage of the `fill` and `stroke` methods to provide the values for the `fill` and `stroke` properties. We set a static `radius` of 8 for the circle style.

```
$('#js-stroke-width').slider({
    min: 1, max: 10, step: 1, value: 1,
    slide: function(event, ui) {
        $('#js-stroke-width-value').text(ui.value);
        setStyles();
    }
});
```

Let's take a look at just one of the jQuery `slider` setups for the stroke width. Once you're familiar with this `slider` function, you'll be able to ascertain how the other `slider` function for the `fill` opacity fits into the implementation of this recipe yourself.

We've limited the width to lie between 1 and 10, inclusive (with the `min` and `max` properties), and the default width is 1. We register a handler for the `slide` action that displays the updated value in the (`$('#js-stroke-width-value').text(ui.value)`) sidebar; this does not influence the style of the actual features against the map yet.

We then call our `setStyles` method, as we want the latest styling to be immediately reflected on the map.

```
$('#js-stroke-color, #js-fill-color').spectrum({
    color: 'black', change: setStyles
});
```

The other widget type that we'll cover in this chapter is for the color picker (we won't cover the handler for the stroke style `select` menu as it should be easy enough to follow).

Within the jQuery selector, we selected both `color` input elements for `fill` and `stroke`, passing in a default color of `black` and a handler that calls our `setStyles` method when a new color is selected.

```
var fillStyle = function() {
  var rgb = $('#js-fill-color').spectrum('get').toRgb();
  return new ol.style.Fill({
    color: [
      rgb.r, rgb.g, rgb.b,
      $('#js-fill-opacity').slider('value') / 100
    ]
  });
};
```

The fill color (from the color picker) was retained by Spectrum when we initialized the widget from the DOM element and whenever it's updated by the user. To dynamically retrieve the latest color, we access the same DOM element and call the `get` method followed by the `toRgb` method—both from Spectrum, storing the result in the `rgb` variable. The result is an object with the red value assigned to the `r` property, and so on for the green and blue values.

We both instantiate and return an instance of `ol.style.Fill`, which accepts a single object property of `color`. This value can be an array of OpenLayer's type `ol.Color` ([red, green, blue, alpha]). We retrieve and populate the array with the RGB values, followed by the alpha value.

The alpha value is taken from the jQuery UI slider DOM element (`slider('value')`). This number is transformed into a float. For example, 55; in this case, we divide 55 by `100` (0.55). This is important, as the `ol.Color` type array expects the alpha to be a float value from 0-1, inclusive.

As we saw earlier in this recipe, our `setStyles` method uses the `fillStyle` method to populate some of its properties.

```
var strokeStyle = function() {
  return new ol.style.Stroke({
    color: $('#js-stroke-color').spectrum('get').toHexString(),
    width: $('#js-stroke-width').slider('value'),
    lineDash: $('#js-stroke-style').val() === 'solid'
      ? undefined : [8]
  });
};
```

Similar to our `fillStyle` function, an instance of the stroke style constructor (`ol.style.Stroke`) is both returned and instantiated at the same time. More properties are available for stroke styling, from which we populate the `color`, `width`, and `lineDash` properties with values.

For the `color` property, we once again utilize Spectrum to retrieve the value of the latest color picker DOM element, but this time, we pass it through the `toHexString` library method, producing the color in string hex format. The `color` property for `ol.style.Stroke` can also accept an `ol.Color` array as well.

For the `width` property, we simply grab the value directly from the jQuery `slider` DOM element.

The value for the `lineDash` property is inferred from the user's selection. If a user has selected **None** (which has an `option value` of `solid`) from the `select` menu, then we pass in `undefined`, which means that no dash is required for the `stroke` instance. Otherwise, we pass in an array with a single number entry of `8`.

When you pass in an array of numbers, you're defining a dashed pattern. The numbers represent the length of the alternating dashes and gaps. So, `8` on its own, as we've done here, is the equivalent of [8, 8] (the gap is assumed to be the same length as the dash).

You can design far more complex patterns at your own discretion. I encourage you to play around with other options. Mozilla has a useful guide on stroke dash arrays at `https://developer.mozilla.org/en/docs/Web/SVG/Attribute/stroke-dasharray`.

The `ol.style.Stroke` constructor accepts other properties, such as `lineCap`, and `lineJoin`, that you may find interesting.

There's more...

A question that can arise here is, what takes precedence when styling, a rule applied to a vector layer or styles applied directly to a single feature?

The answer is that styles go from bottom to top. This means that if we have specified a style directly on a feature, then this will be used to render it. Otherwise, any styles assigned to the vector layer will be applied to its features.

See also

▶ The *Styling based on feature attributes* recipe
▶ The *Styling interaction render intents* recipe

Styling features based on geometry type

We can summarize that there are two ways to style a feature. The first is by applying the style to the layer so that every feature inherits this styling, as seen in the *Styling layers* recipe. The second is to apply the styling options directly to the feature, which we'll see in this recipe.

This recipe shows us how we can choose which flavor of styling to apply to a feature, depending on the geometry type. We will apply the style directly to the feature using the `ol.Feature` method, `setStyle`.

When a `point` geometry type is detected, we will actually style the representing geometry as a star, rather than the default circle shape. Other styling will be applied when a geometry type of line string is detected.

The source code can be found in `ch06/ch06-styling-features-by-geometry-type`, and the output of the recipe will look like the following screenshot:

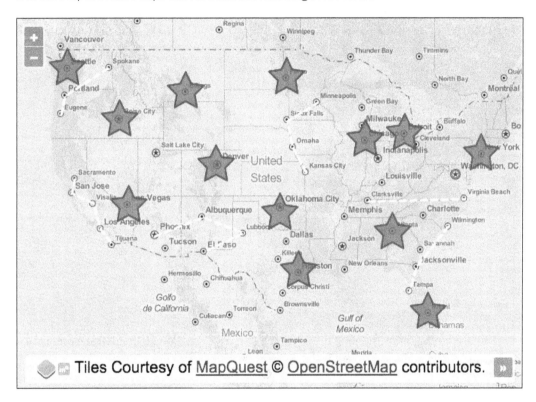

How to do it...

To customize the feature styling based on the geometry type, use the following steps:

1. Create the HTML file with OpenLayers dependencies, the jQuery library, and a `div` element that will hold the `map` instance:

2. Create a custom JavaScript file and initialize a new `map` instance, as follows:

```
var map = new ol.Map({
    view: new ol.View({
```

```
      zoom: 4, center: [-10732981, 4676723]
  }),
  target: 'js-map',
  layers: [
    new ol.layer.Tile({
      source: new ol.source.MapQuest({layer: 'osm'})
    })
  ]
```

3. Create a new vector layer and add it to the `map`. Have the source loader function retrieve the GeoJSON file, format the response, then pass it through our custom `modifyFeatures` method (which we'll implement next) before adding the features to the vector source:

```
var vectorLayer = new ol.layer.Vector({
  source: new ol.source.Vector({
    loader: function() {
      $.ajax({
        type: 'GET',
        url: 'features.geojson',
        context: this
      }).done(function(data) {
        var format = new ol.format.GeoJSON();
        var features = format.readFeatures(data);
        this.addFeatures(modifyFeatures(features));
      });
    }
  })
});
map.addLayer(vectorLayer);
```

4. Finish off by implementing the `modifyFeatures` function so that it transforms the projection of `geometry` and styles the feature based on the geometry type:

```
function modifyFeatures(features) {
  features.forEach(function(feature) {
    var geometry = feature.getGeometry();
    geometry.transform('EPSG:4326', 'EPSG:3857');
    if (geometry.getType() === 'Point') {
      feature.setStyle(
        new ol.style.Style({
          image: new ol.style.RegularShape({
            fill: new ol.style.Fill({
              color: [255, 0, 0, 0.6]
            }),
            stroke: new ol.style.Stroke({
```

```
                width: 2, color: 'blue'
              }),
              points: 5, radius1: 25, radius2: 12.5
            })
          })
        );
      }
      if (geometry.getType() === 'LineString') {
        feature.setStyle(
          new ol.style.Style({
            stroke: new ol.style.Stroke({
              color:  [255, 255, 255, 1],
              width: 3, lineDash: [8, 6]
            })
          })
        );
      }
    });
    return features;
  }
```

How it works...

Let's take a brief look at the `loader` function of the vector source before we make a closer examination of the logic behind the styling:

```
loader: function() {
  $.ajax({
    type: 'GET',
    url: 'features.geojson',
    context: this
  }).done(function(data) {
    var format = new ol.format.GeoJSON();
    var features = format.readFeatures(data);
    this.addFeatures(modifyFeatures(features));
  });
}
```

We saw how this type of source loading worked in *Chapter 3, Working with Vector Layers* in the recipe, *Reading features directly using AJAX*, but as a quick reminder of some of the aspects in relation to this recipe, we'll discuss the `done` promise content once the AJAX response has been received.

Our external resource contains points and line strings in the format of GeoJSON, so we must create a new instance of `ol.format.GeoJSON` so that we can read in the data (`format.readFeatures(data)`) of the AJAX response to build out a collection of OpenLayers features.

Before adding the group of features straight to the vector source (`this` refers to the vector source here), we pass the array of features through our `modifyFeatures` method. This method will apply all the necessary styling to each feature, then return the modified features back in place, and feed the result to the `addFeatures` method. Let's break down the contents of our `modifyFeatures` method:

```
function modifyFeatures(features) {
    features.forEach(function(feature) {
        var geometry = feature.getGeometry();
        geometry.transform('EPSG:4326', 'EPSG:3857');
```

The logic begins by looping over each feature in the array using the JavaScript array method, `forEach`. The first argument passed to the anonymous iterator function is the feature (`feature`).

Within the loop iteration, we store this feature's geometry in a variable, namely `geometry`, as this is accessed more than once during the loop iteration.

Unbeknown to you, the projection of coordinates within the GeoJSON file are in longitude/latitude, projection code `EPSG:4326`. The map's view, however, is in projection `EPSG:3857`. To ensure that they appear where intended on the map, we use the `transform` geometry method, which takes the source and the destination projections as arguments and converts the coordinates of the geometry in place.

```
    if (geometry.getType() === 'Point') {
      feature.setStyle(
        new ol.style.Style({
          image: new ol.style.RegularShape({
            fill: new ol.style.Fill({
              color: [255, 0, 0, 0.6]
            }),
            stroke: new ol.style.Stroke({
              width: 2, color: 'blue'
            }),
            points: 5, radius1: 25, radius2: 12.5
          })
        })
      );
    }
```

Next up is a conditional check on whether or not the geometry is a type of `Point`. The `geometry` instance has the method `getType` for this kind of purpose.

Inline of the `setStyle` method of the `feature` instance, we create a new `style` object from the `ol.style.Style` constructor. The only direct property that we're interested in is the `image` property.

As the default, point geometries are styled as a circle. Instead, we want to style the point as a star. We can achieve this through the use of the `ol.style.RegularShape` constructor. We set up a `fill` style with a `color` property and the `stroke` style with the `width` and `color` properties.

The `points` property specifies the number of points for the star. In the case of a polygon shape, it represents the number of sides.

The `radius1` and `radius2` properties are specifically to design star shapes for the configuration of the inner and outer radius, respectively.

```
if (geometry.getType() === 'LineString') {
  feature.setStyle(
    new ol.style.Style({
      stroke: new ol.style.Stroke({
        color:  [255, 255, 255, 1],
        width: 3, lineDash: [8, 6]
      })
    })
  );
}
```

The final piece of this method has a conditional check on the geometry type of `LineString`. If this is the case, we style this geometry type differently to the point geometry type. We provide a `stroke` style with `color`, `width`, and a custom line dash. The `lineDash` array declares a line length of 8, which is followed by a gap length of 6.

See also

▸ The *Styling interaction render intents* recipe

▸ The *Styling layers* recipe

▸ The *Creating features programmatically* recipe in *Chapter 3, Working with Vector Layers*

Styling based on feature attributes

So far, in this chapter, we took a look at styling features at the layer level using the `setStyle` method from `ol.layer.Vector`. We've also looked at styling individual features based on their geometry type, and then we applied the styles using the `setStyle` method from the `ol.Feature` class.

For this recipe, we'll look at a different way to style features at the feature level using a styling function at the `ol.layer.Vector` level. The vector layer class has a property named `style`, which not only accepts an instance of `ol.style.Style` or an array of various `ol.style.Style` instances, but it also accepts an `ol.style.StyleFunction` method. This method is called whenever a feature is rendered on the map, and the result of this method must return an array of `ol.style.Style` instances.

As part of this new styling technique, we'll determine how some of the styles will be applied, based on the feature attributes.

We will load a GeoJSON file of some USA cities and provide a default style for these features. The user will be able to search for a city by name from an input field, and on doing this, the cities will be filtered on the map so that matching cities stand out, while the cities that don't match the search query will be be less visible.

The source code can be found in `ch06/ch06-styling-features-by-attribute`, and we'll end with something that looks like the following screenshot:

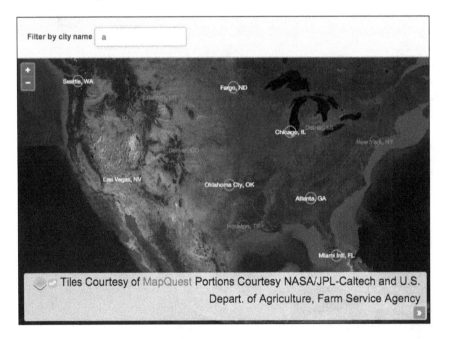

How to do it...

Learn how to style features based on feature attributes by following these instructions:

1. Start by creating a new HTML file and add the OpenLayers dependencies and a `div` element to hold the `map` instance. In particular, add the HTML for the search form, as we reference this within the JavaScript:

```
<form>
  <label for="js-search-query">Filter by city name</label>
  <input id="js-search-query" placeholder="Enter city
      name...">
</form>
```

2. Create a custom JavaScript file and initialize the `map` instance with a `view` instance and a satellite tile raster layer:

```
var map = new ol.Map({
  view: new ol.View({
    zoom: 4, center: [-10987364, 4109254]
  }),
  target: 'js-map',
  layers: [
    new ol.layer.Tile({
      source: new ol.source.MapQuest({layer: 'sat'})
    })
  ]
});
```

3. Cache the search input field DOM element and subscribe to the `keyup` event. Have the handler trigger a change event on the vector layer:

```
var searchQueryElem = document.getElementById('js-search-query');
searchQueryElem.addEventListener('keyup', function() {
  vectorLayer.changed();
});
```

4. Implement the style function that will be applied to the vector layer:

```
var styleFunction = function(feature) {
  var cityName = feature.get('name');
  var searchQuery = searchQueryElem.value;
  var opacity = 1;
  if (searchQuery &&
    cityName.search(new RegExp(searchQuery, 'i')) === -1) {
    opacity = 0.3;
  }
  return [
```

```
        new ol.style.Style({
          image: new ol.style.Circle({
            radius: 10,
            stroke: new ol.style.Stroke({
              color: [74, 138, 168, opacity], width: 2
            })
          }),
          text: new ol.style.Text({
            text: cityName,
            fill: new ol.style.Fill({
              color: [255, 255, 255, opacity]
            }),
            stroke: new ol.style.Stroke({
              color: [0, 51, 0, opacity], width: 1
            }),
            font: '11px "Helvetica Neue", Arial'
          })
        })
      ];
    };
```

5. Create the vector layer, assign the style function to the `style` property, and have the vector source fetch the GeoJSON file. Finally, add the layer to the map:

```
var vectorLayer = new ol.layer.Vector({
  source: new ol.source.Vector({
    url: 'cities.geojson',
    format: new ol.format.GeoJSON()
  }),
  style: styleFunction
});
map.addLayer(vectorLayer);
```

How it works...

As we've often done, much of the HTML and all of the CSS here has been omitted for brevity. Please view the accompanying source code for a complete understanding of the structure and styling:

```
searchQueryElem.addEventListener('keyup', function() {
  vectorLayer.changed();
});
```

Rather than waiting for the user to submit a search request via a form submission, we have opted for a more immediate reaction by subscribing to the `keyup` event from the `input` element. When this `keyup` event is published, we call the `changed` method on our vector layer. The `changed` method increments the internal revision counter for the layer and dispatches a change event, which, in turn, calls our `ol.style.StyleFunction` for each and every feature in the vector source.

It's important to force a rerender of the feature styling from this published event because our feature styles are partly based on the city filtering requirements of the user.

Now, let's move on to the bulk of the code by looking over some of the `styleFunction` implementation:

```
var styleFunction = function(feature) {
  var cityName = feature.get('name');
  var searchQuery = searchQueryElem.value;
  var opacity = 1;
```

When OpenLayers internally calls this function in order to determine the feature styles, it passes in the `feature` in question as its first argument. It also provides a second argument, representing the view's resolution, which we've left out because we don't make use of it.

Each feature from the GeoJSON file contains the city name within the `name` attribute. We use the `get` method from `ol.Feature` to retrieve this value and store it in the `cityName` variable. We get the latest search query value from the input field and store it in the `searchQuery` variable. We also set up a default `opacity` of 1, which gets used in the feature styling customization.

```
if (searchQuery &&
  cityName.search(new RegExp(searchQuery, 'i')) === -1) {
    opacity = 0.3;
  }
```

We check to see whether the value of the input field is not blank (if it's blank, then the `searchQuery` variable will be false. If it's not blank, then it infers that the user has entered a search query of some sort, and we wish to filter the cities as requested by the user.

This brings us to the next condition: the city name from the feature (`cityName`) is checked against the search query from the input field. The search query is converted to a case insensitive regular expression (`new RegExp(searchQuery, 'i')` and passed to the JavaScript `search` method. This searches the string for the contents of the regular expression. For example, the city name 'New York, NY' from the feature attribute will match a search query of `'york'`, or regular expression of `/york/i`.

If there's a match, then the index of where the match began is returned; otherwise, `-1` for no match is returned. If this feature doesn't match the search query, then we set the `opacity` variable to `0.3`. This will make the cities that don't match less visible to the user, in turn, highlighting any cities that do match, which will retain the opacity of `1`.

The rest of our style function returns an array with one item containing an `ol.style.Style` instance to satisfy the function contract that `ol.style.StyleFunction` requires. The configuration within this will look familiar to earlier recipes, and it doesn't require further explanation. You'll notice that the `opacity` variable is used for the alpha part of the `color` property array values, for example, `color: [74, 138, 168, opacity]`. This is the dynamic result of whether or not the city or feature matches the search query.

You'll also notice that the `cityName` variable is assigned to the `text` property of the `ol.style.Text` instance. The city name forms the visible geometry label.

When the vector layer is instantiated, we assign our style function to the `style` property.

See also

- ▶ The *Styling layers* recipe
- ▶ The *Adding text label to geometry point* recipe in *Chapter 3, Working with Vector Layers*
- ▶ The *Using point features as markers* recipe in *Chapter 3, Working with Vector Layers*
- ▶ The *Removing or cloning features using overlays* recipe in *Chapter 3, Working with Vector Layers*

Styling interaction render intents

There are some map interactions, such as **Draw** and **Select**, which change the style of the feature depending on its current state, that is, if it is currently being drawn or selected. There are also other interactions that create temporary geometries, such as the `DragZoom` interaction, which draws out a rectangle over the map representing the extent that you wish to view.

This recipe shows us how we can modify the styles used for each of these render intents to change the look of our applications.

We will create a panel above the map that allows the user to enable the draw or select interactions. They will be able to perform `DragZoom` whenever they like. The source code can be found in `ch06/ch06-styling-interaction-render-intents`, and the styling for the **Draw** interaction render intent will look like the following screenshot:

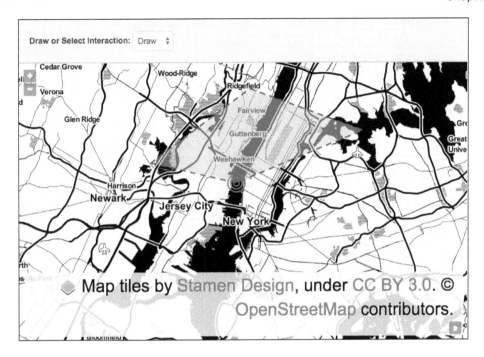

How to do it...

Find out how to style interaction render intents by following these instructions:

1. Create a new HTML file and add the OpenLayers dependencies, including the `div` element to hold the `map` instance. In particular, create the `select` menu that the JavaScript will be accessing, as follows:

```
<select id="js-draw-or-select">
  <option value="draw" selected>Draw</option>
  <option value="select">Select</option>
</select>
```

2. In a separate CSS file, add the following declaration to customize the style of the `DragZoom` interaction:

```
.ol-dragzoom {
  border: 3px dotted white;
  background: rgba(50, 186, 132, 0.5);
}
```

3. Set up the vector layer and the `map` instance, as follows:

```
var vectorLayer = new ol.layer.Vector({
  source: new ol.source.Vector()
});
var map = new ol.Map({
  view: new ol.View({
    zoom: 11, center: [-8238306, 4987133]
  }),
  target: 'js-map',
  layers: [
    new ol.layer.Tile({
      source: new ol.source.Stamen({layer: 'toner'})
    }), vectorLayer
  ]
});
```

4. Create a function that will generate an instance of `ol.style.Circle` with a dynamic `radius`:

```
var imageCircle = function(radius) {
  return new ol.style.Circle({
    stroke: new ol.style.Stroke({
      color: 'red', width: 2
    }), radius: radius
  });
};
```

5. Create the draw interaction with custom styling, as follows:

```
var drawInteraction = new ol.interaction.Draw({
  style: [
    new ol.style.Style({
      fill: new ol.style.Fill({
        color: 'rgba(153, 202, 255, 0.5)'
      }),
      stroke: new ol.style.Stroke({
        color: 'blue', width: 2, lineDash: [8, 10]
      }),
      image: imageCircle(15)
    }),
    new ol.style.Style({
      image: imageCircle(10)
    }),
    new ol.style.Style({
      image: imageCircle(5)
    })
  ],
  type: 'Polygon',
  source: vectorLayer.getSource()
});
```

6. Create the select interaction with custom styling, as follows:

```
var selectInteraction = new ol.interaction.Select({
  style: new ol.style.Style({
    fill: new ol.style.Fill({
      color: 'rgba(255, 255, 31, 0.8)'
    }),
    stroke: new ol.style.Stroke({
      color: 'rgba(255, 154, 31, 0.9)', width: 4
    })
  })
});
```

7. Add the following `Draw` and `DragZoom` interactions to the map:

```
map.addInteraction(new ol.interaction.DragZoom());
map.addInteraction(drawInteraction);
```

8. Subscribe to the `change` event on the `select` menu and remove or add the `Draw` or `Select` interactions, accordingly:

```
document.getElementById('js-draw-or-select')
  .addEventListener('change', function() {
    var oldInteraction = (this.value === 'draw')
      ? 'select' : 'draw';
    map.removeInteraction(window[oldInteraction + 'Interaction']);
    map.addInteraction(window[this.value + 'Interaction']);
  });
```

How it works...

We've excluded showing all the CSS and HTML, but please view the book source code for the complete implementation. The parts that have been included should offer enough in isolation in order to follow along just fine.

You may have observed that the `DragZoom` interaction (`ol.interaction.DragZoom`) does not have a `style` property like the other two interactions in this example. This is because when the `DragZoom` interaction draws out an extent over the map to zoom to, the rectangle is actually an HTML element rather than part of the map canvas. With this in mind, it should make sense as to why the box is styled with the following CSS:

```
.ol-dragzoom {
  border: 3px dotted white;
  background: rgba(50, 186, 132, 0.5);
}
```

We chose to style the border as a dotted white line and applied a semitransparent turquoise color for the background. It's a good idea to put custom CSS that overrides the OpenLayers defaults within a separate style sheet for easier maintenance down the line.

Unlike `DragZoom`, the `Draw` and `Select` interactions do have a `style` property that we must take advantage of in order to customize the style of the render intent. Let's take a closer look at how they're implemented:

```
var imageCircle = function(radius) {
  return new ol.style.Circle({
    stroke: new ol.style.Stroke({
      color: 'red', width: 2
    }), radius: radius
  });
};
```

For the `Draw` interaction, we decided to construct the point image (the point is used to identify where the next geometry point in the feature is going to be placed) with a combination of three circles so that it looks like a target. As the `ol.style.Circle` constructor will be called multiple times but with a varying `radius` size, we've captured it within a reusable function, namely `imageCircle`. Each circle image contains a simple red-colored stroke with no fill color. The result of this is displayed in the following screenshot:

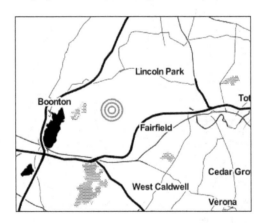

```
var drawInteraction = new ol.interaction.Draw({
  style: [
    new ol.style.Style({
      fill: new ol.style.Fill({
        color: 'rgba(153, 202, 255, 0.5)'
      }),
      stroke: new ol.style.Stroke({
        color: 'blue', width: 2,
        lineDash: [8, 10]
```

```
    }),
    image: imageCircle(15)
  }),
  new ol.style.Style({
    image: imageCircle(10)
  }),
  new ol.style.Style({
    image: imageCircle(5)
  })
]
```

We chopped off the last few properties of the `Draw` interaction instantiation in this code, as it will look familiar to other recipes. We want to draw your attention to what we assigned to the `style` property.

We actually created three `ol.style.Style` instances within the array. The first main style contains the styling for the polygon fill and stroke and also the first outmost ring of the point styling, which is generated from our `imageCircle` function. The `fill color` property is a string in the form of RGBA—another variate that OpenLayers accepts.

The following two styles in the array create the other inner rings of the point. All `image` properties are assigned the result of our `imageCircle` function; each passes in a differently-sized radius, producing the target effect that we wish to achieve.

It's useful to understand that styles can be built up within an array. You can design some very creative styles should you ever have the need or desire to do so.

The `Select` interaction is also supplied with some of its own styles via the `style` property in order to color selected polygons with a bright yellow fill and a thick dark orange stroke.

```
document.getElementById('js-draw-or-select')
  .addEventListener('change', function() {
    var oldInteraction = (this.value === 'draw') ? 'select' : 'draw';
    map.removeInteraction(window[oldInteraction + 'Interaction']);
    map.addInteraction(window[this.value + 'Interaction']);
  });
```

This last piece of code that we'll discuss in this recipe does the grunt work behind switching the active interactions to or from `Draw` or `Select`.

When the `select` menu option changes, the new value is one of two possibilities: `draw` or `select`. From this, we can ascertain what the previously active interaction was on the map. We remove this interaction using the map's `removeInteraction` method, as the two interfere with one another.

The interaction variables are properties of the `window` object, either `window.drawInteraction` or `window.selectInteraction`. Using array notation for the object lookup, we can dynamically remove or add the applicable interaction. For example, if the user switches to the **Select** interaction from the `select` menu, then the `oldInteraction` variable will contain the `'drawInteraction'` string and the interaction to be applied becomes `'selectInteraction'`. So, `window['selectInteraction']` is the same as `window[this.value + 'Interaction']` in this scenario.

There's more...

In case it's not immediately obvious, the `DragZoom` interaction is activated when you hold down the *Shift* key on the keyboard and then left click to start dragging.

The `DragZoom` interaction has a property called `condition` that can be provided with a different event in order to enable dragging instead of using the *Shift* key. The default condition value is `ol.events.condition.shiftKeyOnly`, but feel free to explore others that may suit your application better.

See also

▶ The *Styling features based on geometry type* recipe

▶ The *Modifying features* recipe in *Chapter 5, Adding Controls*

▶ The *Styling layers* recipe

Styling clustered features

When working with lots of feature points, it is common to use the cluster strategy to avoid the overlapping of points and improve the rendering performance. We've previously covered the clustering strategy in detail in the *Using the cluster strategy* recipe in *Chapter 3, Working with Vector Layers*, and although we introduced some custom styling in that recipe, we'll look at some more styling options to enhance the appearance of the clusters in this recipe.

We are going to load two separate GeoJSON files containing around 100 point geometries, each within a concentrated area, displaying the benefits of what a clustering strategy provides to this type of data. We will render these two sets of features on different layers, each layer with a unique style.

As an added extra, for one of the vector layers, we are going to include an icon of an arrow that points to a cluster with a high amount of points beneath it. You can see what we mean by viewing the following screenshot.

The source code can be found in `ch06/ch06-styling-clustered-features`, and here's what it'll look like (as you can see, clustering can be completely transformed into a style that best matches your application):

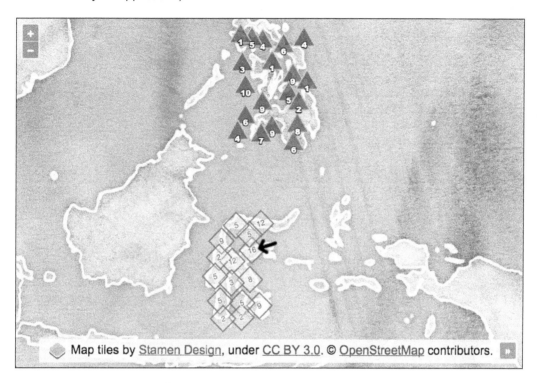

Map tiles by Stamen Design, under CC BY 3.0. © OpenStreetMap contributors.

How to do it...

In order to create uniquely-styled clustering that can complement your own particular map application, follow these steps:

1. Create an HTML file with OpenLayers dependencies and a `div` element to hold the map.

2. Within a custom JavaScript file, instantiate an instance of `ol.Map`:

```
var map = new ol.Map({
  view: new ol.View({
    zoom: 5, center: [13565432, -577252]
  }),
  target: 'js-map',
  layers: [
    new ol.layer.Tile({
```

```
            source: new ol.source.Stamen({layer: 'watercolor'})
        })
    ]
});
```

3. Create the first vector layer style function, as follows:

```
var style1 = function(feature) {
  var length = feature.get('features').length;
  var styles = [
    new ol.style.Style({
      image: new ol.style.RegularShape({
        radius: 20, points: 4,
        stroke: new ol.style.Stroke({
          color: [1, 115, 54, 0.9], width: 2
        }),
        fill: new ol.style.Fill({
          color: [255, 255, 255, 0.3]
        })
      }),
      text: new ol.style.Text({
        text: length.toString(), rotation: -0.3,
        font: '12px "Helvetica Neue", Arial',
        fill: new ol.style.Fill({
          color: [1, 115, 54, 1]
        }),
        stroke: new ol.style.Stroke({
          color: [255, 255, 255, 1], width: 2
        })
      })
    })
  ];
  if (length > 15) {
    styles.push(new ol.style.Style({
      image: new ol.style.Icon({
        src: '../../assets/images/arrow-left.png',
        rotation: -0.3, scale: 1.2,
        anchor: [-0.2, 0.5]
      })
    }))
  }
  return styles;
};
```

4. Create the second vector layer style function:

```
var style2 = function(feature) {
  var length = feature.get('features').length;
  return [
    new ol.style.Style({
      image: new ol.style.RegularShape({
        radius: 20, points: 3,
        stroke: new ol.style.Stroke({
          color: [255, 188, 17, 0.9], width: 2
        }),
        fill: new ol.style.Fill({
          color: [173, 10, 43, 0.7]
        })
      }),
      text: new ol.style.Text({
        text: length.toString(), offsetY: 9,
        font: '12px "Arial Black"',
        fill: new ol.style.Fill({
          color: 'white'
        }),
        stroke: new ol.style.Stroke({
          color: [0, 0, 0, 1], width: 3
        })
      })
    })
  ];
};
```

5. Set up a method that can instantiate a new clustered vector layer:

```
var createClusteredLayer = function(url, style) {
  return new ol.layer.Vector({
    source: new ol.source.Cluster({
      distance: 25, projection: 'EPSG:3857',
      source: new ol.source.Vector({
        url: url,
        format: new ol.format.GeoJSON({
          defaultDataProjection: 'EPSG:3857'
        })
      })
    }),
    style: style
  })
};
```

6. Finally, add two clustered vector layers with different source URLs and styling functions:

```
map.addLayer(createClusteredLayer('points1.geojson',
    style1));
map.addLayer(createClusteredLayer('points2.geojson',
    style2));
```

How it works...

Much of the code here should look familiar to the earlier recipes in this chapter. Let's take a closer look at some of the newly utilized properties and custom JavaScript that is implemented in this recipe.

We will begin by breaking down what the `style1` function does of type `ol.style.StyleFunction` (a method of styling we saw earlier in the *Styling based on feature attributes* recipe):

```
var style1 = function(feature) {
  var length = feature.get('features').length;
  var styles = [
    new ol.style.Style({
      image: new ol.style.RegularShape({
        radius: 20, points: 4,
        stroke: new ol.style.Stroke({
          color: [1, 115, 54, 0.9], width: 2
        }),
```

We store a reference of the feature length (cluster count) in a variable, namely `length`. This is what gets used for the text label.

We create a new instance of `ol.style.Style` and assign a customized `ol.style.RegularShape` instance to the `image` property. We used this type of styling in order to create a star geometry for the *Styling features based on geometry type* recipe. However, this time we use it to create a square geometry (`points` is assigned as 4—the number of polygon sides).

```
text: new ol.style.Text({
  text: length.toString(), rotation: -0.3,
```

This snippet is also plucked from the `style1` function. We can see that when we instantiate a new instance of `ol.style.Text` (for the cluster label), we use the count from the `length` variable, being sure to convert it to type string, as well as setting the text rotation to something nondefault, via the `rotation` property. The value is in radians, and produces a slanting effect.

```
if (length > 15) {
  styles.push(new ol.style.Style({
    image: new ol.style.Icon({
      src: '../../assets/images/arrow-left.png',
```

```
            rotation: -0.3, scale: 1.2,
            anchor: [-0.2, 0.5]
        })
    }))
}
```

The last major part of the `style1` function is the preceding conditional check on the feature count for the cluster.

If the number of features within the cluster is greater than 15, then we push another instance of `ol.style.Style` in the array before returning the completed styles array. We instantiate an instance of `ol.style.Icon` to provide this cluster feature with an icon of an arrow. Just like the text label, we rotate the icon by `0.3` radians, and we also scale up the icon by 20% of its original size (`1.2`).

The `anchor` property contains the *x,y* anchor points for the icon using fraction units (you can adjust it to use pixel units via the `anchorXUnits` or `anchorYUnits` properties). The default uses the fraction units of [0.5, 0.5]. We modified this so that the arrow is offset over to the right of the cluster's center, with `-0.2` instead of `0.5`.

Let's move on to take a look at the `style2` function by extracting just a few portions of the method for discussion:

```
image: new ol.style.RegularShape({
    radius: 20, points: 3,
```

Again, we've used an instance of `ol.style.RegularShape` to customize the geometry that is used for the cluster feature. With the `points` property assigned a value of `3` sides, it produces a triangle.

```
text: new ol.style.Text({
    text: length.toString(), offsetY: 9,
    font: '12px "Arial Black"',
```

This snippet is the last snippet of the `style2` function that we'll look over. It creates an instance of the text style constructor. The newly-introduced property is `offsetY`, which is used to vertically align the text label (cluster feature count) towards the bottom of the triangle. The typography used is a thicker style of font (`Arial Black`).

```
var createClusteredLayer = function(url, style) {
    return new ol.layer.Vector({
        source: new ol.source.Cluster({
            distance: 25, projection: 'EPSG:3857',
            source: new ol.source.Vector({
                url: url
                format: new ol.format.GeoJSON({
                    defaultDataProjection: 'EPSG:3857'
```

```
        })
      })
    }),
    style: style
  })
};
```

We created a function to return a customized instance of a vector layer. The function accepts the parameters of `url` for the source URL, and `style` for the style function to be used by the layer.

We specified the projection as `EPSG:3857` on the cluster instance (`ol.source.Cluster`) via the `projection` property, and we have also been explicit about the projection when formatting the GeoJSON via the `defaultDataProjection` property.

The style function is applied to the vector layer `style` property, which means that the layer styling rules will be applied to every feature within the layer.

See also

- The *Styling interaction render intents* recipe
- The *Styling features based on geometry type* recipe
- The *Using the cluster strategy* recipe in *Chapter 3, Working with Vector Layers*

7

Beyond the Basics

In this chapter, we will cover the following topics:

- Working with projections
- Creating a custom control
- Selecting features by dragging out a selection area
- Transitioning between weather forecast imagery
- Using the custom OpenLayers library build
- Drawing in freehand mode
- Modifying layer appearance
- Adding features to the vector layer by dragging and dropping them
- Making use of map permalinks

Introduction

OpenLayers is a big and complex framework. Advantageously, such a powerful and mature framework allows us to work with many GIS standards, read from many different data sources, render on different browser technologies, and so on. This capability does come at a cost, complexity, and download size to name a few.

As when learning anything else, spending time with OpenLayers will result in a familiarization of the library concepts, and we'll look at how to reduce download size in the *Using the custom OpenLayers library build* recipe, which is especially useful for mobile users or situations where network limitations may be unavoidable.

The implementation of OpenLayers 3 has less homegrown utility functionality, as seen in OpenLayers 2. OpenLayers 3 leans on the Google Closure library for this reason. With Google Closure embedded in the library core, OpenLayers is theoretically a self-contained library with no other dependencies required.

In this chapter, we'll take a look at some more practical examples to create full-featured mapping applications. We'll demonstrate recipes that will help you out with mundane day-to-day tasks (*Working with projections*) and other recipes that will further enhance your applications (*Making use of map permalinks*). In places, this chapter may be better suited for more experienced JavaScript programmers, but please don't let this deter your reading if you don't meet this criteria.

After completing this chapter and the preceding chapters, we hope that you'll be confidently ready to take on any other product requirements that you may need to implement at work.

Working with projections

As we've learned in previous recipes in this book, OpenLayers has built-in support for the EPSG:4326 and EPSG:3857 projections. Of course, this is very useful, but it is also rather limited when you need to work with other projections worldwide. Offering more built-in projections would add bloat to the library, and transforming between projections is not a simple task.

Instead, OpenLayers outsources this task to other libraries dedicated to transforming projections from one to another. One such library is called *Proj4js* (http://proj4js.org), which OpenLayers integrates with seamlessly.

So, when we want to work with projections other than EPSG:4326 and EPSG:3857, we look to the help of Proj4js.

Teaching you about projections is outside the scope of this book. The EPSG codes are simply a standardized way to classify and identify a great amount of available projections. EPSG:4326 corresponds to the **World Geodetic System (WGS84)**, and EPSG:3857 is the Spherical Mercator projection.

For this recipe, we'll show you how to integrate Proj4js with OpenLayers and how easy it is to make use of it. The idea is to create an application that shows the coordinates of the location that's been clicked or tapped. The source code can be found in ch07/ch07-projections, and we'll end up with something that looks similar to the following screenshot:

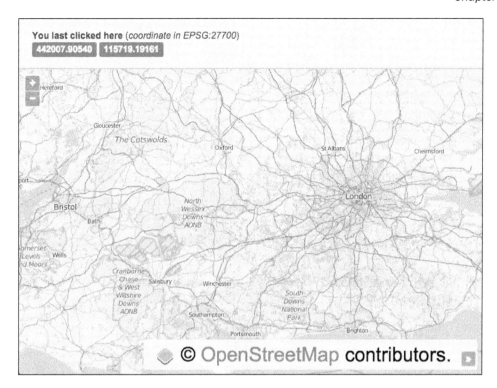

Getting ready

We must, of course, include the Proj4js library, which can be found at `http://proj4js.`
`org`. Download a copy of this library via the website, or link to a CDN copy (for example,
`http://www.cdnjs.com/libraries/proj4js`), or through other means, and include
this in your HTML file.

How to do it...

1. Create an HTML file and add the OpenLayers dependencies, the Proj4js library
    (as explained in the *Getting ready* section of this recipe), and a `div` element
    to hold the map. In particular, add the following markup in order to display the
    coordinate after a click or a tap:

    ```
    <span id="js-coordX">n/a</span>
    <span id="js-coordY">n/a</span>
    ```

2. Create a custom JavaScript file and define the Proj4js string definition for our chosen projection, which will be `EPSG:27700`:

```
proj4.defs(
  'EPSG:27700',
  '+proj=tmerc +lat_0=49 +lon_0=-2 ' +
  '+k=0.9996012717 +x_0=400000 +y_0=-100000 ' +
  '+ellps=airy ' +
  '+towgs84=446.448,-125.157,542.06,0.15,0.247,0.842,-20.489 ' +
  '+units=m +no_defs'
);
```

3. Create an `extent` instance, which covers the range of the `EPSG:27700` projection:

```
var extent = ol.proj.transformExtent(
  [-8.74, 49.81, 1.84, 60.9], 'EPSG:4326', 'EPSG:3857'
);
```

4. Initialize the `map` instance with a `view` instance and a raster layer and restrict the view's `extent` to the bounds of the `EPSG:27700` projection validity:

```
var map = new ol.Map({
  view: new ol.View({
    zoom: 8, center: [-177333, 6626173], extent: extent
  }),
  target: 'js-map',
  layers: [
    new ol.layer.Tile({source: new ol.source.OSM()})
  ]
});
```

5. Cache the DOM elements that'll be used to display the transformed coordinate:

```
var coordXElem = document.getElementById('js-coordX');
var coordYElem = document.getElementById('js-coordY');
```

6. Finally, subscribe to the map's `click` event, `transform` the coordinate, and display this in the HTML:

```
map.on('click', function(event) {
  var coordinate = ol.proj.transform(
    event.coordinate, 'EPSG:3857', 'EPSG:27700'
  );
  coordXElem.innerHTML = coordinate[0].toFixed(5);
  coordYElem.innerHTML = coordinate[1].toFixed(5);
});
```

How it works...

As we've often done, the complete CSS and HTML implementation has been omitted for brevity, but please view this book's source code to see it in full.

Let's jump into the JavaScript to see how we've used our chosen projection:

```
proj4.defs(
  'EPSG:27700',
  '+proj=tmerc +lat_0=49 +lon_0=-2 ' +
  ...
);
```

When we include the external Proj4js library in our web page, the library exposes the `proj4` global namespace to work with. Proj4js isn't yet aware of our chosen projection, so we must first define it. This particular projection definition string can be found at the useful resource, `http://epsg.io/27700`. This website contains many other projections too; it's a great resource to bookmark.

Alternatively, you can link directly to the definition setup from a `script` tag at this URL: `http://epsg.io/27700.js`. Now that the definition is set up (using the library's `defs` method), we've successfully enabled Proj4js to be utilized so that it can convert this projection to or from other projections.

```
var extent = ol.proj.transformExtent(
  [-8.74, 49.81, 1.84, 60.9], 'EPSG:4326', 'EPSG:3857'
);
```

 Note that Proj4js does have some definitions built in, such as `EPSG:4236` and `EPSG:3857`. If, however, you need to convert projections to or from other types, then you'll need to define these other projections too.

As the `EPSG:27700` projection isn't a worldwide projection but a projection that is only accurate for the UK, we set up an extent that covers this region, which we will later apply to the view in order to restrict the panning appropriately.

The `extent` variable of the projection validity is provided in `EPSG:4326`. Our view, however, will use the `EPSG:3857` projection as the default, which we want to retain. So that it's compatible, we use the `ol.proj.transformExtent` method. This method expects an array of the `ol.Extent` type, which follows the pattern [minX, minY, maxX, maxY]. The second and third parameters are the source and destination projections, respectively.

This successfully provides us with an `extent` in the `EPSG:3857` projection.

```
map.on('click', function(event) {
  var coordinate = ol.proj.transform(
    event.coordinate, 'EPSG:3857', 'EPSG:27700'
  );
  coordXElem.innerHTML = coordinate[0].toFixed(5);
  coordYElem.innerHTML = coordinate[1].toFixed(5);
});
```

We subscribe to the map's `click` event and convert the view coordinate (`event.coordinate`) currently in the `EPSG:3857` projection to our desired projection of `EPSG:27700`. We saw that we defined `EPSG:27700` with Proj4js, but how does this magically work with OpenLayers?

Well, OpenLayers makes use of the Proj4js code internally if it's available on demand. When the `ol.proj.transform` method is called for the first time (via click or tap), OpenLayers calls the `ol.proj.get` method. Our `EPSG:27700` projection isn't known by OpenLayers yet, so OpenLayers checks the Proj4js library for the definition by referencing the code. If it's been defined with Proj4js, which it has been, a new projection instance is created via the `ol.proj.Projection` constructor. This stores the projection internally in the `ol.proj.projections` object. This means that the projection won't need to be reinstantiated the next time that its usage is required.

The `ol.proj.transform` method works just as we've seen in earlier recipes, taking the parameters of the source coordinate, the source projection, and, finally, the destination projection to transform into. The result is stored in the `coordinate` variable.

We finish by adding the `coordinate` variable to the HTML, restricting the number of decimal places to 5, with the JavaScript `toFixed` method.

There's more...

As we saw in this recipe, OpenLayers implicitly created the `EPSG:27700` projection object for us on demand. However, there may be times where you need to explicitly set up the projection yourself, with an `extent` array too. When you provide an `extent` array to the projection, OpenLayers can determine the view resolution for zoom level 0, which could be valuable in some scenarios.

Here's how we'd set up the `EPSG:27700` projection ourselves (after setting up the definition with Proj4js first):

```
var proj27700 = ol.proj.get('EPSG:27700');
proj27700.setExtent([0, 0, 700000, 1300000]);
```

Or for whatever reason, if you want to call the projection constructor yourself, you can do the following:

```
var proj27700 = new ol.proj.Projection({
  code: 'EPSG:27700',
  extent: [0, 0, 700000, 1300000]
});
```

See also

▸ The *Playing with the map's options* recipe in *Chapter 1, Web Mapping Basics*

▸ The *Creating features programmatically* recipe in *Chapter 3, Working with Vector Layers*

Creating a custom control

OpenLayers has plenty of controls and interactions that address a broad range of needs. However, the requirements that we could have to build a new web application inevitably demand the creation of a new one or the extension of an existing one.

OpenLayers 2 came with a layer switcher control that's not made it to OpenLayers 3. This is not a problem, as for this recipe, we're going to create our own layer switcher control. Apart from enabling the user to switch between a list of layers, this control will demonstrate how to extend the base control class (`ol.control.Control`) to utilize some default control behavior and then build on top of the base control to deliver an interactive control the user can click or tap to change the layer.

The source code for this recipe can be found in `ch07/ch07-custom-control`, and here's a preview of our custom control placed at the bottom-left of the map:

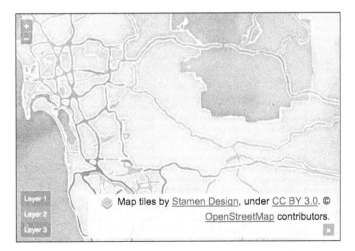

How to do it...

1. Create an HTML file with the OpenLayers dependencies and a `div` element to hold the map.

2. Create a custom CSS file and add the following to style the control:

```css
.ol-layer-switcher {
  bottom: 0.5em; left: 0.5em; }

.ol-layer-switcher ul {
  background-color: rgba(0,60,136,0.5);
  border: none; border-radius: 2px; color: #fff;
  margin: 0; padding: 0; list-style: none; font-size: 0.9em; }

.ol-layer-switcher li {
  display: block; padding: 8px; }

.ol-layer-switcher li:hover {
  background: #7b98bc; cursor: pointer; }

.ol-layer-switcher .active {
  background: #7b98bc; }
```

3. Create a custom JavaScript file and set up our custom control constructor:

```javascript
var LayerSwitcher = function(options) {
  options = options || {};
  var className = options.className ?
    options.className : 'ol-layer-switcher';
  var cssClasses = className + ' ' + ol.css.CLASS_UNSELECTABLE +
    ' ' + ol.css.CLASS_CONTROL;
  var layers = options.layers;
  var list = document.createElement('ul');
  layers.forEach(function(layer, index, layers) {
    var li = document.createElement('li');
    li.setAttribute('data-layer-ref', ++index);
    li.innerHTML = 'Layer ' + index;
    if (index === layers.length) li.className = 'active';
    list.appendChild(li);
  });
  var controlDiv = goog.dom.createDom('div', cssClasses, list);
  controlDiv.addEventListener('click', function(event) {
    if (event.target.nodeName.toLowerCase() === 'li') {
      var itemNumber = parseInt(
```

```
        event.target.getAttribute('data-layer-ref'), 10);
      list.querySelector('.active').className = '';
      list.querySelector('[data-layer-ref="' + itemNumber + '"]')
        .className = 'active';
      itemNumber--;
      layers.forEach(function(layer, index) {
        layers.item(index).setVisible(index === itemNumber);
      });
    }
  });
  ol.control.Control.call(this, {
    element: controlDiv
  });
};
```

4. Have our custom control inherit the base control class, as follows:

```
ol.inherits(LayerSwitcher, ol.control.Control);
```

5. Set up a `map` instance with a `view` instance and three raster tile layers to switch between, as follows:

```
var map = new ol.Map({
  view: new ol.View({
    zoom: 10, center: [-12987415, 3851814]
  }),
  target: 'js-map',
  layers: [
    new ol.layer.Tile({source: new ol.source.Stamen({
      layer: 'terrain'
    })}),
    new ol.layer.Tile({source: new ol.source.Stamen({
      layer: 'watercolor'
    })}),
    new ol.layer.Tile({source: new ol.source.Stamen({
      layer: 'toner'
    })})
  ]
});
```

6. Instantiate our control, passing in some layers, and add it to the `map` instance:

```
map.addControl(new LayerSwitcher({
  layers: map.getLayers()
}));
```

Apart from a `div` element to hold the map, the HTML remains very basic because the control markup is generated from our JavaScript. We've shown you a small amount of CSS that's needed to style our control, demonstrating how easily this can be achieved. You'll notice that we've inherited a lot of the default styling that OpenLayers provides.

As should be expected, the heart of this code surrounds the custom control setup, spanning around 30 lines, so let's split it into chunks for explanation purposes:

```
var LayerSwitcher = function(options) {
  options = options || {};
  var className = options.className ?
    options.className : 'ol-layer-switcher';
  var cssClasses = className + ' ' + ol.css.CLASS_UNSELECTABLE +
    ' ' + ol.css.CLASS_CONTROL;
  var layers = options.layers;
  var list = document.createElement('ul');
```

Like any other OpenLayers control, we have designed this to be somewhat customizable. Any user-defined options for this control will be present inside the `options` argument.

The first of the customizable options can be the class name, which will be used as the styling hook for CSS rules. If a class name has been provided, use it; otherwise, we default to our own class name of `ol-layer-switcher`.

When we create our control HTML wrapping element, we will combine the custom class name with a few defaults from OpenLayers that are used with other controls. It's useful to know about `ol.css.CLASS_UNSELECTABLE` and `ol.css.CLASS_CONTROL`, which respectively reference the `ol-unselectable` and `ol-control` strings, which apply some essential CSS rules to our control.

We store a reference of `options.layers` in a variable named `layers`, create an unordered list (`ul`) DOM element, and store this in the `list` variable.

```
layers.forEach(function(layer, index, layers) {
    var li = document.createElement('li');
    li.setAttribute('data-layer-ref', ++index);
    li.innerHTML = 'Layer ' + index;

    if (index === layers.length) li.className = 'active';
    list.appendChild(li);
});
```

For each layer that is supplied to our control, we create an `li` DOM element for it. We set an attribute of `data-layer-ref` that identifies the layer with a number, and then we add some text to the element in conjunction with the `index` array, for example, layer 1.

If this is the final iteration of the loop, we set the last layer with a class name of `active` by default. We finish within the loop by adding this list item to the parent list element. We've successfully converted our list of layers into an HTML list that will shortly be ready to be switched.

```
var controlDiv = goog.dom.createDom('div', cssClasses, list);
```

For demonstration purposes, we've used the Google Closure library to create our wrapping `div` element with the previous method. Remember that OpenLayers ships with many utility methods from Google Closure that you may find useful to exercise yourself.

This method takes the type of element that it has to create as its first parameter, then the CSS classes to apply to this element, and then a variable number of child elements to append to the parent element. In our case, this is the `list` of layers.

The `controlDiv` variable ends up with the following content (the following is a screenshot from the browser dev tools):

```
▼ <div class="ol-layer-switcher ol-unselectable ol-control">
  ▼ <ul>
      <li data-layer-ref="1">Layer 1</li>
      <li data-layer-ref="2">Layer 2</li>
      <li data-layer-ref="3" class="active">Layer 3</li>
    </ul>
  </div>
```

We then bring our control to life by adding some interaction capabilities:

```
controlDiv.addEventListener('click', function(event) {
    if (event.target.nodeName.toLowerCase() === 'li') {
      var itemNumber = parseInt(
        event.target.getAttribute('data-layer-ref'), 10);

      list.querySelector('.active').className = '';
      list.querySelector('[data-layer-ref="' + itemNumber + '"]')
        .className = 'active';
      itemNumber--;

      layers.forEach(function(layer, index) {
        layers.item(index).setVisible(index === itemNumber);
      });
```

We begin by checking whether one of our `li` elements was the source of the `click` event before taking any action. Once this has been affirmed, we store the layer reference in the `itemNumber` variable.

We reset the list by removing the active class from the currently active list item. Then, we query the list again via an attribute selector so that we select the layer `li` item that's been clicked, and we set this item with the class name of `active`.

The `itemNumber` number is then decremented, as the `index` values in the array of layers we're about to iterate over start at index 0. For example, layer 1 from the list correctly becomes associated with index 0 from the list of layers.

When we loop over the list of layers (an `ol.Collection`), we use the `item` method to select the layer. We then set `visibility` to `true` or `false` by evaluation of whether or not the layer in iteration corresponds to the selected layer.

```
ol.control.Control.call(this, {
    element: controlDiv
});
```

Finally, when this control gets instantiated, as in the last step, we call the base control class with our custom element assigned to the configuration object. This calls the base `control` constructor in order to set up our control with the OpenLayers defaults.

```
ol.inherits(LayerSwitcher, ol.control.Control);
```

The `ol.inherits` class is just an alias for `goog.inherits`, which inherits the prototype from the base `ol.control.Control` constructor in our custom `LayerSwitcher` constructor. For example, one such prototype method that's inherited is `ol.control.Control.prototype.getMap`, which gets the instance of the `map` that the control is attached to.

We are ensuring that our custom control closely resembles the default OpenLayers control behaviors that developers may be accustomed to, making our control familiar, extendable, and easy to work with.

We'll skip over the section that creates the map, as this will look very familiar. After this comes the instantiation of our custom control:

```
map.addControl(new LayerSwitcher({
    layers: map.getLayers()
}));
```

While adding this to the `map` instance, we instantiate our control with a configuration object and set the `layers` property to the value of all the layers from the map (our three raster layers from the Stamen source).

This layer switcher certainly isn't foolproof. However, with the help of this boilerplate, you'll be able to invest quality time in your own custom controls for OpenLayers.

Here's an open source layer switcher implementation that you may find interesting for OpenLayers 3: `https://github.com/walkermatt/ol3-layerswitcher`.

- ▶ The *Adding and removing controls* recipe in *Chapter 5, Adding Controls*
- ▶ The *Listening for vector layer features'* events recipe in *Chapter 4, Working with Events*
- ▶ The *Adding WMS layer* recipe in *Chapter 2, Adding Raster Layers*

Selecting features by dragging out a selection area

One common action when working with features within a vector layer is its selection, and, of course, OpenLayers has some feature selection controls that are available to us. We've already seen this demonstrated in earlier recipes, such as the *Removing or cloning features using overlays* recipe in *Chapter 3, Working with Vector Layers*. This recipe showed us how to select one feature at a time with a click or tap gesture.

This recipe will show you how to select multiple features at once using a combination of interactions. The `ol.interaction.Select` class is for the render intent and grouping of selected features, and the other is `ol.interaction.DragBox`, which is used to enable the user to drag out a rectangle over the map. The joint effort of these two controls will produce a multiselect capability.

Once these features have been selected, we'll display the selected count and enable the user to delete the selected features from the sidebar.

The source code can be found in `ch07/ch07-dragbox-selection`, and this will look like the following screenshot:

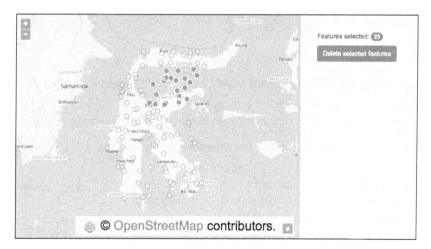

Without further ado, let's put this functionality all together.

How to do it...

1. Create an HTML file and add the OpenLayers library dependencies and a `div` element. In particular, ensure that you've got the following markup, which will be used to display the selected feature count, as well as a delete button:

```
<p>Features selected: <span id="js-selected">0</span></p>
<button id="js-delete" disabled="disabled">Delete selected
    features</button>
```

2. Create a custom JavaScript file and instantiate the `map` instance with a `view` instance and a raster layer:

```
var map = new ol.Map({
  view: new ol.View({
    zoom: 6, minZoom: 6, maxZoom: 6, center: [13484714, -266612]
  }), target: 'js-map',
  layers: [
    new ol.layer.Tile({source: new ol.source.OSM()})
  ]
});
```

3. Next, set up a vector layer with a source that fetches a local GeoJSON file and add it to the `map` instance:

```
var vectorLayer = new ol.layer.Vector({
  source: new ol.source.Vector({
    url: 'points.geojson',
    format: new ol.format.GeoJSON({
      defaultDataProjection: 'EPSG:3857'
    })
  })
});
map.addLayer(vectorLayer);
```

4. Cache some DOM elements that could be frequently accessed, as follows:

```
var selectedCount = document.getElementById('js-selected');
var deleteButton = document.getElementById('js-delete');
```

5. Instantiate the instances of our two interactions and add them to the `map` instance:

```
var select = new ol.interaction.Select();
map.addInteraction(select);
var dragbox = new ol.interaction.DragBox();
map.addInteraction(dragbox);
```

6. Create a reusable function that'll reset some UI state and clear the feature selection down:

```
var reset = function() {
  select.getFeatures().clear();
  selectedCount.innerHTML = 0;
  deleteButton.setAttribute('disabled', 'disabled');
};
```

7. Subscribe to some events from the `DragBox` interaction and update the UI when there's a selection of features:

```
dragbox.on('boxstart', reset);
dragbox.on('boxend', function() {
  var extent = dragbox.getGeometry().getExtent();
  var count = 0;
  vectorLayer.getSource()
  .forEachFeatureIntersectingExtent(extent, function(feature) {
    select.getFeatures().push(feature);
    count++;
  });
  selectedCount.innerHTML = count;

  if(count > 0) {
    deleteButton.removeAttribute('disabled');
  } else {
    deleteButton.setAttribute('disabled', 'disabled');
  }
});
```

8. Subscribe to the `click` event on the delete button element and remove any features that have been selected:

```
deleteButton.addEventListener('click', function() {
  select.getFeatures().forEach(function(feature) {
    vectorLayer.getSource().removeFeature(feature);
  });
  reset();
});
```

How it works...

We've used the Bootstrap CSS framework to handle the styling of this recipe, but much of the HTML and all the CSS have been omitted. Please view the accompanying source code for the complete implementation.

Let's turn our attention towards the newly introduced concepts of this code:

```
var select = new ol.interaction.Select();
map.addInteraction(select);
var dragbox = new ol.interaction.DragBox();
map.addInteraction(dragbox);
```

We've created the two interactions that will perform their duties in unison. Both of them are sub-classes of the `ol.interaction` class. Remember that interactions in OpenLayers don't come with a physical DOM element that's placed over the map.

```
var reset = function() {
   select.getFeatures().clear();
   selectedCount.innerHTML = 0;
   deleteButton.setAttribute('disabled', 'disabled');
};
```

When this `reset` function is called, any features stored within the select interaction (`select`) are retrieved (`getFeatures`) and then thrown away via the `clear` method from the `ol.Collection` array.

The UI is then updated to put the count of features back to zero and to disable the delete button (as no features are selected). The UI will reflect that the user can select more features again. This function will make more sense when you view it in the context of the code execution flow.

```
dragbox.on('boxstart', reset);
```

When the users begin dragging a box over the map, the interaction publishes the `boxstart` event. We subscribe to this event and ensure that the UI is returned to the `reset` state by assigning our `reset` function as the handler.

```
dragbox.on('boxend', function() {
   var extent = dragbox.getGeometry().getExtent();
   var count = 0;
   vectorLayer.getSource()
   .forEachFeatureIntersectingExtent(extent, function(feature) {
      select.getFeatures().push(feature);
      count++;
   });
   selectedCount.innerHTML = count;
```

Here's the first half of the `boxend` event subscription handler. This event is published when the user releases the mouse button. We retrieve the geometry of the last drawn box from the interaction instance and get the extent (`dragbox.getGeometry().getExtent()`). This is especially useful, as it allows us to construct a query against the vector source.

We're about to see how many features reside within the bounding box of the dragged out rectangle, so we set the count to zero.

The vector source has a method called `forEachFeatureIntersectingExtent` that (rather in a self-explanatory fashion) queries the source and returns any features that intersect with the extent. There's also a similar method available called `forEachFeatureInExtent` that behaves slightly differently, in that it returns true if a feature's bounding box is within the extent, rather than whether or not the feature's geometry actually intersects with the extent. You can read more about the differences over at the OpenLayers documentation (`http://openlayers.org/`).

The `forEachFeatureIntersectingExtent` method expects the first parameter to be the `extent` (the extent of our drag box) and the second parameter to be the iterator function that is passed the `feature` in iteration as its first parameter. We add the `feature` into the selection array of the select interaction (`select.getFeatures().push(feature)`). By doing this, the `select` interaction keeps track of the selected features and also styles them with the appropriate render intent.

As the `count` variable has been incremented on every run of the loop (`count++`), we inject the final sum of selected features in the DOM for display.

```
if (count > 0) {
    deleteButton.removeAttribute('disabled');
} else {
    deleteButton.setAttribute('disabled', 'disabled');
}
```

The final half of the event handler checks whether `count` exceeds 0. If this does, this infers a selection of features has been successful, so the delete button is enabled by removing the `disabled` attribute from the HTML. If the user wants to, they can negate the removal of the features from the vector source.

On the contrary, if the count does not exceed 0, we ensure that the `disabled` attribute on the button is set (as the user can't delete anything).

```
deleteButton.addEventListener('click', function() {
    select.getFeatures().forEach(function(feature) {
        vectorLayer.getSource().removeFeature(feature);
    });
    reset();
});
```

Finally, we subscribe to the `click` event on the button. When clicked, we fetch the features held within the `select` control and then loop over each `feature` in the collection. For each `feature`, we retrieve the vector source and chain on the `removeFeature` method, passing in `feature` during iteration. This instructs the vector source layer to remove `feature`.

After the looping and removing feature, we update the UI to the reset state to reflect the changes, and are then ready for the next selection to take place.

There's more...

You may notice that the `DragBox` interaction is activated as soon as you click on the map. This is probably an undesirable default behavior for most applications. To trigger the activation or deactivation of the interaction from a UI element (for example, a button), you can call the `setActive` interaction method and pass in `true`/`false` (or remove or add the interaction from the map) to toggle the interaction.

Alternatively, you can decide to enable dragging only when a particular key on the keyboard is being pressed in combination with a `click` gesture. For example, as in the following interaction:

```
var dragbox = new ol.interaction.DragBox({
  condition: ol.events.condition.shiftKeyOnly
});
```

The preceding `DragBox` interaction is only activated when the *Shift* key is held down in conjunction with a `click` event.

See also

▸ The *Creating a custom control* recipe

▸ The *Styling interaction render intents* recipe in *Chapter 6, Styling Features*

Transitioning between weather forecast imagery

When working with geographic information, its geometrical representation in space is not the only important thing. There's also the dimension of time that we can take into account. People are increasingly interested in up-to-date information or data based around particular moments in time.

This way, visualizations can show us how data changes over time: city population, disease outbreaks, weather forecasts, and so on.

In this recipe, we're going to show you how we can create an animation on the client side by transitioning between weather forecasts at different times of the day.

We're going to use a WMTS service from the Met Office (`http://www.metoffice.gov.uk`), showing the rain evolution at different time instants (as shown in the following screenshot), and we will create an animation by making the previous forecast fade away and the new one fade in. The time of day that the visualization represents will be displayed at the top-right of the map.

The source code can be found in `ch07/ch07-weather-forecast-imagery`.

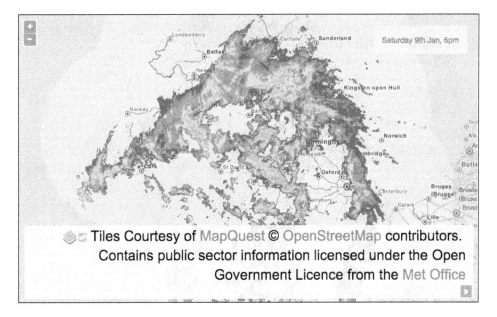

Getting ready

During this recipe, we will work with dates in JavaScript in order to request data at specific times. To help with this and also to assist in formatting times into strings for display, we've used a very good library that is specifically designed for this type of manipulation, which is called *moment*, and it can be downloaded from `http://momentjs.com`.

We will be connecting to a WMTS service from the Met Office (`http://www.metoffice.gov.uk/datapoint/support/documentation/inspire-layers-detailed-documentation`) that requires an API key for usage, just like we saw with Bing Maps in the *Using Bing imagery* recipe in *Chapter 2, Adding Raster Layers*. Go and register (for free) at `http://www.metoffice.gov.uk/datapoint`; on registration, you'll be able to attain your API key. It's a very quick and automated process.

How to do it...

1. Create a new HTML file and add the OpenLayers dependencies and also add the JavaScript date library, `moment`, as discussed in the *Getting ready* section of this recipe. Add a `div` element to hold the map, and in particular, some markup to display the time:

   ```
   <span id="js-time"></span>
   ```

2. Create a custom JavaScript file and manually generate `resolutions` per zoom level based on the `EPSG:4326` projection:

```
var proj4326 = ol.proj.get('EPSG:4326');
var proj4326Extent = proj4326.getExtent();
var size = ol.extent.getWidth(proj4326Extent) / 256;
var resolutions = [], matrixIds = [];
for (var z = 0; z < 11; ++z) {
  resolutions[z] = size / Math.pow(2, z);
  matrixIds[z] = z;
}
```

3. Produce a list of times, starting from the last hour and going back five hours from now:

```
var times = [], count = 0;
while (count <= 5) {
  var time = moment().startOf('hour');
  time.subtract(count, 'hour');
  times.push(time);
  count++;
}
```

4. Assign your API key to this variable (refer to the *Getting ready* section of this recipe for more details):

```
var apiKey = 'YOUR_API_KEY_HERE';
```

5. Create a function that'll return a new instance of our WMTS layer:

```
var createWMTSLayer = function(time) {
  return new ol.layer.Tile({
    opacity: 0.7,
    source: new ol.source.WMTS({
      attributions:   [new ol.Attribution({
        html: '<br>Contains public sector information licensed' +
          'under the Open Government Licence from the ' +
          '<a href="http://www.metoffice.gov.uk">Met Office</a>'
      })],
      url:'http://datapoint.metoffice.gov.uk/' +
        'public/data/inspire/view/wmts?' +
        'key=' + apiKey + '&TileMatrix=EPSG:4326:6&' +
        'time=' + time.format('YYYY-MM-DDTHH:00:00') + 'Z',
      layer: 'RADAR_UK_Composite_Highres',
      matrixSet: 'EPSG:4326',
      format: 'image/png',
      style: 'Bitmap 1km Blue-Pale blue gradient 0.01 to 32mm/hr',
      projection: proj4326,
      tileGrid: new ol.tilegrid.WMTS({
```

```
          origin: ol.extent.getTopLeft(proj4326Extent),
          resolutions: resolutions, matrixIds: matrixIds
      })
    })
  });
};
```

6. Instantiate a new `map` instance with a `view` instance that is restricted to zoom level 6 and a raster tile layer for the background mapping. Call `createWMTSLayer` in order to add the weather forecast layer based on the first time in the list:

```
var map = new ol.Map({
  view: new ol.View({
    zoom: 6, minZoom: 6, maxZoom: 6, center: [-354667, 7254791]}),
  target: 'js-map', layers: [
    new ol.layer.Tile({source: new ol.source.MapQuest({
      layer: 'osm'
    })}), createWMTSLayer(times[0])]
});
```

7. Cache the DOM element that holds the time representing the currently visible data on the map. Add the first time from the list to the element:

```
var timeElem = document.getElementById('js-time');
timeElem.innerHTML = times[0].format('dddd Do MMM, ha');
```

8. Set up some variables that'll be used during the forecast transitioning process:

```
var rotateCount = 1, oldLayer, newLayer;
```

9. Create the function that'll make the previous weather forecast imagery fade out and remove it:

```
var fadeAndRemoveLayer = function() {
  var opacity = oldLayer.getOpacity();
  if (opacity > 0) {
    oldLayer.setOpacity(opacity - 0.1);
    setTimeout(fadeAndRemoveLayer, 100);
  } else {
    map.removeLayer(oldLayer);
    timeElem.innerHTML = times[rotateCount].format(
      'dddd Do MMM, ha'
    );
    if (rotateCount !== times.length - 1) {
      rotateCount++;
    } else {
      rotateCount = 0;
    }
```

```
          setTimeout(rotate, 7000);
      }
  };
```

10. Create the function that'll make the new weather forecast imagery fade in:

```
var showLayer = function() {
  var opacity = newLayer.getOpacity();
  if (opacity < 0.7) {
    newLayer.setOpacity(opacity + 0.1);
    setTimeout(showLayer, 100);
  }
};
```

11. Create the function that'll rotate the weather forecast imagery:

```
var rotate = function() {
  newLayer = createWMTSLayer(times[rotateCount]);
  newLayer.setOpacity(0);
  map.addLayer(newLayer);
  oldLayer = map.getLayers().item(1);
  setTimeout(function() {
    fadeAndRemoveLayer();
    showLayer();
  }, 3000);
};
```

12. Finally, schedule the weather forecast imagery to begin transitioning in 10 seconds:

```
setTimeout(rotate, 10000);
```

How it works...

As you can see, there's a lot of code to cover here. We won't go into any details about how the HTML and CSS is implemented, but please view the book source code to find out more. We're going to focus on the newly introduced concepts of the JavaScript:

```
var proj4326 = ol.proj.get('EPSG:4326');
var proj4326Extent = proj4326.getExtent();
var size = ol.extent.getWidth(proj4326Extent) / 256;
var resolutions = [], matrixIds = [];
for (var z = 0; z < 11; ++z) {
    resolutions[z] = size / Math.pow(2, z);
    matrixIds[z] = z;
}
```

When we use this WMTS service, we need to manually set up the resolution for each zoom level based on the capabilities of the service, which you can discover at `http://datapoint.metoffice.gov.uk/public/data/inspire/view/wmts?REQUEST=get capabilities&key=YOUR_API_KEY_HERE`. As you can see, your API key forms part of the URL, so make sure to add it in.

The WMTS service supports the `EPSG:4326` projection, which as we know, OpenLayers supports by default, so this makes the implementation a bit easier.

From the retrieval of the projection's extent (`proj4326.getExtent()`), we can divide this by `256` (the pixel width of a tile). The next task is to assign a resolution based on the size for each zoom level (this WMTS service supports `11` zoom levels, starting from `0`). On each iteration of the loop, the relevant resolution is applied to that zoom level.

If the zoom level is 7, the base number 2 is raised by the exponent of 7 (`Math.pow(2, 7)`). In other words, *2*2*2*2*2*2*2*. This equals 128, which the size of the zoom level divides by, giving a resolution of 0.010986328125 for this matrix ID of 7.

This information is used when we set up the tile grid for the WMTS source. We demonstrated a similar tile grid construction for the *Setting the tile size in WMS layers* recipe in *Chapter 2, Adding Raster Layers*.

```
var times = [], count = 0;
while (count <= 5) {
  var time = moment().startOf('hour');
  time.subtract(count, 'hour');
  times.push(time);
  count++;
}
```

We collect six timestamps that will form part of the WMTS service request. The service usually provides data in 15-minute intervals, backing up until midnight of the previous day. However, we have decided to collect data hourly. The `moment` library allows us to conveniently start from the beginning of the last hour (`moment().startOf('hour')`). For example, if the current time is 3:28 p.m., the list will begin with a timestamp of 3:00 p.m. and finish with a final time entry of 10:00 a.m. The `moment` method, `subtract`, uses the `count` value (incremented on each iteration) to subtract the relevant number of hours from the starting hour.

```
var createWMTSLayer = function(time) {
  return new ol.layer.Tile({
    opacity: 0.7,
    source: new ol.source.WMTS({
      ...
      url: 'http://datapoint.metoffice.gov.uk/' +
           'public/data/inspire/view/wmts?' +
           'key=' + apiKey + '&TileMatrix=EPSG:4326:6&' +
```

```
        'time=' + time.format('YYYY-MM-DDTHH:00:00') + 'Z',
      layer: 'RADAR_UK_Composite_Highres',
      matrixSet: 'EPSG:4326',
      format: 'image/png',
      style: 'Bitmap 1km Blue-Pale blue gradient 0.01 to 32mm/hr',
      projection: proj4326,
      tileGrid: new ol.tilegrid.WMTS({
        origin: ol.extent.getTopLeft(proj4326Extent),
        resolutions: resolutions,
        matrixIds: matrixIds
      })
    })
  });
};
```

For brevity, we haven't included the entire code for this method, as we don't need to explain every part of it at this stage in the book.

Our `createWMTSLayer` function takes one parameter, `time`. This is because the URL is partly formed from `time` so that we can fetch the weather forecast for a specific time. You'll see that, within the value for the `url` property, we format the time into a string (`time.format('YYYY-MM-DDTHH:00:00') + 'Z'`) using the moment library, which is the structure required by the WMTS service; for example, 2016-04-15T11:00:00Z.

 Custom URL parameters need to be concatenated to the URL string, as `ol.source.WMTS` doesn't provide a `params` property for this, unlike `ol.source.TileWMS`, which does.

The `url` property doesn't contain the entirety of the URL, as the other properties `layer`, `matrixSet`, `format`, and `style`, are also combined in the URL string by OpenLayers. If we wanted to, we could have added these key/values to the URL string ourselves and avoided extra properties.

The `tileGrid` property is assigned a new instance of `ol.tilegrid.WMTS`, which sets up the grid pattern for us. This means that a tile can be correctly requested from the WMTS service with the relevant matrix details, such as the tile column and tile row, which are added to the URL as `TileCol=66&TileRow=13`, for example.

You can see that our resolutions and matrix IDs are used to structure the tile grid that OpenLayers creates for us via the `resolutions` and `matrixIds` properties, respectively.

```
var fadeAndRemoveLayer = function() {
  var opacity = oldLayer.getOpacity();
  if (opacity > 0) {
    oldLayer.setOpacity(opacity - 0.1);
```

```
    setTimeout(fadeAndRemoveLayer, 100);
  } else {
    map.removeLayer(oldLayer);
    timeElem.innerHTML = times[rotateCount].format('dddd Do MMM, ha');
    if (rotateCount !== times.length - 1) {
      rotateCount++;
    } else {
      rotateCount = 0;
    }
    setTimeout(rotate, 7000);
  }
};
```

This method gracefully makes the old WMTS layer fade away and then removes it from the map. It begins by retrieving the latest opacity value of the layer and checks to see whether it's above 0. If this is the case, this infers that it's still visible; so, we take away another 0.1 from the opacity level (further making this fade out) and call this function again in 100 milliseconds using the JavaScript setTimeout method.

When opacity isn't greater than 0 anymore, we remove the old WMTS layer from the map. We then update the HTML time display to the new time and format it accordingly. The time is gathered from the list of times, which are based on the value inside the rotateCount variable. We keep the rotateCount variable up-to-date within the preceding conditional block.

If rotateCount is still less than the last index of the list of times, we increment the value, as it infers that we've not transitioned every time entry yet. On the contrary, if rotateCount is equal to the last index, then we reset the value to zero so that we cycle from the beginning of the list again. It's an infinite loop of the time entries.

We finish off by scheduling the next rotation to start in 7 seconds, with setTimeout(rotate, 7000).

```
var showLayer = function() {
  var opacity = newLayer.getOpacity();
  if (opacity < 0.7) {
    newLayer.setOpacity(opacity + 0.1);
    setTimeout(showLayer, 100);
  }
};
```

On the flip side, to fade and remove, this function makes the new weather forecast imagery fade in. Following a similar logic, but reversed, we get the latest `opacity` value and check to see whether it's below `0.7` (this is the final opacity level that we wish to achieve). If it's lower than this, then we increase it by `0.1` and call this function again in `100` milliseconds. This continues until the layer has gracefully faded into view at the desired `opacity` value.

```
var rotate = function() {
    newLayer = createWMTSLayer(times[rotateCount]);
    newLayer.setOpacity(0);
    map.addLayer(newLayer);
    oldLayer = map.getLayers().item(1);

    setTimeout(function() {
        fadeAndRemoveLayer();
        showLayer();
    }, 3000);
};
```

The `rotate` function, which gets kicked off in 10 seconds when the application first loads, coordinates the transitioning between forecast imagery.

This first creates the new WMTS layer, which is based on the next time entry in the list. The reference to the new layer is stored in the `newLayer` variable, which is how the `showLayer` animation method has access to it. The opacity of the layer is set to zero and then added to the map. We do this because setting the opacity to zero doesn't prevent the tiles from being requested and loaded in the map, they just won't be visible yet.

The current layer (which has to be removed) is stored in the `oldLayer` variable, which is how the `fadeAndRemoveLayer` gains access to it. The 'old' layer is always the second item in the `ol.Collection` array of map layers, so we can access it via `item(1)`.

The final instruction for this method triggers the transitioning of the layers in 3 seconds time. We delay it by an arbitrary amount in order to give the new tiles a chance to load before making them fade in.

See also

- The *Creating an Image layer* recipe in *Chapter 2, Adding Raster Layers*
- The *Changing layer opacity* recipe in *Chapter 2, Adding Raster Layers*

Using the custom OpenLayers library build

In places throughout this book, we've credited the full functionality that OpenLayers offers out of the box with its capacity to help build powerfully capable web-mapping applications. We've also been consciously aware of the fact that this well equipped capability comes with the price of a larger download size.

However, this recipe will show you how to construct a custom minified build of OpenLayers that will include only the code from the library that's fundamental for your specific application requirements.

To demonstrate this, we'll create a custom build, which is made suitable to run an earlier recipe from this book: *Creating a simple full screen map* in *Chapter 1, Web Mapping Basics*.

The source code for this recipe can be found in `ch07/ch07-custom-openlayers-build`.

Getting ready

The OpenLayers build tools has two dependencies that need to be installed on your machine: Node.js (`https://nodejs.org`) and Java 1.7 SDK (`http://www.oracle.com/technetwork/java/javase/downloads/jdk7-downloads-1880260.html`). More recent versions of Java should be okay too.

We're going to perform the following steps from the command line. So, this is via Terminal on Mac or Linux or through the Command Prompt on Windows.

How to do it...

1. From the command line, navigate to the location of your web application code; for us, this is inside `ch07/ch07-custom-openlayers-build`:

   ```
   cd ch07/ch07-custom-openlayers-build
   ```

2. Use the `npm` package manager to install OpenLayers, which will contain all the necessary source files to construct a custom build, which creates the `node_modules/openlayers` directory on installation:

   ```
   npm install openlayers
   ```

3. Create a build configuration file in the JSON format (ours will be called `build-config.json`), which will outline the customization of our own OpenLayers library build:

   ```
   {
     "exports": [
       "ol.Map",
       "ol.View",
   ```

```
      "ol.layer.Tile",
      "ol.source.OSM",
      "ol.control.defaults",
      "ol.Collection#extend",
      "ol.control.FullScreen"
    ],
    "compile": {
      "externs": [
        "externs/oli.js",
        "externs/olx.js"
      ],
      "define": [
        "goog.DEBUG=false",
        "ol.ENABLE_DOM=false",
        "ol.ENABLE_WEBGL=false",
        "ol.ENABLE_PROJ4JS=false",
        "ol.ENABLE_VECTOR=false",
        "ol.ENABLE_IMAGE=false"
      ],
      "compilation_level": "ADVANCED",
      "output_wrapper": ";(function(){%output%})();",
      "manage_closure_dependencies": true
    }
  }
```

4. Finally, run the OpenLayers build file and pass in our custom build configuration file and the output file as arguments to node:

```
node node_modules/openlayers/tasks/build.js build
    -config.json custom-ol3-build.min.js
```

How it works...

The npm package manager is installed with Node.js by default (one of the dependencies listed in the *Getting ready* section of this recipe). When we run npm install openlayers, this downloads the latest version of OpenLayers from the npm registry (https://www.npmjs.com/package/openlayers) and places it inside the node_modules/openlayers local directory. This creates the node_modules directory if it doesn't already exist. This download of OpenLayers includes all the source files that are needed to run the custom build.

Before we explain the contents of the build configuration file that we just created, let's take another look at the application code:

```
var map = new ol.Map({
    view: new ol.View({
```

```
    center: [-15000, 6700000], zoom: 5
  }),
  layers: [
    new ol.layer.Tile({source: new ol.source.OSM()})
  ],
  controls: ol.control.defaults().extend([
    new ol.control.FullScreen()
  ]), target: 'js-map'
});
```

With this in mind, let's breakdown the configuration JSON into separate pieces for explanation, as follows:

```
"exports": [
  "ol.Map",
  "ol.View",
  "ol.layer.Tile",
  "ol.source.OSM",
  "ol.control.defaults",
  "ol.Collection#extend",
  "ol.control.FullScreen"
],
```

The first property of the JSON object, namely `exports`, expects an array of strings. These strings specify the names (symbols) that your application code uses. These strings can also define patterns with the use of * and #. For example, `"exports": ["*"]` will include everything. However, you don't want to do this!

Most of the preceding exports will be self-explanatory from observing what's used in the JavaScript application code. However, it's worth picking up one particular entry that we have in this list, and this is `"ol.Collection#extend"`.

In order to append our HTML5 fullscreen control to the map, we've extended the default list of controls, a list of the `ol.Collection` type. The `ol.Collection` class has a method called `extend`, which, by default, won't be included in our build even if we have an entry of `"ol.Collection"`, as this entry will only export the namespace and constructor, not the prototype methods, such as `extend`.

To include this method, we use the # pattern to export just the `extend` method from `ol.Collection`. If we wanted all the methods, we can perform `"ol.Collection#*"`.

```
"compile": {
  "externs": [
    "externs/oli.js",
    "externs/olx.js"
  ],
```

Next is the `compile` property, which accepts many properties and values other than the ones seen in this example. These options are for the Google Closure Compiler, the workhorse behind this build (the compiler that runs with Java).

The first property that we include is `externs`, which is for external names used in the code being compiled. OpenLayers documents that the inclusion of `oli.js` and `olx.js` are mandatory. You can find a list of all the available `externs` properties inside the `node_modules/openlayers/externs` directory.

```
"define": [
  "goog.DEBUG=false",
  "ol.ENABLE_DOM=false",
  "ol.ENABLE_WEBGL=false",
  "ol.ENABLE_PROJ4JS=false",
  "ol.ENABLE_VECTOR=false",
  "ol.ENABLE_IMAGE=false"
],
```

The `define` property lists some constants that will be used at compile time. This is an opportunity to customize the final output of the build. For us, we exclude as much code as possible to meet our needs and reduce the size of the file.

We are using the default canvas renderer for our map, so we exclude the DOM and WebGL renderers. We are not performing any projection transformations, so we exclude Proj4js integration too. We're also not using vector layers or image layers, so they're excluded as well. There are more feature toggles that are available, and we encourage you to search through the compiled debug version of OpenLayers to discover others that may be of interest.

```
"compilation_level": "ADVANCED",
"output_wrapper": ";(function(){%output%})();",
"manage_closure_dependencies": true
```

Finally, we assign values to three other properties. First, use the most advanced compilation from Google Closure Compiler (this keeps our code nice and minified). Second, specify the JavaScript that wraps the compiled code. Third, ensure that closure dependencies are managed (this is recommended by OpenLayers).

With all this configuration in place, it's time to trigger the build, as follows:

```
node node_modules/openlayers/tasks/build.js build-config.json custom
  -ol3-build.min.js
```

The line begins with `node`, which is the program used to execute the file (`build.js`) passed in as the first argument: `node_modules/openlayers/tasks/build.js`.

The second argument points to our custom build configuration file (`build-config.json`), which is where we've specified the options for the compiler.

The third argument is for the destination of the compiled JavaScript. If this file doesn't exist, it'll be created for us.

It may take a moment to run, but once this has completed the build, we'll have a new file, namely `custom-ol3-build.min.js`, that we can reference from our HTML file.

If you take a look at the normal size of the full OpenLayers library (`node_modules/openlayers/dist/ol.js`), it weighs in at about half a megabyte. However, our custom build weighs in at 109 KB. This is a considerably lower file size, and well worth the extra effort, especially when supporting mobile devices.

There's more...

For the majority of custom builds, modifications to the preceding configuration file properties listed will suffice. However, for full control of the range of compiler options at your fingertips, visit `https://github.com/openlayers/closure-util/blob/master/compiler-options.txt` for more information.

OpenLayers also has some good documentation of the configuration file and related tasks. If you'd like some extra reading to understand the different sections of `config` better, then visit `https://github.com/openlayers/ol3/blob/master/tasks/readme.md`.

See also

▶ The *Creating a simple full screen map* recipe in *Chapter 1, Web Mapping Basics*

Drawing in freehand mode

We showed you how to draw features back in *Chapter 5, Adding Controls* in the *Drawing features across multiple vector layers* recipe. OpenLayers also offers a freehand mechanism to draw features on vector layers using the `ol.interaction.Draw` class. Freehand mode can be defined as sketching something over the map without the defined accuracy and direction that you get when drawing a geometry type without freehand mode.

Having the flexibility to draw with more freedom can be useful in many application requirements. For example, it may be less arduous to create a path along a road with the continuous drawing flow of freehand, rather than having to click to add a point each time on the road as you go. With freehand mode, points are automatically added for you as you move the mouse in the direction that you want to draw in.

OpenLayers supports the freehand drawing of either polygons or lines. In this recipe, we're going to explore drawing polygons in freehand mode. After a polygon has been sketched, we will convert it to a more regular looking shape, either to a circle or a rectangle, based on what the user has selected from the radio inputs (refer to the following screenshot).

By default, the drawing freehand mode is enabled by holding down the *Shift* key, then keeping the mouse button pressed, and moving the cursor. When you're finished, release the *Shift* key and single click to complete the drawing. We'll use these defaults in our recipe.

The source code can be found in `ch07/ch07-freehand-drawing`, and we'll end up with something that looks like the following screenshot:

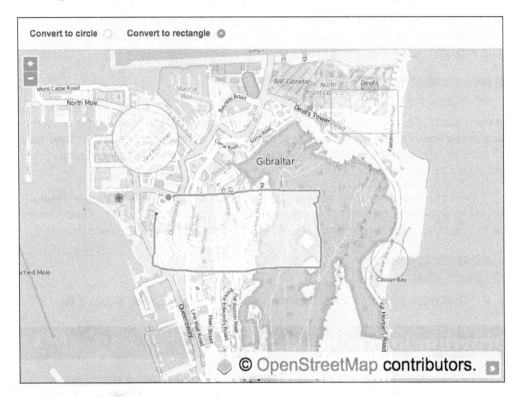

How to do it...

1. Create an HTML file and include the OpenLayers dependencies and a `div` element to hold the map. In particular, have the following HTML for the `radio` inputs:

```
<input type="radio" name="convert" value="circle">
<input type="radio" name="convert" value="rectangle"
    checked>
```

2. Create a custom JavaScript file and instantiate a `map` instance with a `view` instance, a raster layer, and also a vector layer:

```
var map = new ol.Map({
    view: new ol.View({
        zoom: 15, center: [-595501, 4320196]
```

```
  }), target: 'js-map',
  layers: [
    new ol.layer.Tile({source: new ol.source.OSM()}),
    new ol.layer.Vector({source: new ol.source.Vector()})
  ]
});
```

3. Set up the `draw` interaction for the polygon geometry type and add it to the `map` instance:

```
var draw = new ol.interaction.Draw({
  source: map.getLayers().item(1).getSource(),
  type: 'Polygon'
});
map.addInteraction(draw);
```

4. Subscribe to the `drawend` event and convert the sketch to either a `rectangle` or a `circle` geometry:

```
draw.on('drawend', function(event) {
  var feature = event.feature;
  var convertTo = document.querySelector('[type="radio"]:checked').value;

  if (convertTo === 'rectangle') {
    feature.setGeometry(
      new ol.geom.Polygon.fromExtent(
        feature.getGeometry().getExtent()
      )
    );
  } else {
    var extent = feature.getGeometry().getExtent();
    var centre = ol.extent.getCenter(extent);
    var width = ol.extent.getTopRight(extent)[0] - ol.extent.getTopLeft(extent)[0];
    var radius = width / 2;

    feature.setGeometry(
      new ol.geom.Circle(centre, radius)
    );
  }
});
```

How it works...

We've used the Bootstrap CSS framework to help style the top panel content, which we've excluded in the *How to do it...* section of this recipe. Please view the source code for the complete picture.

Most of the code will look similar to you from previous recipes, but we'll of course take a closer look at what's going on within the event hander for the `draw` interaction:

```
draw.on('drawend', function(event) {
  var feature = event.feature;
  var convertTo =
      document.querySelector('[type="radio"]:checked').value;
```

Once a freehand sketch has been completed, the `drawend` event is published, which our preceding handler subscribes to.

The `event` object holds reference to the drawn feature, which we store in a variable, namely `feature`. We store the user's conversion choice in the `convertTo` variable by querying the DOM for the `radio` input that's been selected, and then we retrieve the value of the `input` element. The value will either be `'rectangle'` or `'circle'`.

```
if (convertTo === 'rectangle') {
    feature.setGeometry(
      new ol.geom.Polygon.fromExtent(
        feature.getGeometry().getExtent()
      )
    );
```

If the user has selected this drawing to convert it to a `rectangle`, we update the geometry of the feature in place, using the `setGeometry` method from the `ol.Feature` instance. Inside this method, we provide a new geometry instance.

To create a new geometry instance from the extent of the sketched out feature, we use the helpful method, `ol.geom.Polygon.fromExtent`. This method takes a single parameter of the extent and returns an instance of `ol.geom.Polygon`, which is used as the replacement geometry for the feature.

```
var extent = feature.getGeometry().getExtent();
var centre = ol.extent.getCenter(extent);
var width = ol.extent.getTopRight(extent)[0] -
    ol.extent.getTopLeft(extent)[0];
var radius = width / 2;

feature.setGeometry(
  new ol.geom.Circle(centre, radius)
);
```

However, if the user wants to convert the sketch to a circle, we have a little more manual work to do.

We begin by retrieving the extent of the geometry in the same way as before. With extent, we can estimate what an accurate circle should be from the intention of the sketch. OpenLayers provides a bunch of methods that can be used when working with extents as a part of the ol.extent object.

The first of this is the self-explanatory ol.extent.getCenter method. The centre coordinate that is returned from this method will also be used to define the centre coordinate of our circle.

We then calculate the width of extent by taking the right-most point with the ol.extent.getTopRight method and subtracting it from the left-most point with the ol.extent.getTopLeft method. If we wanted to, we could have alternatively used the ol.extent.getBottomRight and ol.extent.getBottomLeft methods to provide the same desired result.

Both of these methods return a coordinate, an array of the ol.Coordinate type in the *xy* format. We're only interested in width, so we take the *x* values from each array by accessing the first index ([0]). The result, which is stored in the width variable, essentially provides the diameter for our circle.

When we construct a circle geometry, using the ol.geom.Circle constructor, the second argument expects a radius circle, not diameter, so we divide the width variable by two.

We finish by setting the new geometry on the feature in place, just like we did before.

 If you're looking to achieve similar functionality in OpenLayers 2, there's a tutorial at http://codechewing.com/library/create-circles-in-openlayers-using-freehand-mode/.

See also

- The *Drawing features across multiple vector layers* recipe in *Chapter 5, Adding Controls*
- The *Modifying features* recipe in *Chapter 5, Adding Controls*
- The *Styling interaction render intents* recipe in *Chapter 6, Styling Features*

Modifying layer appearance

We already saw how to perform some basic layer appearance modifications in the *Changing layer opacity* recipe in *Chapter 2, Adding Raster Layers*. We also saw how to reorder the layer stack and show or hide layers. This kind of layer modification may be sufficient for the majority of web-mapping applications, but we're going to take a look at some other more advanced techniques for this recipe.

During this recipe, we will modify the appearance of the raster tiles that are returned from the tile service. As we know, raster tiles are returned as images, which means that we can manipulate the color of the images when they're applied through the canvas renderer.

Color manipulation can also be performed on the server (perhaps a proxy server) before returning the modified tiles to the browser. Alternatively, if you're in control of the tile service itself, you could offer the raster tiles in a different color scheme.

We, of course, will look at how this can be achieved in the JavaScript code on the client's side. We will be using the `ol.source.Raster` layer source for the first time in this book. It offers a way to transform input pixel values into different pixel values for output, as specified by us.

We are going to offer the ability to switch the layer between black, white, and other colors. We will also allow the user to adjust the lightness of the layer. The source code can be found in `ch07/ch07-modifying-layer-appearance`. The screenshot of the finished application is displayed next, where the user has switched the layer to black and white mode.

Be mindful of the fact that we are going to be performing operations at a low level for every pixel of a raster tile. This does consume computing power, and performance issues may be noticeable (that is, the layer may take some time to transform from one color scheme to another). Consider the users that you are supporting in your application and appropriately pick the best technology and capabilities for this type of task.

Getting ready

For some of the color manipulations, we are going to convert them between different color spaces (RGB to HCL and vice versa). We are also going to modify the brightness of the colors. We will lean on the great *D3* color library (`https://github.com/d3/d3-color`) to take care of the grunt work for us so that we can focus on the application code. Download the D3 color library, as we'll be referencing it within the HTML.

How to do it...

1. Create a new HTML file and include the OpenLayers dependencies and a `div` element to hold the map. As mentioned in the *Getting ready* section of this recipe, also include the `D3` color library. In particular, we have the following markup for the controls inside the side panel:

```
<form>
  <select id="js-colour">
    <option value="colour">Colour</option>
    <option value="blackAndWhite">Black &amp; White</option>
  </select>
  <button id="js-darker"></button>
  <button id="js-lighter"></button>
</form>
```

2. Create a custom JavaScript file and subscribe to the color select `change` event, forcing the source to rerender:

```
var selectElem = document.getElementById('js-colour');
selectElem.addEventListener('change', function() {
  raster.changed();
});
```

3. Set up the default darker and lighter properties, subscribe to the `click` event on each button, update the relevant brightness properties, and force the source to rerender:

```
var goDarker = { enable: false, level: 0.1 };
document.getElementById('js-darker')
    .addEventListener('click', function() {
        goDarker.enable = true;
        raster.changed();
    });

var goLighter = { enable: false, level: 0.1 };
document.getElementById('js-lighter')
    .addEventListener('click', function() {
```

```
                goLighter.enable = true;
                raster.changed();
            });
```

4. Create the raster source with the pixel operations to modify the layer appearance:

```
var raster = new ol.source.Raster({
  sources: [
    new ol.source.Stamen({
      layer: 'watercolor'
    })
  ],
  threads: 0,
  operation: function(pixels, data) {
      if (pixels[0][0] == 0 && pixels[0][1] == 0 && pixels[0][2] ==
0) {
          return [0, 0, 0, 0];
      }

      var rgb = d3_color.rgb(
        pixels[0][0],
        pixels[0][1],
        pixels[0][2]
      );

      if (data.blackAndWhite) {
        var hcl = d3_color.hcl(rgb);
        hcl.c = 0;
        rgb = d3_color.rgb(hcl);
      }

      if (data.goDarker) {
        rgb = rgb.darker(data.level);
      }
      else if (data.goLighter) {
        rgb = rgb.brighter(data.level);
      }

      return [rgb.r, rgb.g, rgb.b, 255];
  }
});
```

5. Set the correct attributions for the raster source, as follows:

```
raster.setAttributions(ol.source.Stamen.ATTRIBUTIONS);
```

6. Prepare some configuration for the layer manipulation before the pixel operations actually occur:

```
raster.on(ol.source.RasterEventType.BEFOREOPERATIONS,
function(event) {
  var data = event.data;
  data.blackAndWhite = selectElem.value === 'blackAndWhite';

  if (goDarker.enable) {
    data.goDarker = true;
    data.level = goDarker.level;
    goDarker.enable = false;
    goDarker.level += 0.1;
    goLighter.level -= 0.1;
  }
  else if (goLighter.enable) {
    data.goLighter = true;
    data.level = goLighter.level;
    goLighter.enable = false;
    goLighter.level += 0.1;
    goDarker.level -= 0.1;
  }
});
```

7. Instantiate a new instance of `map`:

```
var map = new ol.Map({
  layers: [
    new ol.layer.Image({source: raster})
  ], target: 'js-map',
  view: new ol.View({
    center: [-4383204, 6985732], zoom: 3
  })
});
```

How it works...

We've used the Bootstrap CSS framework to style and organize the HTML, which has been omitted for brevity. Please view the accompanying source code for the full details.

In the UI, there are controls to manipulate the layer appearance. The `select` menu contains two options to transform the tiles between colors or black and white. We subscribe to the `change` event and force the raster source to rerender by calling `raster.changed()` from within our handler:

```
selectElem.addEventListener('change', function() {
  raster.changed();
});
```

By kicking off a render, the pixel operations are performed, which is explained, as follows:

```
var goDarker = { enable: false, level: 0.1 };
document.getElementById('js-darker')
    .addEventListener('click', function() {
        goDarker.enable = true;
        raster.changed();
    });
```

We set up a `goDarker` object, specifying some current state. It tracks whether or not it's enabled and also the current level. Before we perform the pixel operations, we need to know what user action has taken place to trigger the rerender of the layer. In order to achieve this, we keep this object up-to-date accordingly.

If the user presses the darker (minus) button for the first time, the tiles are darkened by an amount of `0.1` of the original, and the level gets incremented to `0.2`. If the user wants to go darker again, the level of increment will be `0.2` this time, making the layer a total of `0.2` darker than the original color, and so on. We can see how the level is incremented in later explanations.

We subscribe to the `click` event on the button, set the `enable` property on the `goDarker` object to true, and trigger the raster source to rerender.

We apply the same setup and logic for the `lighter` button, so we won't go into any more details here, as it should be self-explanatory from the previous discussion.

The raster source setup spans over many lines, so let's break it down into smaller pieces for explanation:

```
var raster = new ol.source.Raster({
  sources: [
    new ol.source.Stamen({
      layer: 'watercolor'
    })
  ],
```

A raster source allows us to perform arbitrary manipulations on pixel values, which is exactly what we want to do. The first property, `sources`, expects an array of `sources` that will provide the input for manipulation. We pass in a source from the `Stamen` tile provider.

```
  threads: 0,
```

The next property is `threads`, which we set to zero. By default, OpenLayers performs the pixel operations in a worker thread for performance gains. In doing so, it introduces some complexities around scope, where functions and values must be passed to the thread context; otherwise, they'll be unavailable. For demonstration purposes, we avoided this complexity. For a good introduction on worker threads, visit `http://www.html5rocks.com/en/tutorials/workers/basics/`. Remember to check for browser support when implementing these advanced capabilities (`http://caniuse.com/#search=workers`).

```
operation: function(pixels, data) {
    if (pixels[0][0] == 0 && pixels[0][1] == 0 && pixels[0][2] == 0) {
        return [0, 0, 0, 0];
    }
```

The `operation` property is provided with the function that'll process the input pixel data and then return the modified pixel data, which will be assigned to the raster source.

The `pixels` argument is an array. The first item of the array contains the RGB values within an array of their own. This is the data that we're most interested in.

If each pixel in the array has a zero value for red, green, and blue, then we `return` early to avoid performing any transforms that may trigger JavaScript `NaN` (not a number) errors. We return an array of zeros, which is the same as the data that was delivered to this operation.

```
var rgb = d3_color.rgb(
    pixels[0][0],
    pixels[0][1],
    pixels[0][2]
);
```

In order to perform some pixel color manipulation with the D3 color library, we first take the pixel input and convert it to a D3 RGB object using the `d3_color.rgb` method and store the result in a variable, namely `rgb`. The `pixels[0][0]` input corresponds to red, `pixels[0][1]` corresponds to green, and so on.

```
if (data.blackAndWhite) {
    var hcl = d3_color.hcl(rgb);
    hcl.c = 0;
    rgb = d3_color.rgb(hcl);
}
```

If the `data.blackAndWhite` property is true, this means that the user has the `select` menu value as **Black & White**. To transform the color to grayscale, we must set the `chroma` attribute of the HCL color space to zero. In order to do this, we first convert the color from the RGB color space to the HCL color space using the `d3_color.hcl` method. Once we have the color in HCL, we update the `chroma` property (`hcl.c`) to zero. We then return back to the RGB color space that OpenLayers expects (`rgb = d3_color.rgb(hcl)`).

```
if (data.goDarker) {
    rgb = rgb.darker(data.level);
}
else if (data.goLighter) {
    rgb = rgb.brighter(data.level);
}
```

 The values are assigned to the `data` object from within the before operations event handler, which we will explain later on.

If the user has requested to go darker or lighter, we assign a new RGB color to the `rgb` variable by calling either the method `darker` or `brighter` on the D3 RGB object and supplying the current brightness level (`data.level`).

```
return [rgb.r, rgb.g, rgb.b, 255];
```

Finally, we `return` an array, with indexes 0-2 forming the manipulated RGB content, retrieved off the D3 RGB object; that is, `rgb.r` is for red.

This completes the setup of our raster source, but we also need to perform some tasks prior to the raster source operations. For this, we subscribe to the before operations event on the raster source:

```
raster.on(ol.source.RasterEventType.BEFOREOPERATIONS, function(event) {
    var data = event.data;
    data.blackAndWhite = selectElem.value === 'blackAndWhite';
```

When the before operations event is published, it provides us with an opportunity to extend the `event.data` object, which is passed to the `operations` method of the raster source (it's called `data` there too, as we've seen).

We attach the `blackAndWhite` property to the `data` object, which is assigned a value of true or false, depending on the evaluation of the condition (whether or not the user has selected the **Black & White** option from the `select` menu).

```
if (goDarker.enable) {
    data.goDarker = true;
    data.level = goDarker.level;
```

```
      goDarker.enable = false;
      goDarker.level += 0.1;
      goLighter.level -= 0.1;
   }
```

If the user has clicked on the minus button to go darker, the `goDarker` property of data is assigned `true`. We also retrieve the current level of the darkness that is to be applied (`goDarker.level`) and assign this value to `data.level` for use inside the operations function.

As these changes (to go darker) will be applied to the next operation but not necessarily to the operation following that one, we must update the `goDarker` object accordingly. We mark it as disabled (`goDarker.enable = false`) and increment the darkness level, which is used for the next step of darkness (`goDarker.level += 0.1`).

Importantly, we also decrement the level of the `goLighter` object. The lightness must be relative to the darkness, so if the darkness has increased, the level of brightness will decrease. This ensures a smooth consistency when adjusting between brightness levels.

We perform similar (but reversed) logic if the user has made the layer lighter, rather than darker. We hope the preceding explanation will cover the details of this as well.

We used the verbose lookup for the event type of before operations: `ol.source.RasterEventType.BEFOREOPERATIONS`. The result is a string of `'beforeoperations'`, which we could have used instead. However, it's interesting to understand where these events are registered in the OpenLayers code.

There is also an after operations event (`ol.source.RasterEventType.AFTEROPERATIONS`). As an idea, if you think your operations could be long running and affect performance, then you could consider displaying a loading graphic on before operations, then hiding the loading graphic once the after operations event is published.

See also

- ▸ The *Changing layer opacity* recipe in *Chapter 2, Adding Raster Layers*
- ▸ The *Creating an image layer* recipe in *Chapter 2, Adding Raster Layers*

Adding features to the vector layer by dragging and dropping them

In this book, we demonstrated many ways to add features to the map, such as with the *Reading features directly using AJAX* recipe in *Chapter 3, Working with Vector Layers*. We also saw an example of exporting features from a vector layer in the GeoJSON format and displaying the result inside a textbox in the *Exporting features as GeoJSON* recipe in *Chapter 3, Working with Vector Layers*. For this recipe, we'll show you how to import a file containing GeoJSON to the map by dragging a file from your computer and dropping it in the web application.

Dragging and dropping is a part of the HTML5 API, an ability, which now has good cross browser support. To read more about the specifications, refer to `https://html.spec.whatwg.org/multipage/interaction.html#dnd`. For a quick run down of browser support, refer to `http://caniuse.com/#search=drag`.

Although there are alternative ways that you can import a file from the user's computer to the map, it's convenient to handle the file import client-side in the browser. For this recipe, the user will be able to drag a file from their computer to the map view. On doing this, they'll be prompted as to whether or not they'd like to proceed with the import, where they can decide to cancel or continue. They'll be shown some details of the import in a modal.

The source code can be found in `ch07/ch07-drag-and-drop-import`, and here's a screenshot of the stage when the user has dragged a file on the map:

For the modal effect in the screenshot, we used the Bootstrap CSS and JavaScript library. Please download a copy at `http://getbootstrap.com/getting-started` or view the accompanying source code for copies of the dependencies.

Bootstrap has its own dependency, jQuery. So, we'll need to pull this in the HTML file too.

1. Create an HTML file and include all the OpenLayers dependencies, jQuery, and a `div` element to hold the map. As mentioned in the *Getting ready* section of this recipe, include the Bootstrap CSS and JavaScript dependencies. In particular, some of the markup for the modal is as follows:

```
<div class="modal-body">
  <p>You're about to import <code id="js-filename"></code>
  which contains
  <mark><strong id="js-count"></strong></mark> features.</p>
  <p>Would you like to proceed?</p>
</div>
<div class="modal-footer">
  <button type="button" data-dismiss="modal">Cancel</button>
  <button id="js-confirmed" type="button" data-
dismiss="modal">OK</button>
</div>
```

2. Create a custom JavaScript file and instantiate the `map` instance with a `view` instance and a raster layer:

```
var map = new ol.Map({
  view: new ol.View({
    zoom: 6, center: [13484714, -266612]
  }), target: 'js-map',
  layers: [
    new ol.layer.Tile({source: new ol.source.OSM()})
  ]
});
```

3. Set up the drag and drop interaction and add it to `map`:

```
var dragDrop = new ol.interaction.DragAndDrop({
  formatConstructors: [ol.format.GeoJSON]
});
map.addInteraction(dragDrop);
```

4. Subscribe to the `click` event on the `OK` modal button and add the imported features to a new vector layer:

```
$('#js-confirmed').on('click', function() {
  var vectorSource = new ol.source.Vector({
    features: featuresToImport
  });

  map.addLayer(new ol.layer.Vector({
    source: vectorSource
  }));

  map.getView().fit(
    vectorSource.getExtent(),
    map.getSize()
  );
});
```

5. Finally, subscribe to the `addfeatures` event from the interaction, update some values for display in the modal, and then present the modal onscreen:

```
var featuresToImport;
dragDrop.on('addfeatures', function(event) {
  featuresToImport = event.features;
  $('#js-filename').text(event.file.name);
  $('#js-count').text(featuresToImport.length);
  $('#js-modal').modal();
});
```

How it works...

Some of the HTML has been omitted for brevity, so please view the accompanying source code for full details of the implementation.

Let's take a look at the newly introduced OpenLayers interaction and the supporting logic:

```
var dragDrop = new ol.interaction.DragAndDrop({
  formatConstructors: [ol.format.GeoJSON]
});
map.addInteraction(dragDrop);
```

We've instantiated a new instance of the `DragAndDrop` interaction from OpenLayers. Behind the scenes, when the `ol.interaction.DragAndDrop` interaction is added to the map, OpenLayers uses the Google Closure library to construct a handler for drag and drop events detected from the map's viewport with the `goog.events.FileDropHandler` constructor. This constructor takes a single argument of the element to listen for drag and drop event types. OpenLayers passes in the map's `div` element to the constructor (`map.getViewport()`).

The `formatConstructors` property takes an array of file format types you wish to accept. Note that you're passing in the format constructor here without calling it. OpenLayers will call the format constructor for you as part of the underlying interaction code when it's processing the imported file.

```
$('#js-confirmed').on('click', function() {
  var vectorSource = new ol.source.Vector({
    features: featuresToImport
  });

  map.addLayer(new ol.layer.Vector({
    source: vectorSource
  }));

  map.getView().fit(
    vectorSource.getExtent(),
    map.getSize()
  );
});
```

We subscribe to the `click` event on the modal OK button. Our handler creates a new vector source and assigns the `featuresToImport` value to the `features` property. The `featuresToImport` variable is populated in the `addfeatures` interaction event handler, which we'll discuss momentarily.

A new vector layer is then created with the new source from earlier and then added to the map.

For user convenience, we recenter the map to the extent of the newly imported features. The `fit` method from `ol.View` takes a first argument of extent, which we derive from the vector source. The second argument is the size (width, height) which we fit the extent into. We provide the total size of the map for these dimensions, as we want it to make use of all the available space.

```
dragDrop.on('addfeatures', function(event) {
  featuresToImport = event.features;
  $('#js-filename').text(event.file.name);
  $('#js-count').text(featuresToImport.length);
  $('#js-modal').modal();
});
```

OpenLayers loops over the list of files that have been dropped on the map's viewport, creates an array of features from the file, and dispatches the `ol.interaction.DragAndDropEventType.ADD_FEATURES` event, which we subscribe to. The `event` object contains the list of features and also some other information, such as the name of the file.

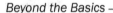

We store the features in the `featuresToImport` variable, as it's referenced in the modal OK click handler. The name of the file (`event.file.name`) is inserted in the DOM, as well as the calculated length of the features to be imported. These values form a part of the modal content.

Finally, we trigger the Bootstrap modal to be displayed. If the user exits the modal without clicking on **OK**, the features are not imported. However, if they click on **OK**, the logic in the `click` event handler executes, adding the features to a new vector layer.

See also

> ▸ The *Exporting features as GeoJSON* recipe in *Chapter 3, Working with Vector Layers*
> ▸ The *Zooming to extent of layer* recipe in *Chapter 3, Working with Vector Layers*
> ▸ The *Listening for vector layer features' events* recipe in *Chapter 4, Working with Events*

Making use of map permalinks

A great feature when browsing the World Wide Web is the ability to bookmark websites that interest you. These bookmarks offer a way for you to save the link and return to the same content at a later date.

Some web pages contain variables in the URL, which identify the particular content that you're accessing. You can share a copy of the URL with someone else, and they can see exactly what you are seeing too. Of course, we can also apply this convenience to web-mapping applications.

Wouldn't it be nice if we could share the URL (the permalink) of a map so that when it's loaded on someone else's device, the same position on the map can be restored? We can achieve this on the client in the JavaScript code, rather than using logic on the server side to help structure the map loading, which is based on the URL.

To demonstrate this, we'll have a URL with a hash of keys and values (a technique that's common with JavaScript applications). These values will tell us the centre of the map viewport, the zoom level, and also the available map controls.

The source code can be found in `ch07/ch07-map-permalinks`, and here's a screenshot of an instantiated map based upon the URL content:

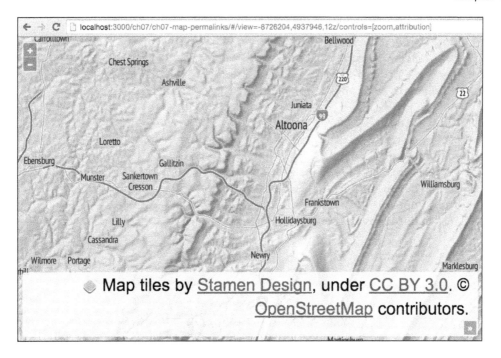

How to do it...

1. Create an HTML file with the OpenLayers dependencies and a `div` element to hold the map.

2. Create a custom JavaScript file and set up the regular expressions to perform matching against the URL, as well as some other default variable assignment:

```
var viewHashRegex = /view=([^z]+)/;
var controlHashRegex = /controls=\[(.+)\]/;
var defaultView = [-8726204, 4937946, 12];
var view, viewArray, controls, controlsArray;
```

3. Instantiate a new `map` instance without `controls` and with a raster tile layer:

```
var map = new ol.Map({
  target: 'js-map',
  layers: [
    new ol.layer.Tile({
      source: new ol.source.Stamen({layer: 'terrain'})
    })
  ], controls: []
});
```

4. Check for the availability of the URL hash content and retrieve the `view` and `controls` details if they are present:

```javascript
if (window.location.hash) {
  view = window.location.hash.match(viewHashRegex);
  controls = window.location.hash.match(controlHashRegex);

  if (view) {
    viewArray = view[1].split(',');

    if (viewArray.length === 3) {
      defaultView[0] = viewArray[0];
      defaultView[1] = viewArray[1];
      defaultView[2] = viewArray[2];
    }
  }

  if (controls) {
    controlsArray = controls[1].split(',');
    controlsArray.forEach(function (control) {
      var name = control.charAt(0).toUpperCase() + control.slice(1);

      if (typeof ol.control[name] === 'function') {
        map.addControl(new ol.control[name]());
      }
    })
  }
}
```

5. Set up the map view based on the provided URL or use the default values, as follows:

```javascript
map.setView(new ol.View({
  center: [defaultView[0], defaultView[1]],
  zoom: defaultView[2]
}));
```

6. Subscribe to the panning and zoom changes on the view of the map and update the URL accordingly:

```javascript
map.getView()
  .on(['change:center', 'change:resolution'], function() {
    window.location.hash = window.location.hash.replace(
      viewHashRegex, 'view=' +
      this.getCenter().join(',') + ',' + this.getZoom()
    );
  });
```

How it works...

To help with the understanding behind the code, let's assume that the value of the hash content in the URL is as follows:

```
#/view=-8726204,4937946,12z/controls=[zoom,attribution]
```

This content in the URL forms part of the map's permalink, and we need to dynamically load the map based on this bookmark.

For the view, the value is preceded with `view=`, followed by the x position, y position, and then zoom number, which is delimited by commas and terminated with the letter `z`. The next character, the slash (`/`), acts as a visual break between this and the next value.

For the controls, the value is preceded with `controls=` and the name of the controls wrapped in square braces (`[]`) and delimited by commas.

Now, let's take a look at how the JavaScript handles this custom URL:

```
var viewHashRegex = /view=([^z]+)/;
var controlHashRegex = /controls=\[(.+)\]/;
```

We store two regular expressions in variables for reuse. The view regular expression looks for the `view=` characters, followed by any character, one or more times, up until (and excluding) the `z` character. The characters between the `view=` characters and the `z` characters are captured in a group of their own (that's what the parenthesis do).

The controls regular expression begins in a similar fashion. It matches the `controls=` characters, followed by a literal `[` character (the backslash ensures a literal match, as the square braces have special meaning within a regular expression), followed by any character one or more times, which is captured, followed by another literal closing square brace (`]`).

Note that these regular expressions have not been battle tested; they are for demonstration purposes only. For more on regular expressions please refer to `https://developer.mozilla.org/en/docs/Web/JavaScript/Guide/Regular_Expressions`.

```
var defaultView = [-8726204, 4937946, 12];
```

We set up an array with a default centre coordinate and zoom level. This gets used if values for the view are not specified as part of the URL.

We won't cover the map instantiation in detail, but note that the `controls` property has been assigned an empty array (`controls: []`).

Let's dissect the content of the core logic within the conditional check:

```
if (window.location.hash) {
    view = window.location.hash.match(viewHashRegex);
    controls = window.location.hash.match(controlHashRegex);
```

We begin by checking to see whether a hash value actually exists within the URL; if this is not the case, we can just create the map based on our defaults.

The result of both the view and controls' regular expressions are stored in the `view` and `controls` variables, respectively.

```
if (view) {
    viewArray = view[1].split(',');

    if (viewArray.length === 3) {
        defaultView[0] = viewArray[0];
        defaultView[1] = viewArray[1];
        defaultView[2] = viewArray[2];
    }
}
```

If a regular expression using the JavaScript method, `match`, does not find any results, then it returns `null`. Otherwise, it returns the matched results in an array. The first value is the whole match, followed by any capture group matches.

Using the example URL from the beginning of this section, we'll be returned an array from `match` with the following values:

```
["view=-8726204,4937946,12", "-8726204,4937946,12"]
```

With this in mind, we run the JavaScript `split` method on the second item in the array, which will convert the `'-8726204,4937946,12'` string, to the following array:

```
["-8726204", "4937946", "12"]
```

We move on to ensure that the array has an expected length of three and override the default `view` array with the custom values discovered in the URL.

```
if (controls) {
    controlsArray = controls[1].split(',');
    controlsArray.forEach(function (control) {
        var name = control.charAt(0).toUpperCase() + control.slice(1);

        if (typeof ol.control[name] === 'function') {
            map.addControl(new ol.control[name]());
        }
    })
}
```

We next check to see whether or not the regular expression for `controls` returned `null`. If we have a match, we once again access the second item in the returned array from `match` and convert the string to an array of `controls`. Using our URL as the example, match returns the following array:

```
["controls=[zoom,attribution]", "zoom,attribution"]
```

Then, once we run `split` on the string inside the second array item, we produce the following array:

```
["zoom", "attribution"]
```

We then loop over each item in the preceding array using the JavaScript `forEach` method. We're expecting the URL to be all in lowercase, meaning that the `ol.control.Zoom` OpenLayers control is identified by `zoom` in the URL.

When we attempt to call the control's constructor, the control name must be capitalized, for example, Zoom, not zoom. To do this, we take the first character (`charAt(0)`), in this case that's 'z', convert it to uppercase, and then concatenate the remainder of the string with the JavaScript `slice` method. Now, we have the value 'Zoom' inside a `name` variable.

We check to see whether this control is available by testing if it's a type of function; if so, we dynamically call the control's constructor and add it to the map.

```
map.setView(new ol.View({
  center: [defaultView[0], defaultView[1]],
  zoom: defaultView[2]
}));
```

Outside of the conditional checks, we finally assign `view` to the map, which will either be the default values or the custom values provided in the URL (which override the default value).

```
map.getView().on(['change:center', 'change:resolution'], function() {
  window.location.hash = window.location.hash.replace(
    viewHashRegex, 'view=' +
    this.getCenter().join(',') + ',' + this.getZoom()
  );
});
```

We finish by subscribing to changes from the map center position (`change:center`), and also any zoom level adjustments (`change:resolution`). Inside our handler, we update the `view` values within the URL (using the same regular expression), based on the current map values. This ensures that our permalink reflects the latest visible map and can be shared once again.

See also

- The *Listening for vector layer features' events* recipe in *Chapter 4, Working with Events*
- The *Moving around the map view* recipe in *Chapter 1, Web Mapping Basics*

Index

modifying 180-183
reading 101
reading, AJAX used 131-134
removing, overlays used 108-114
selecting, by dragging out selection
    area 241-245
styling, based on geometry type 206-211
freehand mode
drawing in 259-263
reference link 263

G

Geographic Information System (GIS) 1
Geography Markup Language. *See* **GML**
GeoJSON
features, exporting as 97-100
geolocation
working with 167-171
geometry points
text labels, adding to 118-122
GeoServer
reference link 54
GML
about 87
layer, adding 87, 88
reference link 122
Google Closure library
URL 2

H

heat map
creating 134-137
HTML5 fullscreen API
using 7-9
Humanitarian OSM 48

I

image layer
creating 74-78
imagery 41
information
obtaining, from WMS server 193-197
interaction render intents
styling 216-222

J

Java 1.7 SDK
URL 255
jQuery
reference link 15

K

keyboard control
customizing, for map 157, 158
Keyhole Markup Language (KML)
about 89
files, reference link 91
layer, adding 89-91
reference link 89

L

layer
appearance, modifying 264-271
data buffering, for improving map
    navigation 70-73
opacity, modifying 66-69
styling 200-206
zooming, to extent 114-117
Leaflet
URL 1

M

map
controls, managing 23-27
controls, placing outside 172-174
extent, restricting 36-38
keyboard control, customizing for 157, 158
navigation 70
options, working with 9-13
stack layers, managing 14-22
map layers
work in progress indicator, implementing
    for 144-147
map permalinks
using 276-281
MapQuest
reference link 54